In the COMPANY *of* REBELS

Also by Chellis Glendinning

In the
COMPANY
of REBELS

A GENERATIONAL MEMOIR
OF BOHEMIANS, DEEP HEADS,
AND HISTORY MAKERS

Chellis Glendinning

New Village Press • New York

Published in the United States by
New Village Press
bookorders@newvillagepress.net
www.newvillagepress.org
New Village Press is a public-benefit, not-for-profit publisher
Distributed by New York University Press

Paperback ISBN: 978-1-61332-095-2
Available also in hardcover and digital formats
Publication Date: May 2019
First Edition

Library of Congress Cataloging-in-Publication Data
Available online at http://catalog.loc.gov

Front cover photo: A protester against the shutdown of the communal
People's Park in Berkeley. Photo credit: Ted Streshinsky. Courtesy of the
film *Berkeley in the Sixties* ©1990.
Back cover and Author page photos: Portrait of Chellis Glendinning, 2010.
Photo credit: Anton Brkic.
Dedication photo of Danny Schechter (opposite): Photo credit and courtesy
of Joyce Ravid.

Cover design: Gayle Grin
Interior design and composition: Jordan Wannemacher

In memory of a shooting star,
Danny Schechter

I believe the most important single thing,
beyond discipline and creativity,
is daring to dare.

—MAYA ANGELOU

CONTENTS

BE HISTORIC

Be strong, be true, be historic.
RICHARD GROSSMAN,
LETTER TO CHELLIS GLENDINNING, 2011

WHY SHOULD WE BOTHER learning about other generations' attempts to bring justice, peace, and beauty into this tattered world—particularly in these times when, for so many, the urgency of immediate survival demands our attention? Why in this razor-edge age of rising flood waters, rising cancers, and rising right-wing lockstep should anyone care about what pre-dated the burning Now?

I admit that, when I was filled with the hubris of youth, I had little interest in what went before. The subject as presented in academia was too often viewed as a big bore, and despite my mother's attempts to awaken me to our ancestors' journeys into the collective timeline, I hadn't yet grasped why anyone would give a hoot. Besides, being young appears to be a time for bursting upon the moment, all the while believing that one is inventing a storyline that has never been thought of before.

While marching in an anti-war demonstration in Berkeley, I caught a glimpse of a familiar campus figure. Bob Mandel was a red diaper baby, student activist, and member of the Oakland Seven who had been charged with conspiracy for organizing Stop the Draft Week in 1967. He was marching alongside his father, Bill Mandel, who had been a staunch Communist in the 1930s, had boldly defied Senator Joseph McCarthy's House Un-American Activities Committee in the '50s, and was a noted expert on the Soviet Union. While a sense of fascination did buzz through my bones at seeing the elder among us, I was too timid to pursue my attraction, and so I discounted it.

But lo these many political winters later, when I hit the age of sixty and suddenly could *see* the decades of history I had lived through, I experienced a dazzling awakening. What can I say? History rocks.

Indeed, in today's climate you and I are witnesses to some crucial moments in human history—one of which, without a doubt, is the flailing exploits of this latest embodiment of state/corporate economics in the U.S. presidency. And yet it comes as little surprise that those benefitting from the marriage of corporate capitalism *cum* government facilitation would finally catapult the most flamingly blatant version of their own into the hotseat of power.

But truly we have to admit that, in its basic template, the contemporary world is really not much different from other periods of history. Like the Neolithic era, when the storing/hoarding of food launched humanity's first Haves and Have-Nots. Or when, three millennia before Christ, kings forcibly cowed their citizens into assembly-line crews to sweat out the construction of the pyramids. Or the era of sixteen-hour days of low-paid/no-breaks toil in the dank factories of the Industrial Revolution; throughout most of history there have been owners and there have been slaves, cognac-sipping generals and human fodder in muddy trenches, the 99 percent and the 1 percent. The difference now is that the technological "advances" that make it possible to reach higher, lower, deeper, and more far-flung have become so expansive, colossal, complex, and out of control that the crisis exists *on every inch of planetary soil and within the cells of every living being.* As we used to say during the anti-nuclear movement of the 1980s: "There's Nowhere to Hide."

Naomi Wolf's brave 2007 book *The End of America* brought attention to a sometimes-latent/sometimes-blatant proclivity festering in the U.S. psyche: the tendency toward despotism. It was once again unleashed into full-blown reality during the George W. Bush administration with its barefaced lunge toward dismissal of democratic rights and the erection of an authoritarian state that enacts whatever it deems necessary to maintain money and power. Wolf's documentation of the tried-and-true methods of controlling whole societies that both elected and non-elected leaders have employed, and are employing, is worth our while to review—and update. As Wolf so clearly demonstrates, things are dire. On top of everything else, we are up against the global emergence of a reworked form of populism—some would call it fascism. If we care about justice, equality, caring, and ultimately our planet's survival, and if we dare to rise to the occasion, both old and young must take seriously the analyses, strategies, and tactics developed in the past—and, perhaps more to the point, take inspiration from the courage, creativity, and clarity of its activists, intellectuals, and artists.

I am taken with Chris Hedges's portrait of the rebel personality in his *Wages of Rebellion*. Hedges describes the rebel as "possessed of 'sublime madness'" á la Reinhold Niebuhr. The dissenter is the one who speaks the truth no matter the consequences. She is the prophet, the poet, the visionary, the defiant one, burning with urgency. He does what is right for its own sake. The rebel refuses to sit on the sidelines of injustice. It is as if paralysis in the face of abuse would constitute spiritual/moral suicide.

I am emboldened as well by the Zapatistas' indigenous/phenomenological/postmodern notion of activism as the awareness of and acting upon *every moment and every manifestation* of injustice—whether a sexually explicit groping in the subway or a Presidential tantrum threatening to push the nuclear button. "Be a Zapatista, wherever you are," they say. The system that now engulfs us has managed to infiltrate each level and every aspect of our earthly lives in what, it turns out, is not at all a "post"-colonial world.

With this purposefully constructed, post-truth/pro-propaganda, "liquid" reality infesting all social perception, the forces-that-be have forged a renewed form of colonialism—and the most recent subjects are *all of us*. And in that "us," as Native peoples have always known, we can include all animals, plants, and microbes; all skies, lands, waters, planets, and stars; all words, images, icons, and idols; even all DNA—anything that can be turned into a profit-making commodity to boast of an economy in the black and boost the lifestyles of the already too wealthy.

The idea to write *In the Company of Rebels* came to me like a lightning bolt flung from a tear-gas-inflamed clash between student radicals and the Berkeley Police. It emerged from a Sunday morning in San Francisco's Café Trieste while opera singers regaled the espresso drinkers; from a bowl of green chile pepper as northern New Mexico's Latino radicals made plans to reclaim the land grants stolen by the U.S. government; from Plaza 14 de Septiembre, Cochabamba, where outraged campesinos burned down city hall.

It is possible that Gurdjieff penned one of the earliest of such appreciative tomes, *Meetings with Remarkable Men,* about a group of spiritual seekers that included his father, a priest, and a prince. Then there was Quentin Bell's *Bloomsbury Recalled,* describing his subversive companions in London; followed by Kay Boyle and Robert McAlmon's *Being Geniuses Together* on the artist-writer community of Paris in the 1920s. Twenty years later came Fritjof Capra's *Uncommon Wisdom,* inspired by the mind-bending pioneers who forged holistic philosophies and practices to challenge old ways of perceiving. I had so recently finished reading Alfred Kazin's *Starting Out in the Thirties* about his era's fête of socialists, actors, writers, and artists in Greenwich Village.

I devoured them all.

But the bolt truly struck—and stuck—when I came upon Ramón Chao's series of essays in *Le Monde Diplomatique* featuring the people he had met as a journalist in Paris in the '50s—folks like Pablo Picasso, Jorge Luis Borges, Julio Cortázar, and Gabriel García Márquez. I used to think of movements, events, and lives of the past as more solid and authentic, and therefore more historic, than those of my own era. At age 60, I came to see that my times have really been no different; we too have been sturdy, creative, courageous catalysts.

I believe it unlikely that anyone can accomplish historically important work without a cadre of fellow trekkers and angels stomping and winging about one's ink well, one's tea kettle, one's canvas, one's camera, one's picket sign, one's gas mask. I personally could not have thought up a single worthy idea without the aerial leaps provided by the rebels, Bohemians, and deep heads* of my day. Too, telling the story of individuals who have participated wholeheartedly in their time and place carries the potential of revealing the spirit—the *alma*, really—of an era.

And so I introduce to you a collection of the fine folk I have worked with and loved—who have enriched my being and that of many others—during a daring, raucous, perilous, and wide-open period of human history. You have in your hands an account of our times told through their lives.

The term 'deep head' comes by way of the family of my political science professor at the University of California, Berkeley, Sheldon Wolin. He was a respected author; a champion of participatory democracy; the founder of the Berkeley school of political theory, where he was extremely popular with graduate and undergraduate students; and the inventor of the term "inverted totalitarianism," meaning the increasing centralization/authoritarianism of the U.S. political system via non-military means. In 1985 his son Clifford lent me the family cabin on the Lost Coast of California to finish my first book. Sheldon's office where he wrote while on vacation lay downstairs; word has it that, when he insisted upon slipping away to the lower depths to work, his family made hay and hilarity by dubbing him Deep Head.

In the COMPANY *of* REBELS

I. BERKELEY:
A LIKELY PLACE TO BEGIN

*I hold that a strongly marked personality can influence
descendants for generations.*

—BEATRIX POTTER, LETTER TO A FRIEND

I AM LAUNCHING THIS book by recalling in my mind's eye the story
of one stellar rebel/historymaker in one historic locale: bookseller/activist Pat Cody of one important hotbed of creative community resistance:
Berkeley, California. Warning to the reader: this chapter is a teaser, a
Circe temptress to lure you into remembering, or learning about, the
history that I and my peers have had the opportunity to live—in the hope
that it might influence *you*.

PAT CODY: IN THE CENTER OF IT ALL
(1923–2010)

I see a world with decent housing, enough food,
no tooth-and-claw struggle like we have now.
I see happier people who aren't going to inflict
emotional injury on one another. No war.
No need for all this high technology . . .

—P.C., IN INTERVIEW WITH CHELLIS GLENDINNING, 1989

Pat Cody exuded Berkeley: she had Berkeley politics, she had Berkeley commitment, she had Berkeley fire in her veins. With her husband Fred, she ran the top independent bookstore on Telegraph Avenue—no, in the city. And her story stands as an example: she was a model of what makes a vital participant in history.

Cody's Books sat on the corner of Haste and Telegraph, its sidewalk-to-roof windows showing off the stacks and tables of books inside. Owning a really first-class bookstore demands more than just knowing what books will sell, how to display the merchandise, who to invite for a book signing, or how to hire and fire; it demands constant and daily attention to the community. It was not only Cody's remarkably complete section on literature and political science, nor its impossible-to-find *Tintin* volumes from France, nor the full collection of Allen Ginsburg's poetry that made the store a legend; above all it was Pat and Fred's willingness to serve. As *San Francisco Chronicle* book review editor Patricia Holt put it on her *Holt Uncensored* blog:

> To Fred and Pat, it didn't matter who walked into the store—a homeless self-publisher (hardly an oxymoron) or a professor of physics from UC Berkeley: Matching the right book with the right customer was the highest act of political engagement they knew. Their first and last job as booksellers, they felt, was to contribute to the experience of quiet solitude that can only happen during the act of reading. When the reader's mind meets the author's mind, they believed, the world will change.

Outside on the ample sidewalk, Fred and Pat allowed vendors to sell their wares, and their presence became a vital part of the burgeoning street life. There was Hassan Faquour, the Iranian whose flower kiosk overflowed with roses and daffodils, azaleas and lilies. A skinny, six-foot-four-inch hippie-type hawked his tie-dyed tee-shirts from an Indian-print bedspread on the sidewalk. You would see Marty Schiffenbauer traversing the corner on his way to the Caffé Mediterraneum for his morning brew and street poet Julia Vinograd in her yellow cap blowing soap bubbles into the air. Inside the store sat Denny Smithson manning the cash register; his show on listener-sponsored KPFA-FM showcased authors and their books.

During the 1950s Pat and Fred boldly vocalized their stance against censorship. In the '60s, while other shops on Telegraph were locking their doors during street battles between anti-Vietnam War protesters and the police, Cody's opened theirs to provide safe refuge. In 1968, as National Guardsmen were tear-gassing and clubbing peace activists, Cody's became a first-aid station for the injured, as well as a place for political meetings at a time when such gatherings were banned on public property. Even the bathrooms—with their blackboards and chalk encouraging personal expression and social commentary—were designed to enhance community.

Every morning around ten, in would traipse Pat Cody. Dressed in sensible walking shoes and a plain skirt—her blonde-white hair in bangs and a little-girl cut—she looked like your typical, plainly dressed, liberal mother. But in reality she was a blaze of radical ideas and action. I know, because she was my boss. In the early '70s, I—a 1969 graduate of UC Berkeley—started working the help desk at Cody's, operating the cash register and keeping track of sales and orders in the Mythology and Occult book sections. The job seemed the right move in my as-yet-undesignated career path, as my boyfriend, a Russian named Misha Besher, who was seriously into esoteric spiritual matters, worked just down the block at Shambhala Books.

Pat was born in 1923 in New London, Connecticut—her father, Jack Herbert, was a railroad station agent, her mother, Rosalia, a homemaker. The Depression and World War II opened her to the political commitment

Pat and Fred in the store, 1970s. Courtesy of Nora Cody.

she would nourish for the rest of her life. She earned a master's degree in economics at Columbia, where she met, fell in love with, and married a handsome, and also very political, activist named Fred Cody. When the FBI knocked on their door and pressed them to testify to the House Un-American Activities Committee—read: to name names of their friends who were members of the Communist Party—they bolted for London and then Mexico. There they met up with folks like Frida Kahlo, Diego Rivera, and Pablo Neruda. As a timid 23-year-old worker at the bookstore, I knew nothing of this courageous and colorful past; truth is, I didn't ask.

But now I know: when the McCarthy era began to lighten up and the HUAC hearings had closed, Pat and Fred returned to California and in 1956 launched the bookstore. At first it was a hole-in-the-wall on Northside, but after a while, they realized that all the political/cultural action was taking place on Southside, so they picked up and moved across campus to Telegraph Avenue. Pat's knowledge of economics found its preferred outlet as she focused on the financial side of the business—endlessly juggling a growing payroll, the accumulating demands for compensation from publishers who were always breathing down their necks, and a burgeoning inventory of the latest and finest of books. Meanwhile, Fred, who earlier had set his sights on becoming a university professor, came face-to-face with the requirement that, to do so, he would have to sign the hyper-patriotic, anti-communist Loyalty Oath. Instead of compromising his values he decided to pursue something else, and in the bookstore he found new meaning in curating the content of the store via creative book ordering.

As a result of the 1964 Free Speech Movement on campus, the couple really dug their heels in to serve the community. They worked with others to found the Berkeley Free Clinic, where Pat also donated her skills as treasurer. And, always attentive to what was needed, she started the group Women for Peace to protest the Vietnam War.

By the late 1980s I had indeed found my career path: I was a writer, and at that moment I was doing interviews with people made ill by dangerous technologies for a book to be called *When Technology Wounds*. The offending technologies included atomic bombs and nuclear power plants, intrauterine devices like the Copper-7 and Dalkon Shield, asbestos, and chlordane, as well as dioxin-based pesticides, oral contraceptives, toxic chemicals, and metals such as those that contaminated Love Canal in Niagara Falls. Another was diethylstilbestrol. DES was a drug prescribed to pregnant women from the 1950s through the '70s to presumably ensure that miscarriage would not take place—until its withdrawal due to medically proven health consequences like breast, testicular, and vaginal cancers, infertility, ectopic pregnancies, and premature births. In the meantime eight million mothers, daughters, and sons had been affected.

When the first studies came to light in 1971, Pat read about them in a *San Francisco Chronicle* article entitled "Drug Passes Rare Cancer to Daughters." At first she ignored this new information, even tried to forget about it. But she could not get around the fact that she had been prescribed DES when she was pregnant with her first child, Martha. In her typical can-do style, she left behind the helplessness one feels about irreversible mistakes of the past and founded the advocacy group DES Action. Starting with little information, she located other exposed mothers to raise consciousness, did research, and collaborated on the first-ever information leaflet about DES. She helped launch a two-year consumer education program and develop a slide show for clinics to show to patients that was called "Ask Your Mother: Finding the DES-Exposed." In time she also served as the organization's program director, newsletter editor, and international liaison.

In the beginning the people in the first kitchen-table group had to learn to read medical journals in order to educate themselves. Then they turned to educate those who had been affected, but soon enough they learned that doctors, medical researchers, and policymakers also knew little about the dangers and needed to be informed. DES Action grew to include chapters in thirty U.S. states, with sister groups around the world; it also became a model for other health advocacy organizations seeking to make an impact.

Once I was writing about DES, I sought Pat out. She was as informed, outspoken, and velvet articulate as ever. "Technological hubris!" she bellowed. "What a price we pay for all the so-called scientific advances!" Needless to say, her interview provided a strong example for my chapter

How true that Cody's was "more than a bookstore"! New owner Andy Ross with Fred Cody. Photo credit: James Pease. Gratitude to the now-defunct *Berkeley Gazette*, July 10, 1981. Courtesy of Andy Ross.

on taking action as a healthy response. "If you get a lemon, make lemon-ade," she affirmed. How strange it felt to realize that she had been going through the pain of realization and doing the work of organizing at the same time that I had been working at Cody's. *When Technology Wounds* came out in 1990, and I had the honor to return to the bookstore to do a presentation not as an employee, but as an author.

In 1977 Pat and Fred sold Cody's Books to fellow book vendor Andy Ross, who kept the store thriving for another thirty-plus years. Pat returned to her writing desk, where she penned a marvelously soulful history called *Cody's Books: The Life and Times of a Berkeley Bookstore.* She also wrote *DES Voices: From Anger to Action* about the political power of effective research, education, and informed action. When Fred died in 1983, her anguish was excruciating—and unbearable. Support for such sorrow and disorientation was hard to find, so she launched the Grief Support Project. It developed a model where groups of the bereaved were led by a trained professional and a lay person who had coped with similar loss.

Her own memorial at Berkeley's First Congregational Church in Octo-ber of 2010 drew a grief-stricken throng of family members, including her four children, Martha, Anthony, Nora, and Celia; former Cody's work-ers; authors; literature enthusiasts; professors; colleagues from the Northern California Independent Booksellers Association; political allies; Telegraph Avenue denizens; and other admirers from all over the world. Nora spoke, saying that in approaching death, the dignity and courage her mother had demonstrated matched that which she had mus-tered in life.

II. EYES ON THE PRIZE
IN CLEVELAND

The rest of the country is perversely wont to
misunderstand Cleveland.

—MARK WINEGARDNER,
CROOKED RIVER BURNING, 2001

BUT DEAR READER: BEFORE we jump headlong into the notorious political uprisings of the 1960s anti-war movement, let's back up in time a couple of decades and focus on my place of origin . . .

Cleveland, Ohio.

Some people call it the "Mistake on the Lake," a term that dates back to 1969 when the chemically polluted Cuyahoga River that slices the city into east and west sides burst into flame. I would guess too that the observation that Cleveland is not worth mentioning on the national news springs from superiority complexes beleaguering both East and West Coasts. As an industrial city situated on the shores of Lake Erie, though, it grew to be a vital port for shipping along the Great Lakes passageway to the Atlantic, as well as becoming the Midwestern residence of J.D.

Rockefeller, Andrew Carnegie, and others of their ilk—thus making it home to a world-class art museum, symphony, and park system.

Such aspects of Cleveland's economic ascent led to its vibrant radical history. After the freeing of African slaves following the Civil War, Blacks left the South to escape the barefaced racism there, and to find work in the industrializing North—for many, in the steel mills along Lake Erie. Then, concurrent with the arrival of thousands of immigrants through Ellis Island came the move west by those who could not make a living along the eastern seaboard. By the 1910s Cleveland featured neighborhoods of Italians, Poles, Russians, Irish, and Welsh, plus a vigorous Jewish community and the Glenville and Hough neighborhoods where African Americans lived. No surprise then: when in the 1930s uprisings of workers were erupting all over the United States, in Cleveland the workforce marched under Communist banners bearing slogans like "Fight, Don't Starve," 2000 hungry men stormed City Hall, and the first national meeting of the Unemployed Leagues took place in nearby Columbus.

March of the Young Communist League, March 7, 1930.
Courtesy of Cleveland Press Collection, Cleveland Memory Project.

Protest against Cleveland Sesquicentennial, July 22, 1971. "Settlers"
had hoped to celebrate until the American Indian Movement
showed up. Russell Means is on the left. Photo credit: Tom Prusha.
Courtesy of Cleveland Press Collection/Cleveland Memory Project.

The '50s and '60s saw the emergence of the civil rights movement—
with Clevelanders, both Black and white, joining Freedom Rides in the
South; eruptions of riots; and the formation of the United Freedom
Movement to desegregate schools. In 1957 the U.S. Bureau of Indian
Affairs established the Employment Assistance Program to relocate
Native Americans from the West to northern cities. When they were
scheduled to begin their migration, the *Cleveland Press* ran an article, in
racist reference to the Cleveland Indians baseball team, "Real Indians
Soon to Call Cleveland Home." Members of Pueblos and of Plains tribes
streamed in, and in 1970 militant activist Russell Means (Dakota/Pine
Ridge) founded the American Indian Movement in the city.

It was in this crucible that my first and most formative remarkable
meeting took place—with my mother. It was from her that, starting in
the second grade, I was given an education in love of beauty and the fight
for social justice.

HOOKER GLENDINNING:
DOING WHAT THERE IS TO DO
(1920-1985)

This *is history!*

—H.G., IN CONVERSATION WITH CHELLIS GLENDINNING, 1964

Mary Hooker Daoust Glendinning had to defend her name just about every day of her life. "The name 'Hooker,'" she would glowingly reiterate with a chuckle, "has its roots in England and came over in 1633 with the Reverend Thomas Hooker who—after an argument over rights to land and voting with Massachusetts Governor Bradford (Hooker being the more equalitarian)—traveled south to become the founder of the Colony of Connecticut." Continuing her introduction to the name Hooker, she would say, "Thomas Hooker's descendant, General 'Fightin' Joe' Hooker, of Civil War fame, was a raving drunk, so his commanders sent him west where he couldn't mess things up for the Union. His troops got bored, and he requested that the army send them 'some women.'" Here my mother would crook her eyebrows and lend a tilt to her head for the sake of suggestion. "Stage coaches of women arrived," she would continue, "and they were dubbed 'Hooker's Girls,' then just 'hookers.'"

Through chance or astrological inevitability, the quirk of ova or karma, this character became my mother. My brothers were Thomas Hooker Glendinning and, taken from our blood line flowing back to the inventor of the telephone, Alexander Bell Glendinning. And so the house on the corner of Edgehill and Kenilworth in Cleveland Heights, Ohio, became the Petri dish for all manner of comedy, calamity, insurgence, and quandary, and the forum for my political education.

Hooker had been the first woman in her family to graduate from college. Connecticut College, of course—where she distinguished herself as a champion fencer and as the art major who painted a picture of a girl boasting tresses blown by the wind in an easterly direction, while a tree above her head displayed branches thrust by the same currents toward the west. She worked as a draftswoman in downtown Cleveland during World War II, and she persuaded the family that she should marry one

My mother Hooker, me, and grandmother "Mimere." Cleveland Heights, Ohio, 1949. Photo credit: Alex Thiel. Courtesy of Chellis Glendinning.

Paul Glendinning, a fellow Clevelander and Harvard graduate. The popular displays of all those shiny post-war refrigerators convinced husband Paul that she should be an in-the-kitchen wife. She was sorry to leave her job, never did like to cook, but like so many of her cohort, she gave in.

As a 1950s housewife, her artistic talents were now funneled toward fabled Halloween costumes, clothes crafted with a Singer sewing machine on the floor of the TV Room, hand-designed Christmas cards, and great ideas for things to do. The union of her parents, Edward Chellis Daoust and Clara Louise Bunts, had spawned backyard theater, and like my mother before me, I too crawled up the back stairs to the attic of grandmother Mimere Daoust's house on Stillman Road to delve into the steamer trunks and don velvet dresses, ankle-length beaver coats, and fairy costumes of past smash hits among the rose bushes.

Hooker also passed on the family Halloween tradition. From its creation in the 1910s, Stillman Road was a bona fide neighborhood, boasting unlocked doors and families sharing garden delights and practical jokes. Come October 31, Hooker and her siblings would stalk the 'hood. If a house had lawn furniture on the front porch, they would heap it in a pile in the yard. The maples and oaks would be strung with toilet paper like tinsel on a Christmas tree. If a garden hose was to be found, one Daoust would ring the bell and aim the nozzle toward the front door while the other would wait to hear the signal that said door had opened and would switch on the faucet. I was encouraged to follow in her footsteps, and I did. And all this is not to mention my made-by-Mom costumes: one year, a window made of canvas complete with curtains and a paper black cat on the sill; the next, a pack of Lucky Strikes.

But the Daousts had also known tragedy. In 1935 Hooker's beloved older brother Buddy drowned in a canoe accident. Her father, Edward Daoust, died in an airplane crash on his way to Washington, D.C., six days before she gave birth to me. Too, there had been World War I, the Depression, and World War II. My upbringing was tinged by the grown-ups' remembrances of these histories.

And there was the tragedy that the brand-new picture box made public. In 1955 Rosa Parks refused to give her seat to a white man on a bus in Montgomery, Alabama, and was hauled to jail for the "crime." My mother was stunned. And upset. Having grown up with the one-liner "Slavery Was Abolished in 1865," she had not been fully aware of the conditions that still prevailed. Suddenly the necessity for contributing to society instilled in her on Stillman Road flared up like a forest fire sparked by a lightning strike. That same year, my father was placed in a hospital in Philadelphia to recover from alcoholism. We rented a house in Swarthmore. There she met Presbyterian minister Joe Bishop and his parishioners, who told her about a nascent movement to demand civil rights. She spent that year learning U.S. history from the perspective of African Americans.

When we returned to Cleveland Heights, Hooker launched the process that would define her life: she stepped up to the plate of social responsibility and became politically active.

Picture our neighborhood: it boasted one humungous Gothic relic left over from the days of Rockefeller and Carnegie—now surrounded by blocks of newer and decidedly smaller middle-class houses, working-class homes, and apartment buildings. It was populated by WASPs, Italians, Jews, Poles, Romanians, Russians, etc. But African Americans were not welcome. The only ones who came up the hill from the Hough Area (seemingly) without fear were the maids.

And so it was something of a scandal when my mother began inviting her Black movement comrades to the house.

She also began to attend meetings in the inner city and to participate in organizing. In 1962 a Cleveland minister practicing civil disobedience against the construction of a segregated school was crushed to death under the treads of a bulldozer. In 1963 a bomb exploded in an Alabama church where civil rights meetings took place; four Black girls were killed. The following year in Mississippi three civil rights activists—one local and two northerners, all of whom had participated in Freedom Summer's campaign to register Black voters—were abducted by Ku Klux Klan members and shot at close range; their bodies were found buried in an earthen dam. Things were on edge. Black Nationalist leader Harllel Jones came to the same meetings that Hooker attended. Sometimes she was appreciated for her intelligence, but other times she was reprimanded for not organizing her own people to quell racist practices and dissolve racist institutions. Fortunately my mother was not burdened by the hubris that she knew everything. She took in criticism, was not uncomfortable with ambiguity—and never once considered dropping out. Following the directive, she sought out like-minded white folk in St. Paul's Episcopal Church in Cleveland Heights, where Clergy and Laity Concerned had been formed.

In the mid-'60s Hooker met an ambitious African American man named Carl Stokes. Son of a laundryman and a cleaning lady, he had dropped out of high school, then after World War II had put himself through Cleveland Marshall College of Law, joining the Ohio bar in 1957. Now he strove for a heretofore unimaginable target: he wanted to run for mayor of Cleveland. After watching my mother in action as a thinker and organizer, he asked her to serve on his campaign committee.

She had what are called blazing blue eyes: they radiated a hue reminiscent of a Canadian ice lake. When impressed by a person or an experience, she had a way of intensifying those blue eyes until they caused painters to abandon whatever style they were pursuing and become colorists. Knowing Carl Stokes and being asked to contribute to his run for office caused her eyes to blaze brighter than the stars in a Van Gogh sky. After all the work to pull off the historic campaign, he won. He *won*! History was made: Stokes was the first African American mayor of a major U.S. city.

I try to imagine my mother's exhilaration at the election night party, as I wasn't in Cleveland. I had gone off to university, first for two years at Smith College, later to the University of California, Berkeley, to do what a college-age woman does: make her own way. And rebel. By the time I got to the West Coast, the generation gap was in full swing. Unfortunately, I didn't have much to rebel against: my brothers and I had been the only children on Edgehill Road allowed to cross the street by ourselves, a sorry privilege because when we got there, all the other kids were stuck on the other side. Later, at Smith, students were not permitted to stay out past 11 p.m., and then only with permission—yet I had grown up with little-to-no nocturnal restrictions. And now, for Chrissake, my own mother was a left-leaning activist!

My political career had begun at age eight—walking around and around the collating table, stapling the resulting information/action packets, stuffing them into envelopes, stamping and organizing them according to postal code. In 1964 my mother picked me up after school on a Wednesday. We met with Blacks and whites in a parking lot in downtown Cleveland and rode all night in a bus to Washington. On Thursday we spent the whole day picketing the White House. We rode all night back to Cleveland, and I missed just one day of school. These sorts of experiences were normal fare for me. So were the mother-daughter chats we had about what she was learning and grappling with, like the one about being a white homemaker in a people-of-color movement. Or the contradiction between sending me to private school while other young people had no school at all.

And there was the conversation about what it meant to be part of history. No excuse for sitting on the sidelines, she said. You have to do what's there to do. First and foremost, my mother was a woman of action. She was dedicated to the electoral process—and for one brief moment I had a focal point for my own personal generation gap. She had grown up under FDR, after all; she was a flaming liberal, a "deluded" believer in working through "the system." I, on the other hand, considered myself a radical. Maladjusted at Smith College, I had transferred to the University of California, Berkeley, and had just been released from jail after the People's Park Mass Bust of 1969, wherein some 400 people had been hauled in opaque-windowed buses to the Santa Rita Detention Center. The phone call from my commune on Vine Street, in which I argued for a revolution and she was heartbroken, was one of just three arguments we had in our entire lives.

In the early '70s Hooker traveled to Paris to stand witness to the peace talks in process and to attend a meeting between North Vietnamese representatives and U.S. peace activists. (Here began a decades-long joke with William Sloane Coffin about a very special British umbrella she had left behind in a shared taxi and he had picked up—which was only resolved after her death via an exchange of letters between him and me about said umbrella, bristling with Daoust/Coffin humor of the madcap sort.) She went on from her civil-rights and anti-war activism to apply her artistic/organizing talents to local and national elections, marches for welfare mothers, efforts to save the endangered Everglades of Florida, and the feminist movement, including bringing Judy Chicago's "Dinner Party" to Cleveland. She (the only non-lawyer) also sat on the board of the Ohio ACLU. In 1978 I swallowed my pride and called her to ask advice about how to navigate the thorny terrain of being a white person in the midst of people-of-color movements.

Around that time, my mother was diagnosed with kidney disease and began a life dependent on dialysis. Plus one failed kidney transplant. In typical form, she mustered her spirit to continue doing what there was to do. She took us kids on two vacations—one to Santa Fe, New Mexico; the other to Michigan. After my father died in 1982, she married her high-school sweetheart, honeymooned carting a home dialysis machine, and in good feminist spirit rejected the idea of changing her last name to his and moving in with him—all the while continuing her political work as best she could.

But, inevitably, the end was nigh. Lying in a coma in Intensive Care at the Cleveland Clinic, she was hooked up to all manner of tubes leading to indecipherable machines flashing digital numbers. A family dispute arose, with her new husband arguing that he wanted her to live no matter what vegetative state she might be in while the doctor was advising us that it was time to pull the machines' electrical cords and let her go. It was Friday, and a brain scan was to be performed on Monday; if it was discovered that she had any brainwaves functioning, the hospital would be legally bound to keep her alive.

I had read Laura Huxley's *You Are Not the Target* about her experience as her husband Aldous lay dying. At his request, she had given him LSD and then gently talked him through the passage. "You are going towards a greater love than you have ever known. You are going towards the best, the greatest love, and it is easy, it is so easy, and you are doing it so beautifully," she had said to him. "Light and free. Light and free. . . . You are going towards the light. Willing and consciously you are going. . . . Go into the light, go into the light," she had repeated until he breathed his last.

I was startled. I felt that I could never do anything as brave as that. I would be too afraid, too frozen. But I did. During my Friday visit, I slipped her hand into mine and, adopting Dr. Elizabeth Kubler-Ross' message that a person in a coma is still aware, I whispered: "You have always lived for others. Through this illness you have begun to do what *you* want to do, for yourself. Now you face the ultimate choice: do you want to live? Or leave? The brainwave exam is scheduled for Monday. If you want to stay, we welcome you. If you want to leave, we are ready. All you have to do is go into the light, go into the light, light and free, go into the light," I said as if some unseen sage were guiding my words. "Mimere is waiting for you on the other side. Pipere is waiting for you. Your brother Buddy is waiting. Martin Luther King. A.A. Milne. C.S. Lewis. Eleanor Roosevelt." As if repeating a mantra, I named the people over whom she had twinkled those blazing blue eyes, who had subsequently passed on.

She left on Sunday morning.

In 1986 my mother was posthumously inducted into the Ohio Women's Hall of Fame—joining other distinguished Ohioans like Annie Oakley, Harriet Beecher Stowe, Lillian Gish, Frances Payne Bolton, Gloria Steinem, Ruby Dee, and Nikki Giovanni.

Psychologists say that the relationship with Mother is the most important in one's life. I still grieve. But thank the Lord: I reside safely on the other side of that blasted generation gap, in full appreciation of all that she was and all that she gave me—not the least of which is a sense of being alive to history.

III. THE PALEOLITHIC AT SMITH COLLEGE

A colleague once defined an academic discipline as a group of scholars who had agreed not to ask certain embarrassing questions about key assumptions.

—MARK NATHAN COHEN, *GOOD CALORIES, BAD CALORIES*, 2007

IT'S NOT THAT I wanted to go to Smith College. It was more like it was something that happened to me. No question: according to going opinion in Cleveland, I was to "go east" where the Ivy League and Seven Sisters colleges were. That much was clear. My idea was the far groovier Sarah Lawrence College north of New York City. My brother Sandy—who was into the likes of Nina Simone, Summerhill, and Segovia before anyone else I knew had ever heard of them—had told me that at Sarah Lawrence an aspiring opera singer would appear unannounced on the balcony of the dorm and belt out an aria. The problem was, I didn't get in. The head mistress of my preparatory high school had gone to Smith and reveled in sending her students to follow in her learned footsteps. So there I was in 1965—a Smithy by somebody else's design.

Students at Smith College, Northampton, Massachusetts, 1964.
Courtesy College Archives, Smith College.

The campus was very much like it had been for the previous fifty years. Students in saddle shoes, kilts, and round-collar blouses bought at Bonwit Teller and Neiman Marcus. Field hockey and rowing. Tea in the living room, bridge in the sitting room. Mixers at Yale. Not allowed to stay out past 11 p.m. People of color few and far between. Lesbians hidden away in the obscurity of their dorm closets.

But my reference to the "Paleolithic" is not a satirical comment about Smith's traditions or student culture. It's about what I studied there.

Paul Shepard's typewriter. Photo credit and courtesy of Anthony Wheeler.

PAUL SHEPARD: SUBVERSIVE ANIMAL
(1925–1996)

The genetic human in us knows how to dance the animal, knows the strength of clan membership and the profound claims and liberation of daily rites of thanksgiving

—P.S., *THE ONLY WORLD WE'VE GOT*, 1996

Paul Shepard dashed into the biology lab in a flurry, the stack of papers in his arms flying up and hitting his blond beard. With such unselfconscious actions, he let us see that he had another life outside the academic domain of microscopes and reptile brains. Little did I know that this absent-minded professor was a genius and a soon-to-become maverick innovator in his field. Perhaps his unfolding as a subversive could have been predicted by the fact that, unlike any biology teacher in high school, he spoke of a little-known area of study called "ecology." But, really, who cared? Biology existed in my life only to fulfill a requirement before I could get on to courses in my major, and my major was definitely *not* biology.

I had no idea, though, that down the line Paul Shepard was to have a major impact on my life's work. At that very moment in 1966 when I took his biology course, he was in fact working on a book called *Man in the Landscape* that he punched out on his portable Olivetti Lettera 32. The book would lay the ground for *his* life's work, while I was just striving to get through the formaldehyde session with the dead frog.

I never saw Professor Shepard again after that semester at Smith College, but some twenty years later I came across his name as the teacher of a workshop in a California Institute of Integral Studies catalog. He was giving a weekend class on animal totems, and the announcement for it sat on the exact opposite page from a session I was offering. Thus began our correspondence—and ultimately his wife Flo's unexpected and most welcome gift to me: the very Olivetti Paul had used to type his books.

Simply put, the gist of Paul Shepard's work is that humans are animals who belong in the natural world just as giraffes and fireflies and manatees do. Whether looked at from the perspective of ecology, psychology, culture, politics, or health, our severance from the world shared by all the other creatures has been a failure. His next book, *The Subversive Science,* introduced the field of ecology, revealing its parameters and prescient of its implications for the survival of life in a world headed toward human-made catastrophe. That same year, 1969, he received a Guggenheim to do ethnographic research on the cultures of hunter-gatherer peoples, studies that would expose the disparities between the looming disaster of civilization and the manner in which our ancestors had survived successfully for more than a million years. Although he had hunted as a child in Missouri, he went on his first bear hunt in 1978; the bear was to become his personal totem and a lifelong fascination. By that time he'd already published *Environ/mental, The Tender Carnivore and the Sacred Game,* and *Thinking Animals.*

Then, in 1979, Paul was appointed a Fellow at the Rockefeller Foundation to write the book that would draw the most attention and create a dedicated group of followers: *Nature and Madness.* I confess to being a member of the fellowship of folks trying to understand why we humans are the way we are. I am also a member of a very specific sub-fellowship of such travelers: the all-out, gung-ho Shepard enthusiasts. In this book

Paul at age two in Kansas City, Michigan, 1927.
Family snapshot. Courtesy of Flo She.

he traces the psycho-historical development of humans from the Paleolithic era through the desert cultures of the Middle East. All the while,
he is revealing the injuries to/adaptations of psyche that produced the
distortions hailed and promoted by Western civilization. By contrast, he
creates a model for understanding the role of the natural world in healthy
psychological development. Based on the fact that humans came to be
humans over the course of the 99 percent of our existence in which we
lived wholly in the natural world, by evolution itself we are dependent
on immersion in nature for our psychic/emotional maturation. He goes
one step farther: he proposes that societies coming after the invention
of sedentary agriculture do not provide that innate and expected immersion, and so many of those born into them become stuck in infantile or
adolescent stages of growth.

"In the ideology of farming," he offers, "wild things are enemies of the
tame: the wild Other is not the context but the opponent of 'my' domain.
Impulses, fears, and dreams—the realm of the unconscious—no longer
are represented by the community of wild things with which I can work
out a meaningful relationship. The unconscious is driven deeper and
away with the wilderness. New definitions of the self by trade and political subordination in part replace the metaphoric reciprocity between
natural and cultural in the totemic life of the hunter-foragers. But the
new system defines by exclusion. What had been a complementary entity
embracing friendly and dangerous parts of a unified cosmos now take on
the colors of hostility and fragmentation."

The unconscious is driven deeper and away with the wilderness! That phrase alone laid the ground for all of my subsequent thinking.

Son of the Midwest, Paul Shepard was born in Kansas City, Missouri, in 1925. His father was Paul Howe Shepard, a horticulturist; his mother, Clara Louise Grigsby. When he was nine, the family moved to Mountain Grove, where his father had been appointed director of the Fruit Experiment Station of the state of Missouri. Paul's future interests already etched into his being, he wrote a weekly newsletter reporting the unfolding of the plant world at the station, and this he delivered to the people of Mountain Grove via a cart drawn by the family dog. With his father he also learned to hunt. He soon had meetings with *his* remarkable people: zoologist Rudolph Bennit, a biologist whose specialty was the life cycle of the bobwhite quail; and Ernest Thompson Seton, originator of the Woodcraft Indians and a founding father of the Boy Scouts, who ran a camp in New Mexico where Paul learned woodsman skills.

He went on to study journalism at Northwestern University; gunning, artillery, and radio through the army's specialized training programs; English literature and wildlife conservation at the University of Missouri; ornithology at Cornell; and he received a Ph.D. at Yale in an interdisciplinary program combining conservation, landscape architecture, and art history.

What lay ahead was a plethora of teaching jobs, grants and studies, hikes and hunts, fellowships—and books. There was no lack of preparation for or imagination expressed in the books that he then banged out on his portable typing machine: *The Sacred Paw,* about the special relationship of humans to bears came out in 1985, followed by *The Only World We've Got, The Others: Animals and Human Being, Traces of an Omnivore, The Eclectic Primitive,* and *Coming Home to the Pleistocene.*

When I realized that the same man with the flurry of papers that blew into the Smith biology lab in 1966 was the savvy leader of an animal totem workshop at CIIS, I wrote him a letter. Perhaps the only way he would remember me was through a rather unfortunate event that had taken place lo these many years ago. He had scrawled "METABOLISM," "CATABOLISM," and "ANABOLISM" on the blackboard and then asked what these words meant. As a card-carrying introvert, I have never been one to speak up in class, but in this case I immediately saw that I had a leg up on everybody else: I had learned these very same concepts from my high-school biology teacher who wore a sari, boasted a red spot on her forehead, and was from India. Mrs. Banerjee also pronounced the words—and thus taught them—with an accent on the *first* syllable (instead of the second). *Met*-a-bolism. *Cat*-a-bolism. *An*-a-bolism. Yes, I became the laughing stock of Bi-*oh*-logy 101 as I pompously enunciated the words aloud as if I myself hailed from the subcontinent. Now, in my letter, the association of that devastating faux pas was good enough for identification—and thanks to Paul's innate kindheartedness, a correspondence began.

He took delight in my memory of the field trip whose purpose, he reminisced, had been to present the question of randomness versus order in nature; all I could think of upon reading his note was the miraculous randomness—or order—in my finding him twenty-five years later. We exchanged letters, sharing books, articles in print, articles under construction, and colleagues. I finally invited him to become what at *The Tao of Physics* Fritjof Capra's think tank the Elmwood Institute was called a Peer, a position that resembled a Fellow. He offered quotes by others to explain his instinct to bow out: "I suppose I am somewhat like my friend, Ivan Illich," he wrote. "Illich says, in effect, 'I have spent my life trying to ask the right questions. As for solving the problems they bear on, it will take all the efforts of highly specialized experts of many different kinds—all beyond my ability.'" He also quoted Edward Abbey, who argued that he might make the right changes in his own life but was not a leader in social action.

In 1993 I received Paul's alarming "Dear Friends" note requesting support, or at least cognizance, regarding the book he had written on his favorite topic: *The Sacred Paw: The Bear in Nature, Myth, and Literature.* As he explained the problem, he had originally conceived of it with his Viking Press editor, and he had written all the chapters on the mythic bear, constellations, archaeology, paleontology, linguistic materials, festivals, rites, and ceremonies of tribal peoples, etc.—while his coauthor had contributed but one chapter, on the bear in literature. "This book," Paul explained, "is part of a lifelong study of animals in culture." His current devastation stemmed from the fact that this coauthor had been proclaiming that it was *he* who had written the bulk of *The Sacred Paw,* and he had actually sold five chapters to another publisher for an anthology, each of which he had rewritten paraphrasing Paul's sources to ensure escape from copyright litigation.

An even more alarming occurrence was Paul's death by lung cancer in 1996. Thankfully, just the year before, I and others had had the opportunity to heap praise upon him in ecologist Max Oelschlaeger's Festschrift *The Company of Others: Essays in Celebration of Paul Shepard.* "The most important thing I can say is [his books] gave the rest of us courage—courage to say what we are saying in our own books," wrote historian Calvin Luther Martin. "I owe everything to Paul Shepard," contributed deep ecologist Dolores La Chapelle.

"Paul was the only college teacher I ever knew to take the class into *the wilds,*" I noted, "all the while seeding our minds with dangerously holistic notions like ecology. Years later, *Nature and Madness* changed my work and days. . . . [Lewis] Mumford's brilliance carved a crystalline picture of what is wrong with mass technological civilization and our lives within it. Shepard sanctioned this view, deepened it with rare psycho-historical insight—and then went on to open the door to what could be right. I remember the moment distinctly. I was lying on the couch in my office, a luscious July breeze blowing in through the door, alternately reading the book and dropping it in my lap to *breathe.*"

A few years later, at a writers conference in Prescott, Arizona, I met Flo Shepard, the woman with whom he had built a wilderness cabin in Wyoming, edited anthologies, and shared that last rich decade of his life. Shortly thereafter I received a letter from her asking if I might like to steward the Olivetti he had used to write his books. Amazingly, it arrived amid crushed newspapers and bubble wrap, a rickety little machine that looked wholly incapable of translating all those enormous thoughts into mere words. I held it in my hands, trying to take in the sagacity and panoramic vista it was still emanating.

IV. MAKE LOVE NOT WAR:
BERKELEY IN THE '60S

LET'S TAKE THE PARK!

—DAN SIEGEL, PRESIDENT, ASSOCIATED STUDENTS
UNIVERSITY OF CALIFORNIA, MAY 15, 1969

A protester against the shutdown of the communal People's Park
in Berkeley—in captivity. Photo credit: Ted Streshinsky.
Courtesy of the film Berkeley in the Sixties ©1990.

THE DEITIES WERE WATCHING over my generation. An acquaintance from Cleveland who was studying at Amherst College—and would soon mutate into a rabid Communist Labor Party militant—said to me, "There's something going on in Berkeley that has to do with our generation. You need to go." The remark sunk in, and just a few days before my twentieth birthday, I threw work shirt, sandals and jeans into a little suitcase, bought a $75 plane ticket from Cleveland to the Bay Area, and made my break.

In 1967, Berkeley was a hub of youth culture and New Left politics—and was located right up Telegraph Avenue from Oakland, where the Black Panther Party was in gestation with its objective of protecting their communities from police violence via its own armed patrols. This was the first place inside the U.S. where I witnessed a flourishing street life, and indeed one of my first observations, at Moe's Books on Telegraph, was how earthy, alive, and laid-back everyone seemed. Old jeans. Navy bellbottoms. Men boasting ponytails. Women in Mexican peasant blouses. Espresso and Gauloises. I heard jazz musicians and 1930s commie pinkos airing their radical sentiments on listener-sponsored KPFA-FM. Mario Savio from the Free Speech Movement was the postman. Richard Brautigan was penning his fish stories up in Bolinas; Julia Vinograd, her street poems at the Café Mediterraneum. Richie Havens belted out "Freedom" in the university's lower plaza. The Free Clinic was overflowing with patients, the Free University with students. Books, books—everyone was devouring books. Karl Marx and Carl Jung. Anaïs Nin. Malcolm X, Eldridge Cleaver, Frantz Fanon. Wilhelm Reich. Simone de Beauvoir. Sylvia Plath. Allen Ginsberg.

I arrived in mid-June, and the tang of the 1966 Oakland Induction Center confrontation with the police lingered like Ripple wine on the tongues of the anti-Vietnam War activists. I found an empty apartment where the landlord let me crash gratis for the summer, got a morning job as a governess, bought a near-see-through dress made of burlap, hitchhiked from Berkeley to L.A., marched with Clevelander Dr. Benjamin Spock at the Century City anti-war demo, and when I took my first drag of marijuana, I saw satyrs galloping through the air. By September I filled out the forms to transfer from Smith College to the University of California, Berkeley.

Activist couple in the 1960s—expressing both their politics and their alternative way of life. Gratitude to the now-defunct *Berkeley Tribe* (1969–1972), which was more radical than the community's original underground newspaper, the *Berkeley Barb*. Vol.1, No. 6, Issue 6, August 15, 1969.

When I got back to Cleveland to collect my things, my mother invited her movement friends to hear me talk about what strange goings-on were erupting in California. I was just delivering my analysis of the Beatles song "All You Need Is Love" when one mother, nearly quaking in fear, asked, "But, but . . . isn't Berkeley just a big cesspool of *sex, drugs,* and *radical politics?*" I paused for a long moment, discombobulated by the alarm in her voice. I hadn't really thought of it that way.

Finally, all I could do was answer: "Yes."

MARTY SCHIFFENBAUER:
MASTER OF POLITICAL INVENTION
(1938–)

I was so unhip, I didn't know Berkeley was hip.
—M.S., LETTER TO CHELLIS GLENDINNING, 2014

I had never been to a real health-food store before. Of course, what with being in Berkeley, I had already been introduced to Adele Davis' food theories, and encouraged to use whole-wheat flour, make my own yogurt, and drink herbal tea. And I'd heard of the Food Mill. At the time—before Wholly Foods opened its doors at Shattuck and Ashby and while the industry remained but a twinkle in the eyes of a few health-food-freak entrepreneurs-to-be—the Food Mill was the Bay Area's only outlet selling organic grains, seeds, and flour.

But I didn't know where it was.

Marty said he would take me. Imagine my awe when he pulled up to the Vine Street commune in a 1963 Chevy II ... *convertible*. To my mind, the car presented a sharp quip of a lampoon of the American Dream our generation was rejecting and, at the same time, was utterly camp in its own right. Off we went—Marty in his trademark shorts and combat boots, with his flaming red corkscrew locks flying in the wind like Gorgonian snakes; me in U.S. Navy bellbottoms, purple Hindu shirt, and long brown braids—cruising along the Eastshore Freeway, past the driftwood/cast-off machinery sculptures constructed anonymously in the mudflats and on to Oakland's MacArthur Boulevard.

In those days it was a good bet you would find all five feet and four inches of Marty as a very tall presence around the political advocacy tables in Sproul Plaza. He was a bit older than most in the anti-war movement and, before the 1974 stock-market collapse, he made his living by buying and selling stocks; it was a feature that I found incomprehensible but also far-out—and that definitely made him the All-American Hippie Weirdo Drop-Out. That he filled his studio apartment with God's Eyes he crafted himself only enhanced my view. Marty kept his Gorgon hairdo for near a lifetime, although it did change color as the years ambled onward; he wore the shorts and boots until the late '70s, when they finally disintegrated and he switched over to athletic get-up. I was standing in front of the Café Mediterraneum on Telegraph Avenue when the tornado of red hair and gym shorts arrived, bubbling over with endorphins and the discovery that if he ran just three miles every day, he could *eat* all he wanted!

Marty grew up in Brooklyn in the apartment behind Berdie's Corset Shoppe. His parents, Berdie and Morris Schiffenbauer, raised him Orthodox Jewish, sending him to yeshivas and keeping the Sabbath every week.

Marty in his Berkeley commune, 1972.
Courtesy of Marty Schiffenbauer.

"My parents were not very political," he reports, "but they loved FDR and always voted Democrat. They were, of course, pro-Israel. Mostly their politics were of the Whatever-Is-Good-for-the-Jews variety."

He first came to Berkeley in 1964, tooling up University Avenue in his Chevy II almost by happenstance. He liked the summer-blue sky, he liked the vibes, he liked the slender blondes—and in his own pre-anti–Vietnam War way he was escaping the draft. In 1962 Marty had opted to join the New York National Guard as the least demanding way to serve his military obligation. By his own admission, he survived six months of active duty but found the subsequent weekly meetings a drag on his time and on taxpayers' money. Presaging the political expression that was to fill the rest of his life, he wrote a scathing letter to the *New York Times*. The captain of his reserve unit happened to read it, freaked out, and proposed that Private Marty move to another state immediately—and one preferably far away. Marty then stumbled upon a summer course in German at UC Berkeley that would satisfy the language requirement for his Ph.D. in experimental psychology at NYU, and voilà! off he went.

By 1967, having completed the bulk of his coursework for the Ph.D., he made the definitive move across country. He launched his political involvement in October Berkeley-confrontation style by joining thousands of others in front of the Oakland Induction Center during Stop the Draft Week. His personal approach, though, did not resemble the serious, organized assemblage of the marchers who had faced down the no-nonsense Oakland Police's Flying Wedge with improvised shields made of garbage-can lids, tire-fed bonfires, and parked cars as barricades. Marty called for a far wackier, Yippie-style Naked Noisy Vigil for Peace. In truth, no one came nude, but a local character named Jefferson "Fuck" Poland showed up strutting nothing more than a jock strap.

Marty was obviously attracted, then, to the Gray-Life Tour of the Suburbs. I was too. This ingenious mirror image of Grayline's tour for suburban people to come to Berkeley to observe the hippies was the invention of the *Berkeley Barb*'s military correspondent, Lee Felsenstein. As if in a zoo, you would be leaning against the steps to Sproul Hall discussing the Camus-Sartre breakup or the nutritional value of alfalfa sprouts or LBJ's role in the escalation of the Vietnam War, when one of these suburban tourists would bold-facedly situate him/herself smack-dab in front of you and rob your soul with a Kodak Brownie. Ergo, one Saturday morning in 1969, two busloads of us (packing Kodak Brownies) veered off the map to Walnut Creek and environs. When we downloaded ourselves to check out the sights on one quaint little Main Street, the terrified storekeepers and restaurant owners bolted their glass doors and pulled down their corrugated metal security gates so fast they looked

In psychedelic style, the poster for the Naked Noisy Vigil for Peace, 1968. Designers: N. Pettitt and Marty Schiffenbauer. Courtesy of Marty Schiffenbauer.

like dominoes crashing down across Southeast Asia. Next stop was a park. Here I got dizzy watching children riding around a pony-giraffe-turtle-festooned carousel, while Marty was approached by some steak-fed teenagers who saw in his wild tresses their possibly best-ever customer; they tried valiantly but unsuccessfully to sell him the acid and marijuana they normally peddled to their high school peers.

The tour was capped off with a visit to the straight people's retirement community, Leisure World. Needless to say, our buses were refused entry to its clipped green lawns and croquet courts, so we hurled our bodies upon the forty-foot erector-set sculpture of planet Earth outside the gate and, freaks hanging from Somoza's Nicaragua and Franco's Spain, flew around and around as the giant globe spun.

Sign of the times: I was at Marty's on Haste Street when the Symbionese Liberation Army crashed and burned in the biggest police shootout in U.S. history. The SLA had first hit the news in 1973; they took down Oakland's popular African American school superintendent Marcus Foster with cyanide-packed bullets for what they misunderstood to be his "support" of compulsory ID cards. (He was, in fact, against them.) They rose up into the public eye again in 1974 when they kidnapped publishing heiress Patty Hearst and her betrothed, Steven Weed, in Berkeley. Now, via the new compact cameras and mobile units, all three TV stations were live-casting the defense of their L.A. "safe house."

The SLA *appeared* to be part of our movement—anti-war, anti-racist, calling the nation's jails "concentration camps" for Blacks. Yet they were different from us for their tactics. This ill-prepared army fancied itself as a self-styled, left-wing revolutionary band and the vanguard of urban guerrilla warfare à la Regis Debray and the Uruguayan Tupamaros. But, as Marty put it, they were nothing but "a violent cult with an egomaniacal leader."

Now, on May 17, 1974—better known to us as the day after Marty's thirty-sixth birthday—the Los Angeles police and fire departments, FBI, and California Highway Patrol were closing in on them. And now, instead of merrily toasting the birthday boy and chowing down on organic carrot cake, we were fixed like the stelae of Stonehenge around the tube. I was too dumbfounded to speak. The men's voices rose and fell in gasps of revulsion as each round was shot and returned, as some inside attempted to break away from the house and were met with law-enforcement gunfire, as the place burst into devouring flames.

For Marty the symbolic protest of street theater gave way to direct action in 1971 when he founded the Berkeley chapter of War Tax Resistance and, applying his expertise in financial matters garnered from playing the stock market, counseled people in federal tax refusal. As the raucous '60s faded from view, he continued to ride this new arc of political action, taking on an issue that would affect all of Berkeley: rent control.

As a long-time tenant, he joined with the city's varied housing organizations as well as its outraged renters—and gave the effort his all. He helped write the bill that in 1972 would make Berkeley the first U.S. city to impose restrictions on unrestrained rent increases and landlord evictions for actions not considered "just cause," while requiring landlord payment of interest on security deposits. In 1976 the California Supreme Court under Chief Justice Wright handed down a landmark decision: he granted victory to the basic principles of rent control, including the right of municipalities to enact their own legislation. At the same time, though, the judge invalidated the Berkeley initiative for its procedural favoring of renters at the expense of the rights of landlords. Ergo, in 1978 Marty and others drafted a new rent roll-back ordinance mandating that eighty percent of landlord property-tax savings be rebated back to tenants as rent reduction. It was approved by the voters. Emboldened, Marty and his allies wrote a comprehensive ordinance in 1980. It too passed. Marty was elected to serve on the first Berkeley Rent Board, and thirty-plus years later the legislation is still in place. Marty is sometimes called the Father of Rent Control, although he likes to clarify by saying: "Well, *maybe* . . . but I was not a single parent."

Rent control easily morphed in his mind into a proposal for limits on house-sale prices. This new wrinkle was formulated in 1989 during a morning run with a friend; the two were kibitzing about skyrocketing prices that divided citizens into the landed class and the forever-renting peon class, thus driving minorities and senior citizens from the community. To Marty, an increase in sale price calculated at the national average of six percent of original cost would be more reasonable and just than the typical increase in chic Berkeley that, in one year, had shot up by *thirty-five percent*—making a $150,000 home sellable overnight at $202,500. Marty's jogging partner revealed the idea in his weekly *East Bay Express* column and from there it went viral, appearing in the *San Francisco Chronicle, Wall Street Journal*, and various venues of the national press. Alarm also went viral, with Marty's progressive friends pronouncing it too radical, and one Berkeley politician withdrawing for fear that her career would go belly-up for association with its "Father." A co-author of the rent-control bill, attorney Myron Moscovitz, proclaimed in a 1989 *San Francisco Chronicle* article, "I don't think the proposal has a snowball's chance in hell." Marty also began to receive hate mail, death threats, and answering-machine messages like "You are scum" and "*Schweinhund*." His response: "We're living in a democracy, and this can be voted on. They don't have to kill me, sue me, or leave hate messages." Just the same, he pulled back.

Walking his talk as a housing activist, Marty lives now in a one-bedroom apartment in the Parker Street Co-op that a collective of twenty-four households formed in 1991. A splendid side effect of going on TV to hype the house-sale proposal was that an old acquaintance, a woman he had once dated, saw the show and called him up. They began what has been, so far, a thirty-plus-year love affair culminating in their 2011 wedding, although—true to form of the inventiveness Marty is known for—they still live in their separate pads. In his, over the kitchen sink, he boasts an R. Crumb cartoon of the infamous 1960s bearded sage Mr. Natural proudly washing dishes. And, indeed, the man "Keep(s) on Truckin'"—as of this writing, launching another controversial campaign, this one to raise Berkeley's minimum wage.

Among those Bohemians, rebels, and deep heads who pursued higher education, the magnifying glass that renders focus to their lives might reveal a vision gone wildly askew in regards to the field in which they majored and what they ended up doing. But as you will see in coming chapters, when all is said and done, Marc Kasky, with his master's in urban planning, indeed spent his life practicing city planning—just in a non-conventional way; while economics major Jerry Mander ended up warning people about the dangers posed to democracy and environment by the corporate-dominated global marketplace. Marty too: though he never held a "real" job in his chosen field, his offerings surely magnify the realm of . . . *experimental psychology.*

TOM HAYDEN: POLITICAL ANIMAL
(1939–2016)

From SDS to Occupy Wall Street, students have led
movements demanding a voice. We believe in not just
an electoral democracy, but also in direct participation
of students in their remote-controlled universities,
of employees in workplace decisions, of consumers in
the marketplace, of neighborhoods in development
decisions, family equality in place of Father Knows
Best and online, open source participation in a world
dominated by computerized systems of power.

T.H., "PERSONAL STATEMENT: FIFTY YEARS LATER,
STILL MAKING A STATEMENT," *THE MICHIGAN DAILY,* 2012

Forty-some years after the fact, round about 2005, I had the chance to tell Tom Hayden that back in the '60s when he lived in a Berkeley commune called the Red Family, I had had a mad crush on him. The truth is I fell into infatuation the moment I heard his voice on KPFA-FM reading the text of his 1962 Port Huron Statement that laid the basis for the peace-justice-equality movements of the 1960s. But it wasn't until the later '60s that he moved to Berkeley. His arrival—much-touted in Bay Area political circles—was almost too much for my twenty-one-year-old hormones to handle. I attended a teach-in on Canada-bound draft avoidance so I could look at him. But there sat his girlfriend on the panel, ever so lovely and sophisticated in her super-wide navy bellbottoms.

I saw him again at a planning meeting at Bill Miller's house in the Claremont district during the citywide 1969 uprising in protest of the university's fencing of a plot of land citizens had crafted into a people's park. Just a handful of us came to the meeting, and Tom reported that he had learned from his Deep Throat within the Berkeley Police Department that a mass bust was in the works. I was spellbound sitting just a breath away from him, listening, taking his presence in. Indeed, I got arrested at the bust along with some 400 others in May of 1969, was carted off to Santa Rita Detention Center in a windowless prison bus, was corralled into a claustrophobia-producing solitary cell with a bevy of some fifty terrified, exceptionally loud, and disorganized women, and in the end was saved from more lengthy prison time by left-wing pro bono lawyer Bob Treuhaft.

Then in June, the month after the People's Park uprising, there was a new demo on the Berkeley campus. That was the moment I realized that we long-timers in the streets had unwittingly, by all appearances through tacit psychic connection, developed a group method in which we would come together, burst apart, come together, then burst apart again depending on if the police were on the attack or not. But this new crop of protesters . . . well, they were proving to be an insipid shade of naïve green. As summer vacation was upon us, they had arrived in our skillful midst from all directions to have their "Berkeley Experience," and they knew exactly jack shit about how to maneuver as a unified mass. Tom was there under the Sproul arch doing his best to direct this herd of cats—with no success at all.

As you can plainly see, I didn't have a lot of quality contact with the object of my adoration in Berkeley. Stay tuned, though: decades later he would change the course of my life. By 2005 he was married to a spirited Canadian actress named Barbara Williams. He'd survived a heart attack and was ever so aware of the fleeting nature of life. He had traveled to New Mexico for a Christmas reunion with his family from the days when he was married to Jane Fonda. We were crossing the parking lot of the Santuario de Chimayó, and I made my confession. We both had a good laugh.

Is Tom most notorious for his role in starting Students for a Democratic Society in 1961? Or for his civil-rights activism in the South and in Newark? Or for being the theoretician of the Chicago 8 along with Abbie Hoffman, Jerry Rubin, Bobby Seale, David Dellinger, Rennie Davis, Lee Weiner, and John Froines? Is he most known for his work as a progressive California State Assemblyman and Senator? Or for his twenty-plus books? Is he most recognized for the ground-breaking work he did with street gangs in Los Angeles? Or perhaps for marrying Jane Fonda? The answer could depend on your politics: some may think his (by 1979) 22,000-page, three-foot-high FBI file is the definition of immortality. Whatever the answer, it is clear that Tom was born to give of himself wholly.

He was, in fact, born in 1939 in Royal Oak, Michigan to Genevieve and John Hayden, both of Irish descent. After graduating from Dondero High School, he went on to the University of Michigan, where he was editor of the *Michigan Daily*. At the time, the National Student Association still held sway with its Cold-War, anti-communist politics. Tom joined with others to found the Students for a Democratic Society, and he was its president in 1962 and '63. During this time, he also traveled through the South as a Freedom Rider to desegregate public areas like train stations, and he was the central drafter of SDS's Port Huron Statement. Its first sentence opened the door to the students and intellectuals who were to burst upon U.S. consciousness: "We are people of this generation, bred in at least modest comfort, housed now in universities, looking

Tom musing at his FBI file in 1979. (Imagine its size by 2015!) First appearance in the *Los Angeles Times* in 1979; later in "The Hunters and the Hunted" by Seth Rosenfeld, *New York Times*, October 5, 2012.

uncomfortably at the world we inherit." Indeed, its ambition was to kick-start "a radically new democratic political movement," one based in participatory rather than representative decision-making. The essay quickly became a founding document of both the emerging student movements and the New Left.

Quite early in the appearance of skepticism regarding United States involvement in Vietnam, in 1965 Tom, Quaker peace activist Staughton Lynd, and Communist Party U.S.A. leader Herbert Aptheker traveled to North Vietnam and Hanoi. The buildup to the U.S.'s eventual full-out participation—at that point mainly via "advisors"—was only just becoming evident, and it was a daring maneuver for citizens, on their own, to not accept what the newspapers reported, but to actually check up on their government's deeds. The trip laid the basis of a primary theme in Tom's life. In 1968 he was one of the main organizers of the anti-war protests outside the Democratic National Convention in Chicago, and six months later the Chicago 8 were indicted on federal charges of conspiracy to inflame violence. Tom was convicted of crossing state lines to incite a riot, but the charges were reversed upon appeal. He went on to found the Indochina Peace Campaign that, from 1972 until the U.S. pullout in 1975, organized protests, and demanded unconditional amnesty for draft dodgers.

I was on a speaking tour in the mid-'90s. Needless to say, I was more than thrilled when Tom and Barbara showed up at my talk on ecopsychology in Los Angeles. My routine was to choose a musician from the community who could improvise an on-the-spot "sound track" for the lecture; I would turn to this person at intervals, and the given task was for her/him to bounce off of my stories using musical expression. The approach had been a wild success at the Prescott College ecopsych gathering in Arizona the year before, where a passionate young singer who sang throughout my presentation brought the house down and we shared a raucous standing ovation. In this case I was directed to a tall Swedish man whose only melodious talent, it turned out too late, was to bang on a chair seat. Afterward, Tom pulled me aside to advise that the talk was great—but the musician . . . well . . . "he had to go."

I agreed heartily, and our post-crush friendship was off to a comical start. What followed was a tour of L.A. with the Williams-Hayden duo, including lunch on the Santa Monica boardwalk amid bathing suits and roller skaters, a peek at the 'hood of his gang friends, an unexpected car breakdown—and superb conversation. What I encountered was a man more multifaceted than I could have imagined or appreciated in the '60s. One might posit that a political animal doesn't need to be or doesn't have time to be reflective—Dan Quail being the best example of what level of intelligence it takes to be successful in Realpolitik; Adlai Stevenson an example of what can happen if one is too much the "egghead." But Tom was swirling with questions and insights, and he wanted to know what I thought. What about this new phenomenon of multiculturalism? What would happen to U.S. society if it truly took hold? How would established religion need to change if it were to embrace ecology? How might one talk to religious leaders to make that happen?

Several years after our time together in Los Angeles, upon flying into the airport in Albuquerque he called to see if he might visit me. And so it was: on the afternoon of Christmas Eve, 2005, Tom drove from Jane Fonda's ranch south of Santa Fe north to Chimayó. We sat for a spell in the Santuario and ate lunch at Rancho de Chimayó, where *sopapillas con miel* reign supreme. My jaw just about spilled the half-chewed delight when he invited me to come to Bolivia—in four weeks. I resisted. It sounded like a preposterous thing to do: the trip was too soon, Bolivia was too far away, it would be too expensive. But Tom gazed at me through those salt-and-pepper eyes. "You *have* to come. After all the dictatorships, they have elected their first indigenous president, a campesino named Evo Morales," he insisted, and then revealing his ever-present awareness that we would not last forever: "Such a thing will never happen again in our lifetimes."

He was right. Bolivia was literally dancing upon its boulevards and dirt paths, people were either crying or singing for joy on street corners, in buses and cafés everyone was feverishly talking politics. Tom stayed for four days to gather information for an article in *The Nation* and then launched off to do interviews in Venezuela, to be followed by his annual jaunt to the L.A. Dodgers fantasy baseball camp in Arizona.

I, on the other hand, was so taken by the spirit of the Bolivian people that I returned—and stayed for the rest of my life.

At a certain point a wrinkle in Tom's and my differing political styles surfaced. Political focus, I believe, is shaped by the Zeitgeist into which we are born, the particular injustice in our midst, and the education that we receive. The wrinkles and labyrinths of our personalities also contribute a great deal to the themes and means of our politics as well—and appear to explain the different paths Tom and I followed.

Tom is the kind of visionary who enacts his ideals for making a better world through concrete acts in society as it exists right now. In the 1970s he and Jane Fonda organized the Campaign for Economic Democracy that, in cahoots with California Governor Jerry Brown, promoted such issues as renters rights and solar energy, and whose most astounding claim to fame was participating in the closure of the Diablo Canyon nuclear power plant in San Luis Obispo, California, via referendum. Despite serving the state legislature under Republican governors for sixteen of his eighteen years in office (twice surviving expulsion hearings propelled by conservatives), he managed to get over 100 progressive measures passed—including achieving equal access to state universities for the disabled, funding for tutors in after-school programs, monies to restore Native sacred springs, requirements for trigger locks on guns, funding for gang-intervention programs, and the largest state park and environmental restoration bond in U.S. history. He also ran as the Democratic candidate for mayor as well as for U.S. Senate.

I cheer such accomplishments, but I am made from a different mold: my work stems from a systemic view of the dysfunction of civilization as a whole and, against the constant onslaught, seeks to preserve the archetypal in the human experience, so rapidly being shredded in this age of capitalist techno-globalization. Too, my sensibility leans more toward the hyper-creative, anarchistic, pre-institutional phase of a social movement; writing/passing legislation and negotiating with government have never been my fortes.

Despite Tom's unsuccessful attempts to convince me that I should join him in a campaign to legalize Bolivia's coca plant for medical use in the U.S., he displayed the wisdom of his long experience in politics: he didn't let disappointment get in the way of our connection. I watched him move like Baryshnikov past the chasm widening between us—and I, with so much more maturity than the flailing tentacles of a mad crush, truly loved him for it.

And the man just kept keepin' on with his commitment. In 2015, at the height of Bernie Sanders' campaign for the Democratic nomination for president, he penned a controversial essay for progressives revealing his support of Hillary Clinton—with hopes that Sanders' effort would swing her to the left. That same year he suffered a mild stroke, but nonetheless showed up at the 2016 Democratic National Convention in Philadelphia as a delegate in support of Clinton's nomination. The Convention was his undoing. He came home to Los Angeles a very ill man.

The morning of October 24th I sleepily padded down to my office in Sucre, Bolivia and opened my email. There I found four red-flagged messages shrieking urgency—from Native American activist Suzan Harjo in D.C., administrator/ecologist Marc Kasky in San Francisco, editor/musician Whitney Smith in Toronto, and non-profit director Lee Cridland in Cochabamba—each passing along a link to an article posted on one media venue or another. Tom had died. Shock gripped my bones, just as the eulogies and accolades poured in. My Goddess! They came from *Huffington Post, New York Times, Scotland Herald, Organized Rage, Aljazeera, The Guardian, Cuba Net,* and on. Los Angeles Mayor Eric Garcetti wrote, "Tom Hayden fought harder for what he believed than just about anyone I have known." Writer/Columbia University professor Trey Ellis said, "As a lifelong believer in the collective, he didn't take credit. He shared. He dedicated his life to good cause after good cause, relentlessly seeking out justice wherever it was lacking."

How lucky we had all been to count him one of our own—and how we, and our movements for justice, miss him.

V. "I'D LIKE TO SAY A FEW WORDS ABOUT THE ENVIRONMENT. AFTER ALL, WHERE WOULD WE BE WITHOUT IT?"

ECOLOGY IN SAN FRANCISCO

If you don't like the news, go out and make some of your own!

—WES "SCOOP" NISKER, "THE LAST NEWS SHOW," KSAN-FM

BY THE 1970S THE San Francisco Bay Area had given New York City a run for its money as the political, cultural, and consciousness Place to Be. Surrounded by ocean and bay, covered in Eucalyptus and Manzanita, burgeoning with tropical and temperate plant life, and just down the foothills from Yosemite National Park and the Sierra Nevada mountains—it was natural that, among the other flowerings going on, the ecology movement would find its most avid escorts in the urban areas cupping both inlet and sea.

The ghosts of John Muir and Ishi haunted the woods of Mount Tamalpais, after all. David Brower was a Berkeley man, lighting a fire under what essentially had been a hiking organization to become the forceful environmental fighting Sierra Club. Under his leadership as president, the San Francisco chapter of the club came to boast one of the national organization's largest and most active memberships. Also, under his guidance, Friends of the Earth, the League of Conservation Voters, and Earth Island Institute were birthed into existence. Meanwhile, architect Zach Stewart launched the River Terminus Expeditions up the Sacramento River so that wannabe and veritable activists could learn firsthand about the watershed of the northern California bioregion, while Marc Kasky took on the then-hippie Ecology Center in North Beach and turned it into a vital hub of environmental awareness and organic muffins.

In 1969 the September issue of *Ramparts* had put out its startling "The Death of the Oceans" essay, by conservation biologist Paul Ehrlich, predicting their demise via pollution and acidification by the year 1979. And there were all those colorful back-to-the-landers with their teepees, Mendocino County communes, organic gardens, compost piles, and Chief Seattle posters . . .

MARC KASKY: THE MADCAP ECOLOGIST
(1944–)

I'd like to say a few words about the environment.
After all, where would we be without it?
—M.K., IMPROVISATIONAL SKIT PERFORMED AT HOTEL
WAWONA, YOSEMITE. HALLOWEEN 1984.

The first year I lived in North Beach with my lover Marc Kasky, he packed up his tent and enough dried food for ten days, and he launched off in his size-thirteen hiking boots to what became a yearly solo hike through the Sierras. That first year, too, he was visited by a hairy spirit in the night. The thing looked like a sort of werewolf-yeti. It appeared at the foot of his sleeping bag, as such creatures have a tendency to do, and crooking its claw in the shape of Little Bo Peep's cane, beckoned Marc to come. It was the dead of night, and the forest was pitch-black. Marc graciously declined, rolled over, and went back to sleep.

I'm not sure if these kinds of visitations were not normal fare for the man. He had, after all, lived a life of wild and hairy ideas. In fact, he had an idea for just about every challenge that lay before him. Consider the

What would happen if everything just . . . stopped? *Positively Fourth Street* mural at Fort Mason Center, San Francisco, 1976. Artists: John Wehrle and John Rampley. Photo credit: Jim Petrillo. Courtesy of John Wehrle.

public TV station he instigated at Franconia College in answer to the school's need to bridge the gap between the insulated student body and the town's working-class community: the communications students made programs about the town and, boasting next-to-nothing funds for a full-time station, set up a camera in the snowy woods through the night when there were no other shows to be had. Or the basketball team he started. Franconia possessed no phys. ed. department, no basketballs, no gymnasium, no outfits, no lanky athletic stars—and so, at the very least, the project was a risk. But it was an ingenious scheme as the town might then get behind its team.

One problem to be hurdled was that the White Mountains of Vermont presented a snow barrier to the other teams that would have to travel north, so they decided to only play, as the saying goes, "away from home." Upon the team's first such bus ride to Hampshire College in Massachusetts, an aghast Marc realized they didn't have a handle. Since basketball courts have a score board that pits "Home" against "Visitors," Marc thought, they could be the Visitors. They actually won that first game—and the national media went feral. *Sports Illustrated*, the *New York Times*, plus newspapers across the country published stories about the Franconia

Visitors, and BINGO! the town—now with its very own TV station and an undefeated basketball team—began to feel very good about its college.

Yes, wild spirits sprouted from the head of Marc Kasky. As a student coordinator of Eugene McCarthy's run for President in 1968, his idea for gaining votes in the all-important New Hampshire primary was not to chuck the campaign's anti-war message down the throats of the voters of Berlin. It was to set up democracy centers where citizens could experience that they were responsible enough, intelligent enough, free enough to debate the issues and come to their own conclusions. The McCarthys were so impressed with this unique approach that they asked Marc to do the same in Grand Island, Nebraska; Eugene, Oregon; and Santa Monica, California. On the night of the primary they invited him to watch the results in their hotel room, and in her memoir *Private Faces, Public Places*, Abigail McCarthy called Marc "a symbol of all that was good in the student involvement in the campaign, all that was good in the new politics, all that was good in the campaign itself."

Later, in the '70s, when he was director of San Francisco's Ecology Center, Marc provided grounding for the churn and swirl of emerging environmental consciousness. The center was on lower Columbus Avenue, below Grant Street, known for its rebel dynamism since the Beat days, and right across from the very symbol of the economic forces that were wreaking corporate havoc upon the Earth: the new pyramid-shaped Transamerica Building.

First thing: in hopes of attracting a few bankers and financial advisors, Marc tore down the burlap wall coverings that hinted at hippiedom and painted the place crisp white. Then he and the staff set up an all-you-can-eat vegetarian restaurant, an eco art gallery, and lunchtime discussions on the city and its quality of life. Sure enough, people from the Financial District poured in. Secretaries. Brokers. Newspaper vendors. Radio commentator Wes "Scoop" Nisker (of "If You Don't Like the News, Go Out and Make Some of Your Own" repute) popped by for coffee. Ponderosa Pine, who for years had trod the sidewalks of San Francisco without shoes, lent his rants on the glories to be had if only the nation could be broken down into self-sustaining bioregions. Stephanie Mills was a regular; she had gained clout when in 1969 she delivered her Mills College valedictorian lecture on the decision not to bear children due to overpopulation. Sierra Club president David Brower made the occasional appearance. And lo and behold for the power of painted white walls, former New York advertising executive Jerry Mander came to discuss his infamous Save the Whales ad campaign.

Architect Zack Stewart's Canessa Gallery sat across the street on Montgomery. Ever the bearded eccentric, Zack enlisted the curious and courageous to join him on a boat trip up the Sacramento River so that the budding environmentalists could get to know what the Bay Area landscape looks like, where the city's water comes from, who is polluting the river, etc.: in essence, to develop a Sense of Place. His River Terminus Expeditions shaped up to be a marine version of the Merry Pranksters' hippie bus. It boasted three houseboats sleeping ten people each for three days. Each boat had a captain and a navigator, but Marc ... well ... he was dubbed Admiral of the whole shebang.

Accompanied by Ecology Center herbal teas and fresh-baked, whole-grain muffins, the All-Species Parade through the streets of the city was launched in 1977. The Rain Dance at the Legion of Honor was spawned to wake up the deities and counter the unforgiving 1976 drought; the ceremony was held on a Friday night, and by Saturday morning (of all rarities in San Francisco), it *snowed*. A block up Columbus, the International Hotel was throwing otherwise homeless, elderly residents into the streets; protest erupted, and the Ecology Center provided childcare for picketers. Then, like some kind of preordained synchronicity, San Francisco's first environmental campaign focused on that concrete behemoth of a building across Columbus with its energy-sucking air conditioners, and its windows that couldn't be opened to let in the Bay's fresh, cool air.

Marc Kasky above Fort Mason Center, 1982. Photo credit: now-defunct San Francisco Food Coop. Courtesy of Marc Kasky.

And since the "straight" drop-ins and non–ecologically minded were confused as to how to live lightly on the land, Marc came up with his how-to-solve-daily-problems-as-if-the-planet-mattered radio show on KPFA-FM called "M.I.N.T." Money Is Not Thrilling. One caller would confess the eco-disastrous temptation to buy a new car, and by the seat of his pants, Marc would advise him to paint the old one, get some new upholstery, add a hood ornament. Another would moan about her gripping desire to own a Kirby vacuum cleaner like the one her neighbor had; Marc would propose sharing machines.

Imagine how life was for me: I lived for seven and a half years with this fount of ingenuity. When I met Marc in 1979, he was director for Fort Mason Center, a World War II army base perched on the edge of the San Francisco Bay, and for 24 years he guided its development from an army base into a people's cultural center. There were non-profit headquarters for the likes of Media Alliance, Magic Theater, and Blue Bear Music School. There were classrooms and museums and performance venues. The Zen Center's Greens restaurant whipped up meals of organic vegetables grown on their Green Gulch ranch in Marin County and, needless to say, served their own baked Tassajara bread. Marc oversaw the building of the 450-seat Cowell Theater; the relocation/restoration of the in-decline eco mural "Positively 4th Street" depicting the reclamation of a defunct freeway off-ramp by plants and animals; and the renovation of the last World War II Liberty Ship, the Jeremiah O'Brian.

When work was finished, the ideas didn't stop. Steeped in the psychological wing of the anti-nuclear movement of the 1980s, I was running an organization called Waking Up in the Nuclear Age. The motivation of WUINA's cadre of mental health professionals was to present lectures on the psychological ramifications of living with the arms race and workshops to help citizens break through the denial and, as psychiatrist Robert Jay Lifton called it, psychic numbing behind the paralysis of the population since the atomic era had begun. We were faced with a U.S. president taunting the opposition with inflammatory phrases like "Evil Empire" and bragging of bold, new weapons systems like Star Wars and Cruise Missiles; the *Bulletin of Atomic Scientists'* Doomsday Clock had been readjusted from its former seven minutes before midnight in 1980 to a hair-trigger three by 1984. Our task was to catalyze a new generation of activists who would plunge into the movement against nuclear proliferation.

After the workshop goers' fear and grief had been excavated and expressed, we would meditate to envision ways to contribute to making a safer world. As far back as 1977, Marc had come up with the Vivatron Bomb, an antidote to the neutron bomb touted by the U.S. government as a military techno-strategy that, upon detonation, would kill all living beings but leave buildings, roads, bridges, vehicles, and airports intact. Marc's notion was to create a bomb that would destroy the buildings, roads, bridges, vehicles, and airports that ecologists were identifying as sources of a lifestyle that was devastating the planet—and leave the people, animals, and plants to thrive anew.

The ways he and I together contributed to making a safer world were to organize protests, march against nearby weapons-research-ing Livermore Laboratory, canvas door-to-door for the Nuclear Freeze, write articles, and do radio interviews. To lend some humor to the effort, we also decided to host a contest toward a citizens' invention of the Vivatron Bomb. *Parade, California Living, Albuquerque Journal,* and *San Francisco Bay Guardian* ran notices for the competition, and letters poured in from all over the United States—five shopping bags of entries stuffed to the brim, to be exact. On the drive to Bolinas where, in a borrowed cottage, we were to read the ideas and determine the winner, I was suddenly struck with the fact that we did not actually *have* the $50,000 prize money we had so frivolously promised. But Marc, of course, had thought all that through: the contest rules stated that the entries had to be not only great ideas for inventions, but also had to have been demonstrated in a major U.S. city. Needless to say, no Vivatron Bomb had yet toppled the Sears Building or set ablaze the New York Thruway—and so we published an article in *California Living* presenting the best of the lot.

This wellspring of ideas was third-generation Russian immigrant: the family surname before hitting Ellis Island had been Kasajovic, which translated to "fur pelt"; his great-grandfather had been a hat maker. The authorities immediately changed it to Kaskowitz; then when, as a Jew, Marc's father set out to play professional baseball, to avoid discrimination he changed it to Kasky. One of Marc's foremost beloveds was the woman who had braved the journey across the Atlantic from Eastern Europe and raised four children alone: Grandmother Rae. From her he learned independence of mind.

His parents were Alice and Dick Kasky. They set about making their home in Stamford, Connecticut, where, upon reaching only the minor leagues, Dick opened a tire store. Marc launched a brief career as what in those days was called a JD (juvenile delinquent)—robbing cars, breaking/entering. Then, suddenly, he made a 180-degree turn-around and became the first in the family to go to college: Connecticut Wesleyan, and later, to Yale for a master's in urban planning. But the times lent themselves more to "drop out/tune in" work than to joining a firm in Hartford. Marc got a job as a community organizer in Jersey City.

His apartment was a third floor walk-up. The Hippie Revolution was in full bloom, although admittedly not that evident in working-class Jersey City, and on his paltry organizer's salary, he had zero cash to spend on fixing up the place. So he gathered a bunch of wooden fruit crates and some enormous slabs of foam rubber, painted them neon orange, and set them in a sort of amphitheater arrangement in the otherwise bare living room.

Imagine Grandmother Rae's visit. Here she had trudged hundreds of miles behind a donkey cart in the dead of winter, braved a harrowing trip across the ocean on a crammed steamer replete with fleas, lice, and the vomit of the seasick, and made her heroic way into a New York City burgeoning with immigrants like herself looking for the same bottom-level jobs. Now at last, *here* was the fruit of her efforts, her grandson who had, by the might of his own intelligence, achieved the American Dream: he had gone to Yale and graduated with a master's degree! The door swung open. Inside: a sweltering walk-up apartment boasting termite-gnawed window sills, chipped linoleum floor—and a (Sears and Roebuck, *not!*) living room set of used cartons and screeching orange foam pads!

Marc's work made an ingenious pivot in the 1990s. A proponent of Richard Grossman's work on the legal "personhood" that bestows the freedoms (read: unimpeded license) corporations use to exploit workers and resources, he and his long-time buddy attorney Alan Caplan cooked up a means to stymie offenders. They launched a series of lawsuits: *Kasky vs. Jolly Green Giant, Kasky vs. Perrier,* and the most infamous, *Kasky vs. Nike Corporation.* The key to each was false advertising. Jolly Green Giant had advertised that its recipe for frozen vegetable dinners was "California style"—yet the product was actually made in Mexico. Perrier had boasted that its water was naturally carbonated underground and bottled at the source—when in fact the spring had dried up years before and the water came out of a tap. Marc and Alan won both cases.

Not once did they request personal remuneration in the settlements. Never short on ideas, Marc requested that Jolly Green Giant donate the money to Second Harvest, a non-profit that distributed to food banks. The Perrier settlement occurred during the riots in Los Angeles, and he proposed—and got—Perrier to supply thousands of water bottles to protestors and looters in the streets!

The Nike case, though—this one thrust him into the limelight of the national financial world, including a five-page feature in *Fortune* called "Nike Code of Conduct," plus stories in the *Wall Street Journal, New York Times, San Francisco Chronicle*, etc. The gist of the suit was that Nike publicized that its workers in Indonesia and Vietnam labored in safe conditions. In reality, according to a report by its own team leaked by a disgruntled worker to the *New York Times*, abuses abounded. Caplan's law firm Bushnell, Caplan and Fielding proved to be too small for the case, and Milberg Weiss of Los Angeles joined up. It went to municipal court, then to appeals court, both of which they lost. In these suits Marc was, of all things, listed as "Private Attorney General" of the State of California so that he could not personally benefit from any gains (a title he regarded as a step down from Admiral of the house boats). His team of lawyers appealed to the State Supreme Court and won. Nike appealed to the U.S. Supreme Court. Amazingly, the decision of *Kasky vs. Nike* went for the plaintiff—and, as a result, millions of dollars went to groups monitoring sweatshop practices around the world. The anti-corporate-globalization movement, of course, was thrilled. Corporations: 0, Visitors: 3.

Marc and I broke up in 1987. A few years later, after much deliberation on the pros and cons of the legal institution of marriage, he and his new love, actress Cat Carr, tied the knot to a full house at the Cowell Theater—with all his former lovers there to give him away. When I visited the Bay Area from my then-home in New Mexico, they always invited me to stay at their house. Marc continues his work to challenge corporate personhood, and each summer he and Cat drive their 1974 Chrysler Commander to the Burning Man celebration in Black Rock, Nevada. There the intrepid Admiral/Attorney General sits—dressed in a blue fake-fur jacket and billowing orange dance pants, eager to share the wisdom of experience with young people at a booth he calls Counsel from an Elder.

Another wild idea . . .

PONDEROSA PINE: SIDEWALK SOLES
(1932-2014)

That's not a new idea, bro. We knew THAAAA-AAAT
like, you know, for-EV-er!
—P.P., *EARTH READ OUT*

Ponderosa Pine was known for the soles of his feet; they had not seen the insides of a pair of shoes since 1968. That year an ecological epiphany struck him as he departed all trappings of the straight life in which his name had been Keith Lampe and morphed into an eco pilgrim named for a tree. Ever since then he had tread the sidewalks of the Haight, the stone paths of Golden Gate Park, and the beaches of Bolinas with neither hide, hair, nor last of footwear.

I got a glimpse of those soles when, fifteen years later, Marc Kasky introduced me to him at Fort Mason Center. They were thick. They were hard. They were the color of the black hole of the universe. Dear reader, we are talking an inch of freshly tarred epidermis contoured by daily deployment to resemble a Vibram sole.

Ponderosa's feet reflected his dedication to the cause. At the other end of his ever-so-lean-from-walking body (he refused to mix his dignity with that of carbon-emitting machines, regularly walking the thirty miles from his home in Bolinas to San Francisco), his mind was devoting its considerable assets to the miserable state of the planet. In her book *Whatever Happened to Ecology?* Stephanie Mills calls him the "grand-daddy of all the bare-knuckles critics of environmentalism," clearly a 1980s moniker from when climate change, ozone depletion, rising seas, dying species, contaminated cities, and ruined ecosystems were not as evident as they are today and even the left-wing intellectuals at *The Nation* thought ecology a bogus concern. Stephanie also calls Ponderosa "a barefoot mendicant chanter and general thorn in the side of people of lesser mettle . . . a guy destined to make us all deeply uncomfortable in our insufficiency of action."

This soleless/soulful pioneer lived so intensely in the Here-and-Now

Pine around 1970 at Marx Meadow in Golden Gate Park. Photo credit and courtesy of James Stark.

that he seemed a man without a past. But in the world of material existence and calculated linear time, Keith Lampe was born in 1932 to Harriet and William Lampe in Wayne, Pennsylvania, the eldest of three
siblings, and he grew up during the Depression. In his early career, he
was both an officer in the U.S. Army during the Korean War and a Par-
is-based reporter for Randolph Hearst's right-wing International News
Service. Upon hearing about the murders of three civil rights workers
in 1964 in Mississippi, though, he chucked his formally sanctioned
career, headed back to the States, and got himself hired by the Student
Nonviolent Coordinating Committee as press agent. Then, in 1966, just
as the Vietnam War was being launched, he burned his discharge papers
and medals on national TV and awoke from his previous life to find
himself on stage in San Francisco's Golden Gate Park, shoeless with his
unkempt beard waving in the ocean wind, speaking to throngs of stoned
hippies about cosmic consciousness, leading group meditations, and
performing improvisational music with drums, lutes, synthesizer, and
belly-dancing women.

The All Species phenomenon took off! Ceremonialist Chris Wells jumped
in and took the event all over the U.S., to Mexico and Sweden. Here,
a gathering dedicated to Turtle Island, the name given to North America
by many Native peoples. Earth Day 1992, Kansas City, Missouri.
Photo credit: Ed Kendrick. Courtesy of Marty Kraft and All Species Project.

Ponderosa was among the first to articulate the importance of an
extremely radical philosophy and politics called bioregionalism. In his
weekly mimeographed publication *Earth Read Out* he spouted its underlying wisdom: for two million years we humans lived in ecological terrains defined by the extent of local watershed and cohesion of flora and
fauna, developing cultures as reflections of the natural world around/
within us. Take, for instance, the obvious differences between traditional
Inuit lifeways and those of the Plains Indians, between the world of
Pacific Islanders and that of the Aymara in the altiplano. The unfortunate
lunge toward expansive survival tactics that has led to imperialism and
finally to economic globalization also created what became the archetypal battle between warring, technological nation-states and in-place,
nature-based cultures. According to Ponderosa, if we are to survive, it is
to this latter state of existence that we must return. Bioregionalism
stands among the various options for breaking down empires and resuscitating archetypal human existence.

As one manifestation of making such a homecoming, Ponderosa—along with his wife Olive Tree—invented the All-Species Day Parade as a dynamic way to build community and consciousness. The first took place in 1978 in San Francisco. Stephanie Mills showed up as a Monarch butterfly. Marc Kasky was there too, dressed as his animal totem, the otter. The eco group Friends of the River arrived with some twenty members dressed as the Tuolumne and Stanislaus Rivers. Fantastic! Scoop Nisker appeared as a primate ancestor, bioregionalists Peter Berg and Judy Goldhaft as forest creatures. Ponderosa came covered in tree bark, twigs, and brush chaotically twisting this way and that.

Another manifestation of Ponderosa's dedication to a return to safe, satisfying, and sustainable living was his stellar political action record:

* In 1965, as a former Army officer during the Korean War, co-founded Veterans and Reservists to End the War in Vietnam;
* 1966, along with other veterans, set fire to discharge papers, service medals, and campaign ribbons on national TV;
* 1966, New York City: protest against Dow Chemical for what he called the company's "obscene manufacture of napalm";
* 1967, Army Induction Center, New York City: during Stop the Draft Week protests, two separate arrests;
* 1968, Hudson River, New York City: civil disobedience to delay the departure of a Navy destroyer to Vietnam;
* 1968, Senate Gallery, Washington, D.C.: arrested for dumping anti-war leaflets on elected officials from balcony above;
* 1968, Pentagon March, Washington, D.C.: arrested with Jerry Rubin, Noam Chomsky, Norman Mailer, Abbie Hoffman, and Stew Albert;
* 1987, World Bank headquarters, New York City: demonstration against funding for a superhighway slated to pass through the endangered Amazon rainforest;
* 2000, White House Rotunda, Washington, D.C.: protest in favor of campaign finance reform—along with climate change activist Bill McKibben, political activist Granny D, etc.

Needless to say, Ponderosa traveled to Chicago in 1968 to protest the

Democratic Party Convention that had given the cold shoulder to the popular anti-war candidate Eugene McCarthy in favor of Old Party machine cog Hubert Humphrey. Here, amid fervent protestors and rampaging police forces, Ponderosa learned that New York City's finest had compiled a dossier detailing his activities on the East Coast and had sent it to their Chicago colleagues. In its forty pages Ponderosa was described as "an especially dangerous leader." The report argued that he advised activists to disobey laws, while he—in typical hippie/yippie fashion—claimed that he had only encouraged people to "Do Your Own Thing."

In 1968 Keith, wife Judy, and daughter Issa made the cross-continental move to Berkeley. Here, perhaps more than ever, amid the glories of the blooming counter culture, he morphed into the activist who would walk the streets barefoot, rename himself "Ponderosa Pine" and—with growing ecological awareness—position his body between "a truck carrying redwood corpses from a nearby tree-slaughter site" and eternity. As humorist Paul Krasner describes the transition: "Hippies became freaks. Negros became blacks. Girls became women. Richard Alpert became Baba Ram Das. High Romney became Wavy Gravy, and his wife became Jahanarah. Yippie organizer Keith Lampe became Ponderosa Pine, and his girlfriend became Olive Tree."

Insisting always on the purity of ideas and actions, Ponderosa fell into the occasional but regular bout of self-righteousness. Or as Stephanie Mills defined that particular stance, making others feel "deeply uncomfortable in their insufficiency of action." To boot, his tone in pointing out said insufficiency was "cranky" and "cantankerous." That's the way Charlene Spretnak put it when she waded into a controversy with "Mr. Pine" that did nothing but let loose said qualities. In May of 1987 she wrote him a letter attempting to inculcate compassion after he had publicly trashed environmentalist David Brower and historian/bioregionalist Kirkpatrick Sale. His complaint was that they (and now Charlene) were mere armchair ecologists/regionalists—"slapstick satirists"—hiding behind foundation grants and typewriters rather than placing their bodies in front of trucks hauling the freshly murdered carcasses of our brothers and sisters, the trees.

Ponderosa published Charlene's correspondence in his newsletter *Deep Bioregional Action-Examiner* and offered up a cranky, cantankerous epistle in response. It included such declarations as "You behave as though you think I *suggested* that David slaughter an indeterminate number of trees to occupy my postal box with junk mail playing on people's fears to suck maximal money from them." In answer to Charlene's contention that his personal put-downs of fellow activists were violent tactics, he wrote: "The violence of *your* tactics is that you've left a long trail of blood behind you by bringing out one two three *four*! books already . . ." Respected feminist Charlene Spretnak had just come out with *Green Politics: The Global Promise* (1984), co-written with physicist Fritjof Capra, the first book about the progressive, neither-left-nor-right Green Party of Germany. He continued his tirade, "I've heard the wide-awake screams of our sisters as the saw rips through their ankles and they tumble to oblivion, Charlene, and I can assure you that you're leading a very violent life."

Plus, the kicker: "I'm grateful to have a copy of that cute photo of us taken at that party in Berkeley. The particular 'party-dress' you're wearing makes you look the demure, ingenuous girl-next-door who has just returned from her junior-year-abroad with a rather good term paper all about environmental politics in Germany."

Nearing retirement in the late 1980s, Ponderosa moved to Chiang Mai, Thailand, where the tropical climate suited him better than that of Bolinas' Pacific coastline and dollars from his Social Security pension went farther towards survival than they would have inside the U.S. I hear tell that his journey to Asia and subsequent return visits heralded the first time since 1968 that he had actually donned a pair of shoes. As the twenty-first century unfolded—particularly after the 2001 Twin Towers attacks and the ensuing Shoe Bomber incident— shoelessness would make passing through airport control faster, but the airlines displayed zero tolerance for the likes of he who now had been reborn and was calling himself Ro-Non-So-Ye. Ro-Non responded to regulations by donning a pair of flip-flops for these transcontinental flights and used the same technique right through his subsequent and final move to the mountains of southern Ecuador.

Here he established the "Double Helix Office in the Global South White House" and relaunched the environmental reporting he had begun so many years before. The former *Earth Read Out* and *Deep Bioregional Action-Examiner* were remade as *A Day in the Life*; its daily accounts— often megabyte-sized, on topics as far afield as the Ebola epidemic, human rights violations, non-ecological education, and climate engineering—were penned, as always, in his emblematic cranky-cantankerous-comedic-flamboyant rant style. Combining the panoramic vista of an informed elder with his bent toward transcendental music and cosmic consciousness, Ro-Non also became something of an eco guru to the *extranjero* community in Ecuador.

But he was not well. Ever since the 1970s when popular thanologist Dr. Elizabeth Kubler-Ross challenged the social taboo against conscious, visible death and dying, we have come to understand that communication about impending death makes its inevitable arrival not any less agonizing or unfathomable—but still somehow easier to bear. Ro-Non gave a great gift to all the folks who loved him when he penned and posted this epistle, sober and yet ever characteristic of the man's originality:

October 31, 2014

Dear Friends and Colleagues,

... I've been severely ill for more than four weeks now. Especially difficult have been frequent episodes of convulsive/spasmodic coughing shaking the inside of my body quite painfully.

My main problem has been my lungs, which constantly fill with phlegm and when added to severe emphysema and asthma cause quite a problem.

I've had two mainstream doctors up here to my mountain retreat but they've been unable to improve my condition.

So Tuesday I asked for a visit from a local shaman whom I've known for a few years now and for whom I have great respect. What he said is quite interesting. Here's one of his most memorable lines: "Too much compassion for plants and animals causes a lung problem." ...

So what I think we should take from this is that a much higher percentage of our current illnesses than we think are psychosomatic (or neurosomatic) rather than simply somatic. For example, we may think we're sick from toxic chemtrail residues when actually we're sick from these plus the neural stress resulting from having to absorb the info that those controlling us are so evil that they perpetrate chemtrails.

Certainly the news of these past four weeks has been more horrendous than that of any similar period I can remember. One of my most aware readers commented a few days ago that "Hell has come to earth."

I've had information sickness several times before but always mildly: two or three days of deep fatigue, then back to okay again. In any case, yesterday morning my housemate came up to my second-floor room just as I was waking and said: "I'm scared. I think you are dying." That same thought had occurred to me just the day before as I wondered how I was going to make it through this at 83. . . .

On the positive side, it's certainly a respectable cause of death: Natural World Hyperconcern (NWH).

And I've already arranged for my death to instigate at least one more really good party. Forty-nine days following it, there'll be a Bardo Party for me at the Bolinas Community Center with excellent live music and potluck food. Yeah, at least my death will have some value. . . .

Power to the Flora,

Keith Lampe, Ro-Non-So-Te, Ponderosa Pine ~ Volunteer

P.S. NYC graffiti a few decades ago: Death Is Nature's Way of Telling You to Slow Down.

VI. THE ROARING INSIDE HER: FEMINISM

A woman needs a man like a fish needs a bicycle.

—FEMINIST AXIOM COINED BY IRINA DUNN, 1970

Women's Strike for Equality, New York City, August 26, 1970.
Photo credit: ©Diana Davies. Courtesy of Diana Davies Papers,
Sophia Smith Collection, Smith College, Northampton, Massachusetts.

ASIDE FROM ALL THE solid sociological, historical, and psychological theories explaining why a movement arises at a particular moment
and not another, perhaps the only believable one consists of one word:
magic. Indeed, beginning in the 1970s, women all over the world were,
in serendipity, gathering together in consciousness-raising groups. The
goal was to share experiences of our psyches/bodies as emblems of sexist society, to uncover the striking universalities—and in the process, to
take control of our lives. The first marches across the Berkeley campus
made little impression on me. Nor did the CR (consciousness-raising)
meeting we attempted in the commune on Vine Street. It was Anne Kent
Rush and Hallie "Mountain Wing" Iglehart Austin who opened my pores
to the necessary tasks at hand.

Even before I read such mindblowers as Kate Millet's *Sexual Politics,*
Germaine Greer's *The Female Eunuch,* and Phyllis Chesler's *Women and
Madness* or delved into the history of the demolition of early wom-
an-originated healing/ritual traditions, their one-liners clinched the
absurdity of dominating women and revealed visions of what should be
or what, before the patriarchy, *was.* Why is the deity touted in today's
religions a man when it is females who enact the definitive creative act
of childbirth? Why is there just one overarching deity and not many as
in indigenous cultures and ancient mythology? And consider this: the
institution of marriage was invented as a way to own and have power
over women. Does the constant threat of rape unconsciously function
to keep women "in their place"? They took away the stars and tried to
divert our distress by giving us diamonds. Is the subjugation of women
a mirror of the oppression of animals and land? Is it because at heart we
are more expressive of nature?

As our minds were pried open from thousands of years of enforced
closure, we began to take action. We demanded equal pay and equal
rights. We marched to legalize abortion and "Take Back the Night" from
rapists, imagined voting for a woman for President, launched wom-
en-owned businesses. We sought out female gynecologists, female Jungian therapists, female architects, female carpenters, female anthropologists, female house painters—all of whom were few and far between.
We bought specula to do our own cervical exams. We became adept at
telling men when they had crossed the line into sexist behavior. Many

women abandoned the male world altogether. We studied prehistory, wrote books, painted canvases, produced what came to be called "women's music," and made our own films. We admired each other, fought with each other, made love to each other.

We became.

Kent, Hallie, and I—along with such stalwarts as Sally Gearhart, Merlin Stone, Barbara Hammer, and Charlene Spretnak—gravitated toward the facet of the movement called "women's spirituality," critiquing world religions that positioned females as foot-washers to Great Men and God, instead reaching into prehistory to create/recreate the rites of female-based sacredness, ancient goddess cults, witchcraft, and pagan herbal medicines. As French visionary Monique Wittig counseled us: "If you cannot remember, invent."

And—ladies, get a grip—who could *not* have experienced instant enlightenment by that first glimpse of a woman in an—oh my Goddess!— all-women rock band, twanging the Man's Machine: *an electric guitar?*

Suzanne Shanbaum, 1970s, then of the Berkeley Women's Music Collective—with electric guitar. Photo credit and courtesy of Irene Young.

SUSAN GRIFFIN:
THE ARDENT INTELLECTUAL
(1943–)

*We are women. We rise from the wave. We are gazelle
and doe, elephant and whale, lilies and roses and peach,
we are air, we are flame, we are oyster and pearl,
we are girls. We are woman and nature.*

—S.G., *WOMAN AND NATURE: THE ROARING INSIDE HER*, 1978

Susan Griffin is a poet, philosopher, playwright, scriptwriter, and champion of The Sensual. Due to a marvelous ability to drape events in irony and comedic insight, she is also a veritable hoot to be around. Early on her writing was associated with a feminist-invented theme: literature springing from everyday female experience such as being a single mother, subjects that were not considered by male critics to be worthy of the paper they were scrawled upon. But when her play *Voices: A Play for Women* was shown on PBS in 1975, she won an Emmy Award. *Woman and Nature: The Roaring Inside Her* came next, in 1978. This was a pioneering prose poem that instigated a feminist interpretation of the relationship of woman and the natural world to patriarchal society; its underlying theme—the connection of female oppression with the exploitation of nature—had not been thought about or discussed before.

It is through this work that Susan became known for the style that she would spend decades developing. She is the mistress of uncommon juxtaposition, reminding us anew that the nature of the human mind is to integrate, to bind together facets and phenomena into the Whole that they in fact make up. Her facile imagination allows her to leap beyond the limits of cause-and-effect logic and reflect how people do in fact experience, think, and make sense of things: as oneiric unfolding.

Each of Susan's subsequent works deepened this approach. In *Pornography and Silence: Culture's Revenge against Nature,* she applied Western culture's identification of woman with nature, coupled with its urge to dominate both, to pornographic literature and imagery. After the

1990 publication of *A Chorus of Stones: The Private Life of War,* she invented the term "social autobiography" to describe the approach taken in this volume, as well as in two subsequent books also combining memoir with history; the expression has since become an accepted category of literature. The next volumes in the trilogy are *What Her Body Thought,* an account of her experience with illness and poverty, and in the wake of 9/11 and the U.S. government's rescinding of civil rights, *Wrestling with the Angel of Democracy,* exploring the psychological qualities necessary to sustain democracy.

During this time she wrote a collection of essays called *The Eros of Everyday Life* and *The Book of the Courtesans.* She also published two volumes of poetry, *Unremembered Country* and *Bending Home;* the script for *Berkeley in the Sixties,* a theatrical piece written in poetry called *Thicket,* and a play to be set to music called *Canto* about massacres in El Salvador.

Susan is a striking woman, her posture presenting both a compassionate sensibility and a sense of purpose. Her blonde (now white) hair often boasts a simple cut with straight bangs, and she possesses a talent for putting together attire that reflects, in her own words, "an understated androgynous style with sudden flares of eccentricity"—like all black covering her body, set off by glasses with brilliant red rims.

She has used this same panache to create a home reflecting her artistic sensibility and love of imagination, filled with mementos of the very themes she has explored in her writing. In the living room a photograph of Sarah Bernhardt performing Camille sits on a bookshelf. Native American art, paintings by her adoptive father Morton Dimondstein, and works by friends adorn the ochre walls. Hand-painted plates from Italy are displayed on a primitive-style cabinet, Moroccan tiles embellish the fireplace, and the French doors invite one to step onto a courtyard shaded by an orange tree.

Most of all, I remember the kitchens in her houses on Hawthorne Terrace and Keeler Avenue. Magical places, these—emanating warmth with their pottery crafted in the 1800s and market baskets bursting with tomatoes and lemons. A heavy wooden table covered by a cloth from the Basque countryside defines the dining area. During a luncheon date, one might imagine that one is in Provence or the American Southwest. Or another century.

To Susan, her house is an art form no different from a poem.

Robert Bly, Yevgeny Yevtushenko, and Griffin, whose poetry appears together in *Love is Like the Lion's Tooth: An Anthology of Love Poems*, 1984. Courtesy of Susan Griffin.

I came to know Susan during the high holy days of the feminist movement. What a time we had, rising up as we did in some gloriously inexplicable way, first in our kitchens, classrooms, and communes with consciousness-raising groups, then erupting into Take-Back-the-Night marches, entry into fields like government, law, medicine, art, construction, fishing, and law enforcement; gynecological self-exams, styles of dress not handed down from fashion designers but all our own; with woman-identified books, magazines, radio shows, films, record albums; and through the union lesbians were forging with the emerging gay men's movement.

It's hard to recall exactly how we met. Her house on Cedar Street had become a hub for women who were coming into their own through the movement, and there activists/artists/writers like Adrienne Rich, Alice Walker, Michelle Cliff, Audre Lord, and Grace Paley passed through for tea, wine, and always good conversation. When I went there, Susan became a model for me; I had never seen someone my age who owned so many books! Plus she had a room of her own: a tiny writing studio framed in windowpanes adorned by the leaves on the neighbors' trees. Then there was the time in 1977 when *Chrysalis* magazine—out of the L.A. branch of the movement—published a chapter of her forthcoming book, *Woman and Nature*. The read was mind-blowing enough to cause a gal to forget all timidity and call someone up.

However it happened that we met, in the years after our first outing—a walk in Berkeley's Tilden Park—we became friends with an affinity so synergistic that we might encounter each other at an anti-nuclear fundraiser or in a Northside café and slip into a laughter that rippled on until our jaws ached.

This bundle of humor, soul, brainpower, and drive began life in Los Angeles in 1943. Her mother Sally Williamson's idea of cooking was often a TV dinner. An alcoholic, twice a week she would cart seven-year-old Susan to bars—mother to go on a bender, daughter to play the pinball machines, sleep on the Naugahyde banquettes, or wait alone and scared in the car. When Sally was drinking at home late into the night, she would sometimes drag her daughter out of bed to level verbal attacks at her.

Susan attributes her familiarity with human dysfunction to this experience, to the constant moving from one family member to the next that resulted from her mother's personal chaos, as well as to the fate of being born just as World War II and the Holocaust were casting their psychic shadows over humanity. She went to live with her father, Walden Griffin, a fireman at the North Hollywood Station. When she was younger he had taken her trout fishing and horseback riding and, as she reached junior high school, to museums. Tragically, while living with him, another shock shook her world: Walden was killed in a car accident.

At this point fate looked kindly upon Susan. She had been babysitting at the home of Gerry and Morton Dimondstein, sometimes staying with them several nights a week. After her father died, they became her legal guardians, and their influence shaped Susan's life. They were bona fide Bohemians—he an artist known for his woodcuts in the tradition of Mexican Realism, she an arts educator. And they were ex-Communists. During the McCarthy years, they had fled to Mexico City, where they hung out in the same circles that Frida Kahlo and Diego Rivera had frequented, and that muralist David Alfaro Siqueiros did at the time they were there.

Susan and friend Roxanne make a stab at sophistication, 1959 or 1960. Courtesy of Susan Griffin.

Susan went on to study at UC Berkeley—where she protested against the House Un-American Activities Committee, picketed Woolworth's, and joined a sit-in at the Sheraton Palace Hotel against racist hiring practices. She worked as a strawberry picker for one scorching summer day so that she could testify to a federal committee on labor about farm worker conditions. Then, after a summer in San Francisco's North Beach neighborhood where the likes of Allen Ginsburg, Lawrence Ferlingetti, and Diane di Prima had downed espresso, written books, and held poetry readings, she transferred across the Bay to complete a B.A. in Creative Writing at San Francisco State. Afterward, she worked at Warren Hinckle's New Left magazine *Ramparts*. She got married, gave birth to her daughter Chloe Andrews (née: Levy), and returned to SF State to complete a master's degree.

Around 1986-87 Susan became ill with a strange, unidentified sickness. Knocked out by exhaustion, muscle aches, and joint pain, she began to spend what would become several years of active affliction, close to or in bed. Other people, particularly women—among them feminists Hallie Iglehart Austin, Phyllis Chesler, Kim Chernin, and Naomi Weisstein— were suffering similar symptoms, and at last, against adamant denial by the medical profession and insurance companies, an alarmed minority of researchers launched investigations to understand this fast-spreading illness. The results of their efforts revealed a host of changes in the bodies of the affected cohort: lowered hypothalamic-pituitary-adrenal axis, brain lesions similar to those found in AIDS and Alzheimer's patients, high levels of protective immunological titers in the blood, and deficiency of the natural killer cells that normally combat viruses. It was speculated that a virus was the culprit, and the disease was termed Chronic Fatigue Immune Dysfunction Syndrome.

During this pained period of Susan's life, I occasionally traveled from New Mexico to the Bay Area and stayed at her house—mingling my work activities with picking up things she needed, cooking, and watching films together on video. Stunningly, her perspective on the tragedy was not just personal, it was global. "In a terrible way, no one who has CFIDS is truly alone," she wrote in *Ms.* magazine. "Sadly, we are all part of this global process. Those who are ill [are] like canaries in the mine—our sickness a signal of the sickness of the planet. An epidemic of breast cancer, the rising rate of lupus, M.S., a plethora of lesser-known disorders of the immune system."

Like a heroine in a mythic tale, despite her infirmity, Susan did not stop participating in life. Postmodernism was just arising as the new interpretation of social reality in computerized mass society. It was hard for me to grasp, living as I was in the more rooted environ of a land-based village struggling to preserve its traditions, but Susan had already digested the essence of the new thinking and begun to critique its assertions in ways that would later be written about by thinkers like Noam Chomsky, Melford Spiro, and Charlene Spretnak. As the illness lost its force and she could concentrate better, ever so emblematic of the feminist axiom "the personal is political," she penned *What Her Body Thought* about the experience.

And she had lovers. "The hope you feel when you are in love is not necessarily for anything in particular," she wrote in *What Her Body Thought*. "Love brings something inside you to life. Perhaps it is just the full dimensionality of your own capacity to feel that returns. In this state you think no impediment can be large enough to interrupt your passion. The feeling spills beyond the object of your love to color the whole world. The mood is not unlike the mood of revolutionaries in the first blush of victory, at the dawn of hope. Anything seems possible." During the early 1980s Susan loved and lived with writer Kim Chernin. In 1989 she fell for *Tikkun* publisher Nan Fink, and they renovated Nan's house—Susan building a light-filled office and bedroom by the back rose garden and Nan using the older front side of the residence.

Needless to say, the humor, soul, brainpower, and drive unfurl still. Susan has finished a novel called *The Ice Dancer's Tale* about an ice skater from California who, with the guidance of a shaman from the Arctic, "creates an ice dance about climate change that transforms the consciousness of anyone who sees it." Her goal for the coming years is to complete an epic poem inspired by the Mississippi River, and, true to her roots in the women's movement, she has begun a nonfiction work about misogyny and the threat of fascism.

LUCY LIPPARD: SOCIAL COLLAGIST
(1937-)

Art must have begun as nature—not as imitation of nature, nor as formalized representation of it, but simply as the perception of relationships between humans and the natural world.
—L.L., *OVERLAY*, 1983

Lucy Lippard sends postcards. By now there must be enough of them—penned in near-illegible scrawl and mailed to the four winds—to fill an exposition at the Brooklyn Museum of Art. Such an exhibit would be emblematic of Lucy's originality. Officially known as an art critic, in fact her roles span from cultural intellectual to street rabble-rouser, from twenty-plus-book author to hands-on curator, from university lecturer to radical political activist. She is a woman so crossover inventive that she has been dubbed not just a bystanding commentator on art—but a "Dada-esque strategist." Or, as she might say, a social collagist.

Aside from her name festooning the masthead of the New York feminist magazine *Heresies*, Lucy became a reality for me in Susan Griffin's living room on Hawthorne Terrace in 1983. Here was her new book, a photographic text—a prose poem, really—revealing the similarities of contemporary women's art with ancient creations of Paleolithic, Neolithic, and indigenous peoples. *Overlay* was about the most relevant piece of research to hit the bookstores I could have imagined. In the women's spirituality wing of the feminist movement, we were focused on unearthing pre-patriarchal times when women were honored and held valued social positions, when the moon as reality/symbol held equal influence as the male-associated sun. We were steeped in the cave paintings of Lascaux, the Venus sculptures, the figurines of matriarchal Catal Huyuk, as well as the circular stone construction at Stonehenge—and now here was evidence of the unconscious mind of the twentieth century reiterating these earlier archetypes in painting, photography, and earth sculpture.

In 1973 Lucy's insights about conceptual art as documented in *Six Years: The Dematerialization of the Art Object from 1966 to 1972* had flung her into the track lighting of the national art scene. Just as her topic was controversial, so was her approach. The book is a photo poem, a bibliography arranged chronologically, between which are inserted fragments of text, interviews, documents, and artworks. Lucy had written five books before: works on Philip Evergood, Dada, Pop Art, and Surrealism, and a collection of her art criticism. By the mid-1970s she was covering such developments as land art, minimalism, systems, anti-form, and feminist art. "Conceptual art, for me," she wrote, "means work in which the idea is paramount and the material form is secondary, lightweight, ephemeral, cheap, unpretentious and/or 'dematerialized.'" Linking changes in American society such as the eruption of the civil rights, women's rights, and anti-Vietnam War movements to their ramifications in artistic

Reminder of Tierra Amarilla Land Grant fight in New Mexico, summer 1998: Lucy's photo of a creative billboard near Tierra Amarilla, which she mailed to me as a postard. Courtesy of Labadie Collection, University of Michigan, Ann Arbor.

Back note on Lucy's photo postcard. Courtesy of Labadie Collection, University of Michigan, Ann Arbor.

expression, her insights offered social context to the task of understanding such otherwise inscrutable artists as Yoko Ono, Robert Barry, Eva Hesse, and Lawrence Weiner.

Meanwhile, Lucy herself was taking to heart a truism of the conceptual art movement: life itself is as much a work of art as a painted canvas or a sculpted chunk of marble. She was plunging into the political movements of the times and has been involved ever since. In a 2006 interview with artist/curator Julie Ault, Lucy wryly recalled, "This was . . . a point in my own life when I couldn't sit down at a table with people without starting an organization." A believer in collaboration whether in art or politics—what she terms "social collage-making"—she was a co-founder of Ad Hoc Women Artists Committee, Political Art Documentation/ Distribution, *Heresies*, Artists Call against U.S. Intervention in Central America, as well as the Women's Slide Registry and two performance-art street troupes.

Lucy was born in 1937 in New York City and raised there as well as in New Orleans, New Haven, and Charlottesville, Virginia—the daughter of Margaret Cross Lippard, an energetic liberal involved in such issues as affordable housing and race relations, and Vernon Lippard, dean of medical schools. The only child of two voracious readers, she decided at an early age that she wanted to be like the people behind the books: a writer. She graduated from Smith College in 1958 and New York University's Institute of Fine Arts with a master's in art history in 1962.

I met this incisive mind when, by happenstance, we both moved to northern New Mexico. She built her tiny eco house in Galisteo in 1993. When I asked her about her vision for such a bold project, she surprised me.

"I built it with no vision whatsoever," she said. "One guy called it 'the shack by the creek.' It has expanded a lot since the original 16' x 24' footprint; there's now a book-and-paper-inundated workroom and a tiny guest room. And the trees I planted have grown. I love the interior—a light-filled room with high ceilings and a sleeping loft. It reminds me of loft living in NYC where, after escaping from East Village tenements in the 1960s, I spent most of my adult life. I'm still off the grid, but I've stopped hauling water now that I finally got on the community system."

The Heretics Collective of *Heresies* magazine, 1977.
Courtesy of Lucy Lippard.

When the house was finished enough to move in, Lucy proceeded to become a member of the partly Hispano, family-oriented desert village. Again boldly, she launched *El Puente de Galisteo*, a newsletter aiming to preserve local identity against the invasively gentrifying forces of economic globalization. Meanwhile, she became a Research Associate at the Museum of Indian Arts and Culture and a member of both the Galisteo Archaeological Sites Protection Act working group and Galisteo's Community Planning Committee and Water Board.

Lucy is a petite, athletic woman, maybe a tad like the roadrunners that speed across the upland desert. Wisps of salt-and-pepper hair fly around her face like ideas leaping into flight, her thick eyebrows add a hint of distinction—and she loves to hike.

One summer day we made a trek under New Mexico's turquoise cathedral of sky to see the petroglyphs in the Galisteo Basin. Dodging red rocks and fissures of erosion, she told me about New York's feminist art movement of the 1970s, a period she described as "one of the most exhilarating ongoing experiences I've ever had, and it changed my life." Aside from working in the *Heresies* collective, she was a founder of the bookstore/gallery Printed Matter. Its purpose was to publish and sell artists' books that would offer "the page as an alternative space," hence lifting art out of the sole domain of educated museumgoers to a wider audience. She was so dedicated to the intention of the project that she refused to include for sale her own "weird little novel" *I See/You Mean* because it didn't fall within the definition of an artist's book. I told her that someone should write her biography, and she shrugged off the prospect with character-istic self-deprecation and humor.

She was always doing that, shrugging off praise. The truth is that, during the years I have known her, she along with partner anthropologist Jim Faris were forever soaring off to give a lecture, receive an award, attend a meeting, or accept an honorary degree. "I'm as hectic as ever. Now we have to go to Australia," she would explain as if the trip were a dreaded burden.

Lucy's Galisteo Fire Department shot, 2001.
Photo credit: Richard Shuff. Courtesy of Lucy Lippard.

But one trip was never a burden. That was the annual jaunt to "sum-mer" in Maine. Lucy has gone to Kennebec Point in Georgetown, Maine every single year of her life. Being the ever-active archivist, she does not just go boating and hiking and read novels like the other "summer peo-ple"; she's become something of a historian of the area as a gift to the generations whose roots are implanted in the seacoast soil.

Her 1997 book *The Lure of the Local: Senses of Place in a Multicentered Society* is a tribute to the paradoxical urge toward having a sense of place while moving from locale to locale in an itinerant society. The book boasts two simultaneously running displays of text plus many illustrations with lengthy captions. The main text consists of a discussion of issues such as historic preservation, mapping, archeology, photography, cultural differences, toxic contamination, and today's public-art movement. Along the top edge of each page runs "the vein of Maine"—Lucy's personal observations about Kennebec Point and how the issues highlighted in the main text play out there. Then, throuout the book, are photographs of place-based art, with captions that relate them to the same issues. The point—and clearly the way she herself integrates the demands on a person who has lived in, come to know, and loved many places—is to be receptive and accountable to the place where one finds one's self.

Speaking of accountability to place, shortly after its publication in 2014 Lucy sent me a copy of *Undermining: A Wild Ride through Land Use, Politics, and Art in the Changing West*. In this essay she uses the same twist of thinking being developed during the days of *Heresies* in which disparate phenomena are linked by history, theme, or place—and thus revealed. The starting point is gravel pits in the U.S. West as a metaphor for the tragedy of what is happening in this portion of the continent. The journey includes Galisteo, Santa Fe, and the Navajo Nation as well as September 11's Ground Zero in New York City, the Nevada nuclear bombing range, and Hoover Dam in Arizona. Each locale is elucidated as a face of contemporary, capitalist-fueled perception of land—what one might call unintentional "art," contrasting with the deliberate land art that poets of imagery are creating to draw attention to the madness of seeing land as inanimate, useful, and disconnected from consequences.

She and I have shared not just place, but time; we both celebrate our birthdays in the spring. Aside from meeting for the occasional goblet of wine at La Fonda Hotel in Santa Fe and the yearly Thanksgiving fests at Sabra Moore's Abiquiú abode, our birthdays bring us together. She was born in 1937, I in 1947—so I look to her for advanced notice of the twists, turns, triumphs, and potholes on the road to aging.

Needless to say, to celebrate, we send postcards.

SABRA MOORE: APRONS AND ART
(1943-)

I grew up with the tinges of historical forces at play
within my own family—racial secrets, violence, war,
labor, sexism and class were background forces that
have motivated me as an artist and activist. . . .

—S.M., LETTER TO CHELLIS GLENDINNING, 2015

Sabra Moore made the same trek from New York to New Mexico as her co-conspirator in the feminist art movement, Lucy Lippard. Specifically, she moved to a desert mesa overlooking Abiquiú where the great (but reluctant) icon of the feminist movement—Georgia O'Keefe—had lived and painted decades earlier. Sabra and her partner, painter Roger Mignon, bought the land in 1989 and made the leap across the continent in 1996, handcrafting their adobe/straw-bale house as if it were a work of art.

I met Sabra at the Española Farmers Market. As director, she cut a striking figure—as tall as a cottonwood tree; boasting beaded earrings dangling to her shoulder bones and long, white-blonde hair with short little bangs across the forehead; nearly hollering in a high-pitched soprano of a voice. In between helping the farmers—the bulk of whom were elderly locals from the various villages of the Española Valley—she sipped Lipton Iced Tea from a metal cup and awaited the welfare recipients who had received vouchers to buy the organic vegetables they normally could not afford. Sabra was rightfully proud of the innovations she had instituted at the market. The voucher system was one of them. Moving from a scorching, rented parking lot to purchasing a grassy field across from Northern New Mexico College was another, then embellishing it with a parachute tent, *horno* oven, and gardens. Perhaps the crowning glory was the annual end-of-summer contest for the biggest pumpkin, chile, apple, ear of corn, squash, etc.—and (the most anticipated award every year) for the *weirdest* vegetable. The contest was followed by a photo of the farmers, which Sabra then made into a postcard. She also displayed photos of the market in a booklet called *A Farming Chapbook,* featuring poems local school children had written about gardens, animals, and insects for the annual poetry contest.

Yes, this Amazon-sized woman was one force of nature. She was also blessed with an innate ability to make you feel at home. She would take out her thermos, pour a spot of Lipton, and invite you to sit under the umbrella to chat about the latest gossip at the market. Where did all this irrepressible creativity come from? Sabra was an artist: a Texas-born/New-York feminist, kick-ass creator of hand-sewn/painted books, wall works, sculptures, and installations.

She was home-birthed in Texarkana, East Texas, second daughter to Louise Christine Moore and Augusta Frank Moore, and grew up in an extended clan of sharecroppers, midwives, healers, quilt makers, railroad engineers, carpetbaggers, loggers, and labor organizers; unionist John L. Lewis was a second cousin. Native Choctaw blood ran through the veins of Grandmother Gladys' side of the family, and one aunt was registered with the Cherokee tribe. Seeing the joy that reading Western novels brought her husband Chester, Gladys taught herself to read by diligently copying the words on a Quaker Oats box and thereafter became an avid bookworm. Sabra herself received a bachelor's degree in 1964, her major the Great Books course at the University of Texas, Austin. She joined the Peace Corps and was sent to Guinea, West Africa, where, as she puts it, "I felt at home, it changed my life. . . . I decided to become an artist." Her subsequent education included the Centre for West African Studies at the University of Birmingham in England, and the Brooklyn Museum Art School.

Proud of her country roots, Sabra's work poses an exploration of women's sensibilities and craft based on the quilt-making traditions of her country grandmothers and the artisan traditions of West Africa. She describes herself as a "literate granddaughter" who translates "the elements of quilt-making (the use of repeated patterns, resonant materials, narrative) into sewn and painted artworks."

A third influence on Sabra's artistry became the feminist art movement in New York City. Despite the swirl of fourteen years at openings of women-oriented galleries and bookstores, all the individual and collective women's art shows, the founding of organizations, and protest actions to end the art world's discrimination against females and people of color, by the time MoMA held its grand reopening on June 14, 1984 after a year of renovations, the vast majority of women and minority artists were still not included in mainstream gallery or museum exhibitions! Where were Louise Nevelson, Faith Ringgold, Alice Neel, Jaune Quick-to-See Smith, Louise Bourgeois? Of the 169 artists featured at the renovated MoMA, less than ten percent were women; all were white.

Feminist artists, curators, critics, and historians in New York City were livid—and thus was born the raucous Women Artists Visibility Event (WAVE) or "Let MOMA Know," timed to coincide with the museum's grand opening. Sabra joined performance artist Betsy Damon and art historian Annie Shaver-Crandell as the event's organizers, and so much enthusiasm erupted that the *Heresies* Heretics Collective, the Feminist Art Institute, and the Women's InterArt Center added support, all working feverishly to pull off a spectacular protest. In the best anarchist fashion no one group held the right to claim officialdom, and instead of using one slogan as the emblem of the protest, all and any slogans were

Roger and Sabra in her hand-built studio in Abiquiú. *A Warhead Doesn't Have a Heart* (2003) stands in the background. The images on the work's panels are faces of Iraqis during the first week of the U.S. invasion. Photo credit and courtesy of Katrina Lencek-Inagaki.

encouraged. Sabra's 2016 book *Openings: A Memoir from the Women's Art Movement, NYC 1970–1990* recounts details of the organizing and the event itself:

There were three demands, that the museum display women's work from their permanent collection, that it feature women in loan exhibitions, and that it establish a policy for acquiring artwork by women. We prepared a two-page alphabetical listing of four hundred prominent women artists from the past decade. This list became an organizing tool for the march. I called Mary Beth Edelson to see if she was coming. She said that no one she knew was coming. I told her about the list. "Is my name on it?" "Yes." She came. We talked about the march in our weekly *Heresies* meeting. Lucy [Lippard] had demonstrated at the Whitney in the seventies; she was coming. "We kept yelling, '*Let us In!*'" Holly Zox was cool to the idea of putting her energies into such a protest. "The museums are elitist." "Yes, but they legitimize culture," I argued. "We need to do this for the issue of fairness and to change how people perceive culture."

On the day of the march, hundreds of women poured into the street in front of the museum wearing yellow sashes emblazoned with names of women artists or bristling with colored show cards. Some of us had met to assemble ribbons that we wore like overgrown suspenders trailing below our knees, defying Virginia Wolf's admonition against wearing medals. We bedecked our ribbons in the images of our collective achievements, usurping the prerogative of the museum to decide which artists were worthy of attention. Some carried signs. Others had printed the names of artists from many countries and women from the past to wear on ribbons across their breasts. Ora [Lerman] appeared wearing a sunbonnet. Patricia Jones held a sign that read "MoMA Doesn't Always Know Best." We hugged. We shouted slogans. "You don't have to have a penis to be a genius!" "MoMA! Where's Mama?"

I had stayed up the night before finishing the *Model MoMA*, a small painted wooden replica of the museum with an opening in the top. I had already trespassed in the model's interior galleries, printing wax transfers of petroglyphs and mirror slogans including "Can MoMA Contain Us?" along its yellow walls. Marchers could write their names on strips of paper and place them inside, becoming symbolically included. Roger

[Mignon] helped me glue the sides, and I constructed a stretcher out of driftwood so we could parade with the *Model MoMA* as the names were added. Ora and Lenora [Champagne] met me to help carry the model, but the driftwood pole broke and the little museum crashed to the sidewalk, spilling its contents. [...] Ora and Lenora helped me push the sides back together and we sat it on the sidewalk on top of a yellow-checkered cloth. It filled with names there.

Some people had read the flier and came prepared with bags of printed names. "Help fill the Model M.O.M.M.A. with names and images of women artists. Make the Model contain us." Others scribbled their names on the cards and narrow strips of paper I had brought. Some stuffed show cards or envelopes lined with names, keeping their promise to friends in other cities to include them. The *Model MoMA* was bulging by the end of the march, unkempt with its heterogeneous offerings, though we couldn't carry it into the museum.

(Sabra Moore, *Openings*, New York, New Village Press, 2016. 109–111)

As she became empowered to express herself with confidence through such solidarity, Sabra also began to open venues for others by curating

W.A.V.E. protest posters pasted on a wall—an art event in itself. New York City, 1984. Photo credit and courtesy of Clarissa Sligh.

large-scale shows. The 1987 Reconstruction Project at the Artist Space Gallery commemorated the four Mayan Codices that survived the Catholic Church's book burning in 1562. Connections Project/Conexus, held at the Museum of Contemporary Hispanic Art in 1987, was a collaboration between 32 women from Brazil and the U.S. She herself has shown her work in New York City, New Mexico, Brazil, and Canada, and her artist's books can be found in numerous museum collections, including the Brooklyn Art Museum and, yes . . . MoMA.

Just as the chile seeds would speckle the fields with new sprouts each spring and photo-postcards would spring from the farmers market in the fall, like clockwork, come November, we New Mexicans would

Lucy and Sabra, March for Women against Trump, New Mexico Roundhouse, Santa Fe, New Mexico, January 21, 2017. Photo credit: ©2017 Sharon Stewart. Courtesy of Sharon Stewart.

trundle out to the Abiquiú mesa to whoop up one hell of a Thanksgiving dinner at Sabra and Roger's. Lucy and anthropologist Jim Faris came. Radio producer Deborah Begel along with woodcrafter Ernesto Ulibarri. Writer/activist Margaret Randall and painter Barbara Byers. Artist May Stevens. Translator Ronald Christ and eco designer Dennis Dollens. One year I brought Taos painter Anita Rodriguez. Another year anthropologists Barbara and Dennis Tedlock showed up.

Sabra's kitchen was a thing to behold. Roger had crafted country cupboards with doors made of screen mesh. One cabinet was an old fruit carton covered with homey ruffled curtains, and a built-in adobe *banco* (bench) in the corner provided space to sit down and chew the fat. An oval table sat smack in the middle of the kitchen festooned with a smattering of second-hand dinner plates, each in its own size, color, and design. And there was the turkey, inescapably emitting its earthen aroma. An ample number of wine bottles was uncorked; we would sit down, toast the day, and pass around serving plates overflowing with stuffing, wild rice, candied yam, tossed salad, string beans, whole-grain bread, cranberry sauce, pumpkin pie, and ice cream—all organic, of course.

This, too, is Sabra's art.

MORGAN ALEXANDER: OUR OWN GERTRUDE STEIN
(1939–2016)

It can take years to find your place, your mission. My place in the world and opportunities led me from one experience to the next and as I look back, I see a pattern: each experience had a place in my life's mission. It was as if I was being directed by some energy other than myself. That is the creative process—just following your nose as best you can; the rest will take care of itself.
—M.A., LETTER TO CHELLIS GLENDINNING, 2015

Morgan: broad of mind, broad of body. Morgan: the lace niceties of female fashion long since hurled into the trash can. Morgan: gray-black tresses flailing in all directions like Medusa's bush, her booming voice crafting bold assertions that either enhance a listener's own ideas or strike terror into the marrow of her bones. Our own Gertrude Stein: irrepressibly clever, wry, persistent architect of vocalized opinions and artistic endeavors that jar stagnant air like claps of thunder.

I must speak of her now in the past tense. She was a documentary photographer and poet. This is not to mention her much-loved mule Mabel, her pursuit along with life partner Kate Mack of beyond-the-expiration-date food via scavenging the trash bin out back of the supermarket, or her dedicated quest for altered states of mind/body through the impossibly trying, warrior-creating Sun Dance of the Lakota Sioux.

I fell in with said warrior in the mid-1990s as she passed through New Mexico on her way home to Ojai, California. She had been to a Sicangu Sun Dance in South Dakota. Author Adele Getty and her husband, Aldous Huxley's nephew Francis Huxley, were hosting British consciousness pioneers Jill Purce and Rupert Sheldrake at their house in Jacona. They insisted Morgan and I would see eye to eye, and thus they sequestered us together in the living room.

They were on target.

I lit up as she shared her poetry book *Vanilla Custard*, as well as one particular poem that had been published in the journal *Floating Island 4*, "Natural Large Puddle," a lyrical replica of instructions for guests she had found tacked onto the wall of a hotel in Chiapas, Mexico:

!Hello to
the friendly here!
We waits for your arrive
with necessary measurements.
Here are some precaucatiuons for your take.

Enjoy all sensation
to take a bath
in the spring water
on our natural large puddle

Please go along the singnalling.

Towels dont only soap ever
and no swallow to the forget.
!Drink Room Bottles Only!

Childrens give adult accompany all ways
in swims
Them importance because
we cannot be sure
you leave you room
if some himself to your satisfy

You drown no hotel response
we find somewhere you body

And tennis call to paddle the porter
No tips in lobby only.

Easy stay to come back
if to prelongs is fine
We care much money.
Checks not but Travelings
The Bank on Sunday. Is
open all week.

Leaving to forget personal belongs
and our dont keys.
Tell friends to message us.
Them too we waits.
Come soon back or front.
    —11 November 1986
    Na Bolom, San Cristóbal de las Casas
    Chiapas, Mexico

Morgan also informed me of her latest wild scheme: what ultimately would become an unpublished poetry/photo book called *Welcome to American Flats*. It featured a carcass of an abandoned cyanide mill in

Nevada that would reveal the lack of human justice and ecological awareness that textures mining history. I was, at the time, deep into the fight
to gain federal support for indigenous miners injured by exposure to
radiation. I invited her to a gathering I was helping to organize south of
Albuquerque at Laguna Pueblo. As she later described it in a letter, "I did
colored slides of Jackpile, the largest open-pit uranium mine in the
world. The road uphill to Laguna Pueblo is paved with low-grade uranium
tailings. Everyone drives or walks on it, and many people living there
have developed cancer from leakage into the water system. I remember
camping with you, [anthropologist] Frances "Fiz" Harwood and [envi-
ronmental-justice activist] Carl Anthony. At one of our crazy campfires,
I accidentally set Carl's pants on fire!"

This descendant of Dadaesque Mind came into the world in Philadelphia,
daughter of stock broker Carlyn Kohn and corporation president Ernest
Alexander, both of German Jewish heritage.

At age four, upon being commanded to eat her watermelon with a knife
and fork, Morgan "knew [she] was in the wrong place"—and from then
on she seemed to know where she was going instead. She preferred the
company of the violets and jack-in-the-pulpits of the forest to that of
country-club golfers. She rode her horse Andy constantly. At the University of Michigan she majored in English Literature, where she met fellow
student Tom Hayden and witnessed the birth of Students for a Democratic Society, and went on to gain a master's degree in Theater. Her
studies were highlighted by the presence of an off-Broadway troupe on
the UM campus. When they left Ann Arbor to return to New York, she
went with them. There she trained with Lee Strasburg and Paul Mann
and worked with the Repertory Theater at Lincoln Center.

Under the direction of actor/director/civil rights activist Ossie Davis,
she also became the only white person in the Theater for the Forgotten,
a program Davis developed to bring plays to prisoners. The troupe traveled to federal and state prisons such as Attica, Auburn, and Bridgeport.
"Prison audiences are so honest," she told me. "If they love you they stand
up and cheer. If not, they boo and scream at you. There were many times
while traveling with three black men that we could not get served
in restaurants."

But then, in 1967 at Lincoln Center, "One short conversation in the dressing room of screen actress Aline MacMahon changed my path in life forever. She said to me: 'You don't want to do this all your life. Look at me, an old woman, still whoring for my next part.' The comment sliced right into my gut. I left the theater soon after that."

Lucky thing, though: the California skies of the 1960s-'70s were bursting like fireworks with new approaches to well-being—from holistic health systems like acupuncture and homeopathy to assorted massages and exercises for releasing chronic tension and improving body alignment. Morgan traveled to the Golden State and became her own firecracker. She studied the subtle Alexander Technique; Jack Painter's more direct methods for manipulating connective tissue, Postural Integration; Gestalt Therapy with Stella Resnick and Jack Rosenberg; plus Ron Kurtz's contemplative form of psychotherapy, Hakomi.

Her creation of art was never far behind. She became a photographer and wrote poetry—with the result of combining images with lyrical readings in far-flung exhibition galleries, from the Universidad de Sonora, México, and San Francisco's Grace Cathedral, to the Los Angeles Center for Photographic Studies and Topanga's Will Geer Shakespeare Theater. Throughout the 1980s El Salvador was wracked by a civil war between the military-led, U.S.-backed government, and a coalition of left-wing guerrilla groups, the Farabundo Martí National Liberation Front. In '88 she photographed there with Medical Aid for El Salvador and the L.A.-based Prosthetics Project that provides artificial body parts to land mine victims. From 1989 to 1994, just as the AIDS epidemic was on the rise, she documented at the Hartford Street Zen Center and Maitri Hospice for People with AIDS in the heart of San Francisco's Castro District. This experience led to "AIDS Affects Us All": an internationally recognized portfolio of intimate photos of gay men in the throes of suffering from the medical effects of the virus.

After two marriages, Morgan finally met the love of her life in the person of Kate Mack, a Russian-speaking, Russophile photographer twelve years her junior who had also attended the university in Ann Arbor. They first laid eyes on each other on a pathway on the Ojai Foundation's forty acres. Kate had just driven cross-country from the likewise educational Omega Institute in upstate New York, and she was to assume a position at Ojai. Morgan was the staff photographer. It was love at first sight.

My initiation into Morgan and Kate's family of two wild women, one mule, dogs and cats, and a bevy of hens occurred in 1996 when, to travel from Malibu up the coast to their Ojai hill retreat, I commandeered an unbeknown-to-me mega-high-end sedan. Upon pulling up the driveway, I encountered no initial greeting; rather, first thing: "Do you know how much this car you are driving flaming... ##!*COSTS!*#?*" Morgan blurted out, pointing to the late-model Mercedes Benz.

"I have no idea. Andrew Beath loaned it to me," I explained. I was staying in Andrew's beach house after speaking at an ecological conference his Earthways Foundation had hosted.

"Well then, I WON'T tell you!" she quipped, and after not seeing each other for a few years, we heartily embraced. And so it was that I had the opportunity to put my feet in the soil of the little farm along the lazy Matilija Creek, meet both Kate and Mabel, catch a gander at aforementioned garbage bin behind the supermarket, and gorge on olives, bread, salmon, and cheese—all one to five days the far side of their expiration dates.

It was my unabashed appreciation for the household comedic sensibility that launched the idea that I should become a member of their heretofore two-person "Bimbles family." The three of us discussed the possibility, and I was rapidly voted in, which bestowed upon me two benefits: 1) that of calling myself by the surname that only we three shared and 2) cascades of laughter.

My christening into the "family" may have also been boosted by the fact that I had invited Ms. Morgan Bimbles to participate in a little caper of my own: the annual Nelson Martinez Christmas Phone Call to the not-clued-in Raymond Bal at Chimayó's El Potrero Trading Post. Nelson Martinez was a popular northern New Mexico singer, native to the village, who had sought fame and fortune in the big city of Albuquerque; forever and a day the trading post had been his favored hometown showcase for CD sales. But one year things went awry. He issued a disc of Christmas songs, and, lo and behold! Raymond found the quality of the recording fatally below the standards of the store; despite decades of unwavering family solidarity and upstanding business relations,

Raymond refused to carry it. A rift between them developed that was never to be bridged.

Now, Raymond is a serious sort who keeps his feelings to himself, and if he knows he is being had by a prank such as this one, he won't let on. I saw the opportunity to play a joke that could go on from one winter holiday season for years to come. And so it was that I asked Morgan to call El Potrero a few weeks before December 25 and request an order of Nelson Martinez Christmas CDs of an unfathomably lofty quantity—like thousands and thousands—the kind of order that, when sold, would allow the store to go on vacation until Easter.

And so was born "Mrs. Banerjee."

Mrs. Banerjee was an entrepreneur from India who, over the years, delved into any number of mega-projects of a religious nature, at which she would highlight the aforementioned CD. For instance, using a clipped Indian accent Mrs. Banerjee would announce to Raymond that she was sponsoring a mass religious gathering in Bangalore, India. It was to be a sort of Hajj pilgrimage to Mecca in miniature, but blending Hindu and Christian traditions. She was expecting some 900,000 of the faithful, and she would be selling the Nelson Martinez CD from 500 strategically located kiosks. Her order: 50,000 copies. Christmas after Christmas, Morgan proved to be an endless wellspring of new situations that promised to attract colossal sums of money to the trading post. Needless to say, in the process Raymond was challenged to feel ridiculous for his clearly faulty business decision to abandon the retailing of his now-alienated compañero's musical endeavor.

But another surprise was in store for us. I made sure to be in El Potrero at the very moment the phone rang, and my report is that, in character, our sober protagonist never cracked a smile or let on that he knew the call from Mrs. B. to be a hoax, his voice alternating between sardonic and naive tones, carrying on as if the whole vignette were for real.

An endless fount of explosive ideas, Morgan moved on to her next project in 2006. She and Kate traveled to Cuba to photograph the murals adorning public walls in Havana's barrios—and so was born "Murales Pintados: Community Projects and Street Art in Havana, Cuba, 2006-2011" that, so far, has shown at the Municipal Administration's Paraiso gallery and the San Alejandro Art Academy, both in Havana; the Gold

Standard in Philadelphia; plus in galleries from Ventura, California to Burlington, Vermont.

In 2014 Morgan learned that she had dermatomyositis and ovarian cancer. True to character and bolstered by Kate's unending compassion, she vowed "to beat this thing." After chemotherapy treatments, surgery, and four more chemo sessions, the cancer went into the hoped-for remission and she declared that she "got off easy." Ten months later, her health went suddenly askew and, as Kate wrote in a letter, she "sailed through brain surgery too" and reiterated that she "got off easy."

On June 13, 2016, with no warning, our dear Morgan collapsed and died in Kate's arms—all in a matter of minutes. The passing of this great spirit—feminist, poet, actress, photographer, Sun Dancer, comic—is a loss we are still reeling from.

Mabel and Morgan, Ojai, 2000. Photo credit and courtesy of Kate Mack.

VII. IRON JOHN: THE MEN'S MOVEMENT

... where a man's wound is, that is where his genius will be.

—ROBERT BLY, *IRON JOHN: A BOOK ABOUT MEN,* 1990

Men drumming at a Men's Leadership Alliance conference in the 1990s. Courtesy of Jason Geoffrion, Men's Leadership Alliance.

THE MEN'S MOVEMENT AROSE in the 1980s, some say, as a sincere response to feminism. Men, after all, were the rapists, wife beaters, and war generals—and women had been excruciatingly vocal about this. For these observers the men's effort began as an inquiry into the question "Why?" and an attempt to socialize out of such behaviors. Classes to teach women how to defend themselves against attack, attempts at rehabilitation of offenders, and serious soul-searching were among the practices of the approach.

For others, the movement came about to understand and support men in a time of rampant technological expansion, increasing social fragmentation, and changing gender roles. A true-to-form expression of psychological wisdom popular at the time, this wing of the men's movement revealed that men were not in fact the standard of what it meant to be human, as society projected and so many women believed; but rather they too had been terribly wounded by child-rearing practices/excesses stressing suppression of feelings, harshly constricting gender roles, and the competitiveness inculcated in both sports and military training. Some even proposed, as did public policy investigator Clifford Cobb, that men who have been socialized into contemporary mass techno-societies may be the most estranged souls on the planet today.

If there was one book that lay the ground for what became a vibrant and far-reaching social movement in the 1990s, it was Robert Bly's *Iron John: A Book about Men*. In it he blends Brothers Grimm fairy tales and archetype-based poetry with sociological and historical knowledge to analyze the sources of frustration, defeat, and rage so often found in the modern man. He traces radical distortions of men's roles to changing work structures during the industrial revolution, the resulting break between father and son, estrangement from the natural world, and the loss of initiation rites into manhood—and thus solidarity among men. The book lay the ground for what became the mythopoetic men's movement, and it struck a resonant chord: it was on the *New York Times* Best Seller list for sixty-two weeks.

The simultaneous uprising that arose fostered men's support groups, drumming circles, ecological practices, health-awareness education, and recovery of an archetypal sense of fatherhood with an emphasis on the healing brought about by renewed camaraderie among men. Enthusiasts looked to the knowledge of leaders, healers, and wisdom keepers of ancient cultures, such as Malidoma Somé of the African Dagara people, while many, like Michael Mead and Bly, researched and practiced the rites and rituals of their own cultural roots—Mead, those of Ireland; Bly, of Norway.

The consequence was a bold redefinition of what it means to be a man.

SHEPHERD BLISS: RETURN TO THE ROOTS
(1944–)

Mythopoeisis means re-mythologizing. . . . [It appears]
at times of cultural chaos such as we have now. . . .
Mythopoetic images arise when you break through
and articulate new images.

—S.B., "INTERVIEW WITH SHEPHERD BLISS," *MENWEB*

At a meeting of anti-nuclear activists in 1982, Shepherd was a theatrical sight to behold. He was writhing across the nubby fibers of a carpet, intently imitating moves of the symbolic larvae we were inviting to inhabit our bodies. He flipped awkwardly over—*CLUNK!*—arranging the act so that his arms clung stiffly to his torso; all the while the surrounding circle of observers to this enactment were shrieking with merriment. They had, after all, just determined that we humans must morph from the psychological straitjackets proffered by the nuclear arms race into newly birthed beings capable of making and maintaining peace. In the 1980s, we were all awakening chrysalises; Shepherd and I shared that moment during the heyday of the nuclear freeze movement, and it became both symbol and guide for our friendship.

To me, it was also a symbol for Shepherd himself.

Proud, decisive, scholarly, and devoted to his unfolding as a contributor to life's well-being, he is a man who stands with military spine. His snowy hair, moustache, and beard give evidence to a lengthy history— spanning from the Southern army family that Fort Bliss, Texas was named for, to subsequent military service, and on through to his leadership in the men's movement and his reclamation of an Earth-friendly heritage as an organic farmer in the berry-producing marshlands of Sebastopol, California.

Plus all the writhing explorations and winged offerings in between.

Shepherd was born one year before World War II's atomic finale. His father, Walter Shepherd Bliss, was a captain in the U.S. Air Force; he would call each of the five children by their numerical place in the birth order—"Number One, Front and Center!" for Shepherd—and each child would have to answer "Yes, Sir!" and march in formation around the yard.

His mother, Alice Miller Bliss, was a Midwestern farmer's daughter and homemaker. She was compliant and caring; to Shepherd's mind, the stronger of the two. He spent his first years on military bases in Florida, North Carolina, Texas, Nebraska, Kansas, New Jersey, Illinois, etc., the family changing location every three years. In an unpublished essay entitled "The Making of an American Radical," Shepherd writes of arriving at a new base: "When you go to school, one of the boys comes up to the new boy in town and says, 'Wanna fight?' The others gather around, shouting 'Fight! Fight!' There is only one correct answer to the question, or one is considered to be a coward."

This hectic and upsetting period was broken by two life-changing moves, the first being to Panama. The experience of living in a different culture marked Shepherd in two crucial ways: he learned about the existence of other traditions of thinking, and he learned about the healing quality of the natural world, in this case of the jungle, with its abundance of wild animals. A second revelation came when, due to a cancer operation his mother went through when Shepherd was a young teen, he was sent to his Uncle Dale's Iowa farm where he lived among cows, pigs, and chickens, with no electricity, an outhouse, a windmill, and a woodstove. A formative event in terms of what it might mean to be a man happened the morning of Shepherd's first stab at maneuvering the tractor by himself: he proceeded to veer smack into the chicken coop, its wooden boards crackling like toothpicks and crashing to the ground. As Shepherd writes in "The Making of an American Radical," "My father would have killed me." But Uncle Dale just doubled over in laughter.

From 1962 to 1966 the Bliss son enrolled in college at the University of Kansas, treading in his father's footsteps by taking ROTC and going to boot camp at Fort Riley, where the famous fighting force the 1st Division was housed. With the goal of becoming a general like his forbearers, he signed up to go to Vietnam. But, as John Lennon sang, "Life is what happens to you while you're busy making other plans." At U.K. Shepherd was affected by three men who offered a glimpse of masculinity distinct from that which his father was modeling. One was Martin Luther King, Jr. Shepherd had been invited by his girlfriend to attend a Methodist Student Movement conference. The keynote lecturer was King. Two other speakers came to Kansas as well: poets Allen Ginsberg and Robert Bly.

Awake dear sleeper!
Enjoy the ebbing darkness,
before the morning light appears.
Praise the night.

Arise slowly!
Don't charge up the mountain yet.
Stay down in the valley.
Night is for soul-making.

What followed the presentations of the three mentors was what Shepherd understood at the time to be a nervous breakdown, but what today might be dubbed a spiritual emergency. He realized that he would prefer to be like *these* men—one a minister of the sacred through the pursuit of social justice, the other two radical poet-philosophers. He took on a double major in subjects that grated against the norm of the values that had reigned in the Bliss household: communications and human relations. He graduated cum laude. That same year the U.S. Army commissioned Shepherd a Second Lieutenant, destination: Vietnam. He resigned, and his father disowned him.

Guided only by seat-of-the-pants intuition and the inspiration acquired from meeting Martin Luther King, Robert Bly, and Allen Ginsberg, Shepherd took a giant leap into the unknown. He bucked all family expectation and enrolled at divinity school at the University of Chicago, where he received a master's in theology, then a doctorate in ministry—with emphasis on poetry, spirituality, and education à la Brazilian philosopher Paulo Freire. Post-graduate work included mentorships with Eric Fromm, Paul Goodman, Ira Progoff, and Harry Lasker. He also engaged in activism—joining the Chicago Area Draft Resisters and going to jail during the 1968 protests at the Democratic National Convention.

Shepherd had thrust himself into a process to become who *he* wanted to be.

Birth is bloody,
Something gets torn.
Go ahead—howl, sob,
Release your sound.

Since then he has ministered to various churches, including the Washington Square Methodist Church in Greenwich Village, where he found himself in a hotbed of radicalism and enjoyed a second meeting with Allen Ginsberg. He also went to Chile, studying with Paulo Freire himself. He assumed he would live there for the rest of his life—but the fascist military ousted progressive President Salvador Allende in 1973, and among those tortured or disappeared were both his fiancé and his best friend Frank Teruggi.

After fleeing for his life, Shepherd directed the Harvard/Radcliffe Education for Action program. He also taught at John F. Kennedy University, the Dominican University of California, Sonoma State University, University of Hawaii, and at the University of Denver Graduate School of Professional Psychology. His writing has been published in dozens of journals and newspapers—*Boston Phoenix* and *San Francisco Bay Guardian; Utne Reader, Poetry Flash,* and *Farm Bureau News; Huffington Post, USA Today, Santiago Times,* and *Counterpunch.* Plus in some twenty anthologies like *Veterans of War, Veterans of Peace* and *To Be a Man: In Search of the Deep Masculine.* He has delivered uncountable keynote addresses at symposia such as the 8th Annual European Congress of Humanistic Psychology and the Redwood Men's Center Conference on New Directions in Male Psychology. All along, his passion has been the application of depth psychology to social issues such as war-making and ecological destruction, as well as to changing outlooks on male and female identities in technological society.

Shepherd's entry into what he unwaveringly labels *not* the "men's move-ment" but "men's work" was decisive—for him personally and for the movement as a whole. He claims the change was catalyzed by the teach-ings of mentors like Bly, Michael Mead, and James Hillman. I remember waiting outside an auditorium in Santa Fe, New Mexico, alongside his lover Chicana *curandera* Elena Ávila—we, the only women within sight—as hundreds of men held a symposium inside. We waited a long time, perhaps an hour and a half, all the while chatting about the men's effort to confront difficult issues and reinvent themselves. Finally they poured down the stone steps, and Shepherd emerged, a mentor now himself, surrounded by young and old men in vibrant discussion.

A fervent dialogue was occurring at the time within feminism, giving voice to the vagaries of our situation as oppressed beings through what we called the women's spirituality movement. Via history books and depth psychology, we had found the archetype of the Goddess and a diver-sity of female templates taken from Greek mythology à la Esther Harding and Jean Shinoda Bolen. And so it was among men, too. Attraction to Warrior, King, and Hero archetypes arose as men attempted to reclaim a manhood that was neither domesticated nor repressed.

But Shepherd, with his own extensive background in the realm he called "mythopoetic," saw the issue differently. In a 1995 interview with Bert Hoff of *Menweb*, he distinguished between these popular archetypes he determined harkened back to a more juvenile developmental stage from those he hoped the movement would embrace. "Warrior work is young man's work," the former Second Lieutenant averred. "Some men get stuck there.... As you know, I'm not into this Warrior stuff. Men who are drawn into it need to mature. ... What I associate with the King archetype is ruling, commanding, dominating. I associate generativity with someone who's beyond the King, beyond the Hero.... People came to America to get away from kings. I don't want kings! I want peers, equals, democrats. I want strong men. Powerful men. Men who do good for the community.... Let's go beyond monarchism and feudalism."

And the Hero? "The Hero comes at an early stage in human develop-ment. And it comes early in a man's life. The teenage years, the early twenties, the thirties. We need to be, both individually and in the culture, in a post-heroic time. The mature Trickster is interesting because he works on behalf of the community as a whole. The genuine Elder. The genuine Crone for a woman. The Elder has mastery but he tends to evoke it in a different way."

Shepherd boldly discusses what he terms "the failure of the men's movement" due to its fixation on immature archetypes. "The media picked up these images [the Warrior and the King] and ridiculed us . . . [and] we never dealt with those images and their limitations in a clear way." His prescription? To link up with the environmental movement and its generative Trickster/Green Man figure. To open to movements against racism and in support of land-based/indigenous cultures with their proposals of the diversity, multiculturalism, and multiplicity that mythopoeia suggests.

Shepherd's approach to men's work also mirrored the feminist principle that the personal is political. He champions support groups; no matter what movement he is part of, he leaves behind an abundance of networks of people who have shared their deepest terrors and their wildest imaginings of possibility. He also tends toward the excavation of those issues that others would rather ignore. One example is his bold conversion of the men's movement from a sometimes-guilt-ridden reaction to feminism into a soul-searching exploration of the ways in which men too have been violated. Another is his drive to highlight the wounds of returning soldiers and veterans of not just his generation's war, but also previous and subsequent conflicts: World War II, the Korean War, and the "War on Terror" in Afghanistan and Iraq.

I recall a presentation he gave in the late 1980s. First he drew attention to the ongoing psychological plight of Vietnam veterans. Then, after speaking of the burden of post-traumatic stress disorder that so many have carried since the 1960s and '70s, in typical fashion—for Trickster Shepherd likes to share the microphone—he asked a vet to disclose what hurt him most from his war experience. The answer was a bombshell. The chosen invitee was former U.S. Army Sergeant and Green Beret medic Ray Gatchalian, at that time a captain of the firefighters in Oakland. Clenching his throat to hold back sobs, the clear-eyed Filipino American revealed the deepest ache he still bore. Even worse for Ray than engaging in deadly combat was his homecoming. Upon arrival at

Alameda Naval Base Station, the iron ship carrying hundreds of returning soldiers pulled up to the dock, but instead of a glorious greeting from crowds of U.S. citizens as he had seen in newsreels of World War II, the returning soldiers were confronted by jeering anti-war activists.

My response gripped my throat as well. I had been an anti-war activist, never hostile to the soldiers myself, but certainly neglectful of them. Listening to Ray, I was suddenly overcome by an instinct to jump onto the stage and cry out, "I'm an anti-Vietnam protester and my pain is not giving you the gratitude you deserved. Please, *please* forgive me. I beg you . . . Your courage! Your stamina! The risks! . . . Soldier! . . . *WELCOME HOME!*" As I sat contemplating doing this, I knew that Shepherd would welcome a spontaneous act. *I knew it!*—and yet I had not the courage to break from my passive seat in the audience and offer this gift to Ray. Years later, thinking a welcome home could never come too late, I asked Shepherd how to contact Ray. He told me that, true to the way he lived, he had died during a 2003 mission to shoot a film about street children when the truck in which he was riding careened into a ravine in Chile.

Shepherd's brilliance as a facilitator shined that day. Very much in the background of what was essentially his forum, he created a shared space for Ray to expiate the anguish that lay fixed in his psyche, for the audience to know what had to have been a common experience for the soldiers, and for me to allow my psyche to imagine a healing act—and admit the icy clench of my fear.

Recall your beginning!
Mine was a thick jungle
of crawling about
like a boa constrictor.

Three-clawed sloths
hanging from trees.
Let your panther
roar out in delight.

Shepherd's own healing from growing up inside the strictures of a military family and serving in the army took a leap forward by his 1992 purchase of a farm in the marshlands of Sonoma County. There, amid redwoods, cedar, badgers, coyotes, bobcats, owl, and wildflowers, he took as his guides Helen and Scott Nearing, Wendell Berry, and Michael Pollan, as well as permaculture and the Findhorn Foundation in Scotland. Since then he has created a family-sized endeavor growing boysenberries, apples, raspberries, and plums. He named his little haven Kokopelli Farm for the mythic character of the Pueblo peoples of the American Southwest: the humpbacked flutist, Great Fertilizer, and Wounded Healer.

The farm has become the backdrop to a multiplicity of projects that Shepherd believes fulfill Kokopelli's mission: tours for school children and environmental organizations, activism in watershed groups like the Grange, Village Building Convergence, and Sustainable Sebastopol; founding the Sebastopol Peaceful Air Effort, and mentoring interns through hands-on practice with organic farming. He manages to carve out time to write essays in print media as well as in anthologies like *Ecotherapy: Healing with Nature in Mind* and *Sustainability: Radical Solutions Inspiring Hope.* And he hosts a weekly radio program called "A Better World is Possible." The goal of it all, as he has written in the Kokopelli flyer, is "to farm with nature in mind, rather than against nature."

But the true centerpiece of the farm's offerings springs from Shepherd's dedication to the idea that human-scale farms can be healing

Shepherd and best friend Winnie, 2015.
Photo credit and courtesy of Ernie Carpenter.

places. Based on Stephanie Westlund's *Field Exercises: How Veterans Are Healing Themselves through Farming and Outdoor Activities,* this translates into Shepherd's invitation to war veterans to visit the farm, commune with the chickens, taste the apples, and put their hands in the soil. Once a precious reconciliation occurred at the farm for one homeless, divorced Vietnam vet when his distraught daughter invited both him and her mother to Sebastopol so they could talk honestly with each other. In the serenity of Kokopelli, the tattered family reunited in compassion—with Shepherd pulling weeds in the background.

VIII. THE NEW PARADIGM

Why, sometimes I've believed as many as six impossible things before breakfast.

—LEWIS CARROLL, *ALICE IN WONDERLAND*, 1865

THE NEW PARADIGM IS what theoretical physicist Fritjof Capra dubbed the conversation among quantum physics, holistic biology, ecology, natural medicines, depth psychology, and mystical traditions that began to take shape in the 1970s. From all spheres emerged ideas that crashed like laser rays from a wizard's fingertip through the hyper-categorical principles of Kantian/Cartesian/Lockean thinking.

Consider, for instance, that matter is not an inert solid; it is energy cloaked in ever-changing forms. Mull over this: humans do not reside at the summit of a pyramid of life and Manifest Destiny is but a narcissist fantasy invented to restore lost self-esteem; rather, we are interconnected with all that exists, and—bottom line—all that exists is a miracle and a mystery. Then wrap your mind around the notion that domination over nature has never been the right of humans; try on instead that our role is to participate with all creatures in the miracle. According to Haudenosaunee statesman Leon Shenandoah, the human task is distinct from that of other animals, each of whom is given a special role; ours is to praise Creation. Consider too that mind, body, and spirit are not facets of being to be addressed separately; they are one and the same. The human definition of truth is not absolute; it is relative to upbringing, culture, experience, perspective, or the position from which one views. Reality is ever flowing and ever shifting; change is the basis of existence. From the spin of atoms to the interchanges among beings in a forest, this mystery we call life is, above all, relational.

Max Planck. Albert Einstein. Niels Bohr. Werner Heisenberg. Richard Feynman. Their original perspectives on matter and energy began to pop up in all arenas—psychology, art, literature, television, philosophy, the news. In 2012 Bolivian film critic Pedro Susz proposed in his trail-blazing *Para una filosofía de la insubordinación* that such a way of thinking/being might also be applied to social-change movements. It was a new idea for me, but brilliantly Susz does not tell the reader what that might actually look like. In a review of his book for *Le Monde Diplomatique* (and later in English in *Counterpunch*), I stumbled about trying to imagine such a transfer.

How might we change the current obsession with time? Like a Tibetan Buddhist with her demons and deities, meditate on the forces of destruction, the quality of courage, and proud rebels of the past? Instead of shopping or aimlessly surfing the web, get together with our comrades to *make* history? Like a Luddite with his hammer, sever/ scramble the sources of operation of the media, their satellite dishes, wireless antennas, and computer programs? Re-take art/craft via the traditions/visions of artists and land-based people? Participate in Slow Food and Slow Money? What would Slow Media look like? Slow Technology? . . .

And what of the usurpation of space by the forces of Power? Might we re-dream dignity via the reuniting of mind with body, of human with nature? Launch movements without solo leaders, but with everyone equal and participating? Reflecting the Mariposa Effect, acknowledge that each radical provocation and each creation of sanctuary ricochets to all, thereby multiplying actions like springtime waterfalls? Inspired by India's Salt Marchers and today's cyber-whistleblowers, reject the construction of destructive public works like giant dams, oil pipelines, industrial-size mines, and towers spreading electromagnetic radiation? Join indigenous and secession movements seeking human-scale self-determination? Reclaim places "owned" by Power–farms, buildings, parks, factories, websites, ideas, interpretation—as do the hacienda-claimers in Brazil, the squatters of London, neighbors creating community gardens, hacker-journalists divulging Power's manipulations? . . .

Perhaps the task would require the perception of a shaman balanced between the nature of the cosmos and the laws of this world? Perhaps the result would be a politics like that of the Zapatistas–with its phenomenological confrontation in every moment (Now) in every place (Here)? With its vision of Mexico as a net of horizontal communities and its reconstruction of ancient/horizontal modes of self-government in *caracoles* ("snail shells")? With its dedication to land-based sustainability and celebration of the purity of a "future primitive"? With its Buddhist-like mindfulness and patience?

I am reminded of a conversation I had with a Keres man from Laguna Pueblo/New Mexico who had been elected his village's representative to the tribal council. Sitting on low-slung lawn chairs beneath an August full moon, Stan Lucero told me that his was the only village in the pueblo still not using rational discussion; rather the elders consulted the spirits to determine how to vote. His job was merely to attend the council meeting to register the choice. I was brimming with envy when he turned to me. "You are fortunate," he said. "I am bound by tradition. *You get to create the new ways.*"

Jungian therapist Jean Shinoda Bolen wades into these same unknown waters, proposing in *The Millionth Circle*: "A proliferation of circles with a spiritual center becomes a worldwide healing force by bringing feminine values of relationship, nurturing and interdependency into a global culture in which hierarchy, conflict and competition, power over others and exploitation of the earth's resources are dominant values."

Silent Kolo – Circle Dance from Grebaštica.
Photo credit: ™Vidoslav Bagur, ©Ministry of Culture of the Republic
of Croatia, 2008, with the permission of UNESCO.

"Playing Children," Federico Oliva (Spain, late 19th century).
Public Domain.

"Dancing Secotan Indians in North Carolina," John White, 1585,
British Museum. Public Domain.

FRITJOF CAPRA: THE TAO OF ECOLOGY
(1939-)

Quantum theory thus reveals a basic oneness of the universe. . . . As we penetrate into matter, nature does not show us any isolated "building blocks," but rather appears as a complicated web of relations between the various parts of the whole.

—F.C., *THE TAO OF PHYSICS*, 1975

Fritjof Capra is the perfect scientist. Approaching the world in a state of wonder, he is as curious as a fox squirrel. He knows the field of theoretical physics like the map of his palm and wants passionately to discover connections and patterns in an effort to make sense of the world. Plus, he's an intellectual giant whose thinking is sculpted not by egoism, but by curiosity.

Fritjof made the fateful move from London to Berkeley in 1975, arriving at the high point of the women's spirituality movement. Author Charlene Spretnak first told me that his comparison of the themes defining quantum physics with the ineffable wisdom of Asian philosophies offered wide-ranging implications for our efforts to create a better world. Following up on the innate intelligence that exploded via knowing by intuition during the 1960s, the '70s became a time of digging deeper into what had previously been but a smattering of hunches. Many of us began to question if the long-touted dichotomies that define Western thinking were not dysfunctional at their core and would not be better replaced by a renewed integration of their many seemingly contradictory phenomena. I could not help but note that fellow feminist Charlene was enthusiastic about this new person in the community, but swallowed up as I was in the feminist movement, I did not look into his work. (Indeed Charlene went on to co-author *Green Politics* with Fritjof; seemingly far afield from his scientific research, it enthusiastically describes the rise of the European Green Party with its integrated weave of feminist, anti-nuclear, and pro-justice/equality themes.)

Little did I know at the time that in the years to come this Fritjof Capra would become a force in my own life as well.

Upon meeting him, the first thing one may notice is the Austrian accent that textures his every word. He is tall with curly hair, a beak-like nose, and the formal manner of a Germanic diplomat. And yet, also immediately evident is an endearing vulnerability that manages to coexist with an inner force in pursuit of any cue that might propel humanity forward toward a coherent—and more accurate—grasp of reality. The "New Paradigm" was Fritjof's well-researched gathering of parallel developments in physics, medicine, social relations, psychology and psychiatry, economics, food production, etc. The term comes from the Greek *paradeigma*, or pattern. In his first book, *The Tao of Physics*, Fritjof defines paradigm as "the totality of thoughts, perceptions, and values that forms a particular vision of reality, a vision that is the basis of the way a society organizes itself." All of the above-mentioned disciplines were engaged in a simultaneous breaking away from the Newtonian/Cartesian insistence on the rigidity of mechanistic projections and the fragmentation proffered by linear thinking; all were moving toward a shape-shifting, relational vision in which each facet is neither cause nor effect; rather, all components work interdependently toward the well-being of the whole. As in a mandalic chant. Or a hologram.

In *Uncommon Wisdom*, Fritjof tells the story of his fifteen-year exploration to bring together the emerging assumptions and practices. This trek into unknown terrain ferried him from the latest developments in physics to parallel realizations in fields he had previously been unfamiliar with. He read extensively, of course. But more importantly, he pursued conversations with explorers outside his domain—Gregory Bateson, Stan Grof, R.D. Laing, Charlene, Hazel Henderson, the Simontons, and Indira Gandhi among them. And, to even better understand, he pursued experiences ranging from holistic health practices like acupuncture and meditation to the shamanist breathing technique known as the Grof Method.

His personal account to gain such knowledge reads like a detective novel. Page after page, we go through the same uncertainties and amazements that Fritjof did; we penetrate into the insights of each pioneer,

Fritjof discusses holistic ideas and applications with economist Hazel Henderson, 1982. Henderson's *The Politics of the Solar Age* had just come out. Courtesy of Hazel Henderson.

just as we become more and more admiring of the unreserved honesty of the author.

The immediate result of this journey was *The Turning Point*, Fritjof's masterful account of holistic changes in modes of living, healing, and dying that were congealing into a general philosophy informed by ecology, feminism, Asian mysticism, shamanism, systems thinking, and holistic reworking of the sciences—all of which considered together place one smack dab in the swirl of the mind-bending mysteries of life and the universe, all of which suggest that reality can*not* be described with mere language.

Who is this remarkable explorer? Fritjof was born in Vienna in 1939, one year after the country had been annexed into Nazi Germany, half of all residing Jews had emigrated, and World War II was erupting at the speed of light. His father was a lawyer, his mother a writer—and Fritjof grew up amid conversations about art and philosophy. To escape the day-to-day grasp of the regime, the family moved to the countryside in southern Austria. Fritjof was four years old, and for eight years—his formative period—the family stayed hidden from view while creating their own little world. They lived with Fritjof's grandmother in what became a communal refuge. Here the growing boy experienced a natural matriarchy that would affect what later became, among many men, an unusual sensibility and ability to champion the principles of feminism. He writes in *Uncommon Wisdom*:

> Our household consisted of the extended family—my grandmother, my parents, two aunts and uncles, and seven children—plus several other children and adults who were refugees from the war.... This large family was run by three women. My grandmother was the head of the household and spiritual authority.... My mother's elder sister worked in the fields and provided maternal security. My mother, a poet and writer, was responsible for the education of us children, keeping an eye on our intellectual growth and teaching us the rules of social etiquette....

His mother had to have been a skillful teacher; the young Fritjof went on to the University of Vienna, where in 1966 he earned a Ph.D. in theoretical physics. Clearly an accomplished student, he was hired by the University of Paris to conduct research in high-energy particle physics and systems theory. At the same time he was deeply affected by the 1968 street protests, general strikes, and university/factory occupations in Paris, at their height bringing the entire economy of France to a halt. After two years, he went on to teach at the University of California/Santa Cruz and work at the Stanford Linear Accelerator Center—just in time for him and wife Jacqueline to plunge into the emerging counterculture where the philosophies of Buddhism, Hinduism, and the Tao held particular attraction. The contrast between his "straight" job and the rebel redefinition of values and lifestyle set forth a theme that would come to dominate his thinking and life choices for decades to come.

Back and forth, back and forth across The Pond. Europe, California, Europe, California. In 1971 he and Jacqueline returned to England, this time hired by Imperial College in London, where he had the opportunity to converse with the great physicist Werner Heisenberg about his inkling that the "new physics" known as quantum theory held a mirror to the insights of Eastern religions. Heisenberg revealed that he had noticed the very same thing, as had Niels Bohr. In 1975 Fritjof and Jacqueline left England for yet another job, this time at the Lawrence Berkeley Laboratory in California. In Berkeley, once again he juggled his passion for science with a fascination for philosophies of the Far East. What emerged out of this so-called collision of disparate realms was his first book, *The Tao of Physics: An Exploration of the Parallels between Modern Physics and Eastern Mysticism*. It was an immediate best seller, he became a sought-after speaker—and for the first time Fritjof had enough income to pursue his deepest interests. This new-found freedom, plus the enthusiasm he had generated, led to his explorations of the ways in which other disciplines were also growing beyond the mechanistic conceptions constricting their relevance.

In 1984 he founded a think tank to further elaborate these themes. Round about 1988 I was invited to become a member of the governing council of Fritjof's institute. As I understood its purpose, it was a deepening of that years-long journey he had undertaken in order to write *The Turning Point* and *Uncommon Wisdom*: a purposeful gathering of fellow pioneers to widen the conversation about an emerging New Paradigm. We held private exploratory gatherings to discuss subjects such as recent scientific theories that could be applied to social and psychological practices, the human place in the natural world, and holistic means of stimulating the body/psyche to heal. We put out a fine newsletter as a further exploration, and we put on conferences on related topics for the general public.

Other folks on the board included Ernest "Chick" Callenbach, who had authored the visionary novel *Ecotopia*; psychologist and former president of the Association of Humanistic Psychology Jacqueline Doyle; Sierra Club Books editor Danny Moses; and political organizer Claire Greensfelder. After some years Jerry Mander and Marc Kasky were brought in, and Stan Grof attended some of our in-house meetings. In honor of our shared enthusiasm for place-based bioregionalism, the organization was given the name of Fritjof's neighborhood in Berkeley: the Elmwood Institute.

I felt flattered to be included and, admittedly, a bit dazzled by the stature of these other council members. I hung in, dragging my timidity around with me, and what I recall from my years at Elmwood is the gentle, intellectual, and near-invisible leadership Fritjof provided.

Then there were the special events. One was the 1991 weekend encounter of indigenous thinkers and activists with those of us from the dominant society. This event opened me to new ways of disengaging from my still too-Westernized modes of perceiving reality and making politics—and introduced me to folks who would impact my life in unimagined ways. Then there was the task I was given to organize a conference in New Mexico concerning another encounter: that of artists with New Paradigm thinkers. It was held at the Center for Contemporary Arts in Santa Fe in 1988. In my view a clash of values hindered any resolution of parallels. The problem was this: many of us at Elmwood had been well educated by the various Megatechnology meetings that Jerry Mander, Helena Norberg-Hodge, and Andrew Kimbrell had been putting on, not to mention neo-Luddite books like Mander's *Four Arguments for the Elimination of Television*, Langdon Winner's *Autonomous Technology*, and the works of U.S. scholar Lewis Mumford and French sociologist Jacques Ellul. Ellul's thinking was profound in its insight into the nature of what he termed the "technological bluff"—but Mumford, in particular, *he* was special to me. I first came upon his work in Allan Temko's class at UC Berkeley on architectural history and years later rediscovered him through his "Myth of the Machine" series, in which he described The Machine as the central archetype and template of modern techno-civilization. Some of us, including me, had gone on to make critique of mass technological society a centerpiece of our life's work. On the other hand, the director of the Center of Contemporary Arts insisted that the group of invited artists be dominated by the new digital creators who were all agog about the possibilities offered to them via computer technologies; it was that or lose our use of the center's auditorium. My reading of the resulting conference was that the content somehow drifted up into the New Mexico firmament like wisps of smoke from a near-extinguished bonfire: nothing of great import came out of it, no new ah-ha's, no fresh revelations—not even a healthy clash that would have at least defined the divergence. Fritjof with his unceasing state of wonder, on the other hand, was satisfied with the proceedings, relishing that the New Paradigm had had its day in the sun.

For me, hosting my colleagues on my home turf was the gift. Fritjof and his new partner, Elizabeth Hawk, came to visit me in my trailer plastered over to be an adobe house in Tesuque. And who can forget the hilarious entrance of Chick Callenbach and wife Christine Leefeld—two urgent advocates of the small-is-beautiful ethic—after the car-rental company at the Albuquerque airport upgraded them from a humble compact to . . . a flamingly humongous, white-leather-upholstered, gas-guzzling automotive monster of a *LINCOLN CONTINENTAL*?! Chick broached my desert driveway with ultra apprehension and ever so tenderly maneuvered the behemoth into a space that would have held three times that required for his own car. He then announced the calamitous mismatch with irony and characteristic self-deprecation.

A number of council members left the Elmwood Institute in the mid-'90s. It seemed that the organization had lost its wind, focused as it was on theoretical exploration. At the same time Fritjof was experiencing a change in focus as to what was needed in the world. Elizabeth's and his daughter Juliana was growing up, and he was looking forward toward the world she would inherit. He hired a new executive director of Elmwood named Zenobia Barlow. As a photographer and enthusiast for Eastern philosophies, she brought fresh vision and talents first to our group—and then to the organization that replaced it.

The Center for Ecoliteracy was born in 1995 with a mission of providing hands-on ecological education to young people based in systems thinking and complexity theory. CEL's founders were Fritjof, Zenobia, and lawyer Peter Buckley. Their first project was to donate money to an innovative idea called The Edible Schoolyard, brainchild of founder of Chez Panisse organic restaurant Alice Waters. The earliest such schoolyard garden was planted at Martin Luther King Jr. Middle School in Berkeley in the mid-'90s. With Waters' guidance, an ugly asphalt lot on the campus was torn up and replaced by a luscious garden whose purpose was to involve the students in the growing of the very food they would eat for lunch. It was also for them to learn how to cook in a healthy way, to appreciate organic vegetables and fruit, to experience the natural world, and in the process to build the strength of community that cannot happen in a classroom. Decades later—after generations of raspberries, mustard greens, heirloom tomatoes, and eager young gardener-chefs—the Center for Ecoliteracy still funds the project.

This involvement branched out into CEL's California Thursdays, by which a network of school districts around the state now serves 250,000 children local, freshly prepared lunches each year. The point is that children learn both to favor healthy meals as well as to know where food comes from; at the same time, local farm production is given a boost, and the environment is benefitting from the fact that produce travels via carbon fuels far less distance to reach the lunch room. And in 2017 Fritjof and Elizabeth launched Barrio Solar to bring solar power to Puerto Rico after the devastating hurricanes that wracked the Caribbean.

After a lifetime of investigation, discoveries in theoretical physics and the pursuit of their synchronistic appearance in other disciplines, Fritjof had turned to applying his education into living knowledge and skills for young people. Still, ever the intellectual, he continues to contribute to the well-being of the planet by researching and writing. Since that initial involvement with The Edible Schoolyard, he has written *The Web of Life* (1996), *The Hidden Connections* (2002), *The Science of Leonardo* (2007), *Learning from Leonardo* (2013), and other works. In 2014 he and Italian chemist Pier Luigi Luisi published *The Systems View of Life,* a text for undergraduate and graduate students. In this effort the authors use the recent focus on networks, complexity, and patterns of organization as tip-offs toward identifying scientific—and holistic— conceptions of reality.

Fritjof Capra: ever the "shape-shifter," willing to devote himself to whatever is needed.

JOANNA HARCOURT-SMITH: ADVENTURES IN RELATIVITY
(1945–)

It was a Buddhist moment in which the observer,
the act of observing, and that which is being observed
become one. . . . The Veil lifted and the simplicity of
truth appeared.

—J. H. S., *TRIPPING THE BARDO WITH TIMOTHY LEARY*, 2013

My 1979 Jeep was in one of its recurrent entropic phases, and sure enough, it did just that on the apron of the road by El Niño restaurant in Tesuque, New Mexico. Without hesitation Joanna and her Spanish husband José Luis Gómez Soler jumped into their car and rescued me. Since the day lay before us, we headed north on an adventure, arriving at the Embudo Station restaurant just in time for lunch. We sat down at one of the outdoor tables within toe-dipping distance of the Río Grande and ordered sandwiches.

I surmised the other diners thought we were stoned on grass, acid, or *something*—but the truth is, since her Timothy-Leary days lo these decades ago, Joanna has been in recovery from all mind-altering substances, José Luis is not a stoner, and I hadn't touched the stuff since 1970 when I began a yoga practice. We were just three friends having a hilarious time, each egged on by the others' keenness to expand the possibilities. Blessed we were that day, too, for Joanna was packing her brand-new Samsung Galaxy cell phone, I was toting my three raven hand-puppets, and by happenstance the violinist under the cottonwood tree was providing the perfect sound track for a theater of improvisation.

José Luis and I headed to the river in slow-motion, free-movement mode à la Isadora Duncan. Joanna picked up her phone and began to film. José Luis, in slow motion, brought back stones and, ever so slowly, arranged them in a funeral pyre for a stray banana that Joanna had rejected from her plate—all the while giggling like ravens on a bender. Then, at the table, our feathered friends began to make cogent social commentary, none of which will ever be remembered.

It was our first fumbling venture into the creative realm of home movies. But not our last.

Joanna Harcourt-Smith's spectrum of passion extends from the very heights of ecstasy-in-love-with-ecstasy down to rock-bottom despair— as anyone's would, had they endured the brutality perpetrated upon her childhood body/psyche. Her spectrum of intellect spans from attentiveness to the daily foibles and delights of the material world to informed analysis of the human condition and onward to the implications of quantum physics to psychology. Her personality flexes from the bone-thin vulnerability of a wounded sparrow to in-your-face self-assertion. This exceptional creature became my dearest friend during my last years in New Mexico.

She is best known in public for two things: 1) her Future Primitive podcast interviews with contemporary researchers, thinkers, and teachers like Ralph Metzner, Riane Eisler, and Vandana Shiva, on such topics as soul-making, the future of evolution, urban food growing, indigenous wisdom, and shamanism; and 2) her much-touted marriage to LSD psychologist Timothy Leary during his troubled years of politically motivated persecution and imprisonment. His crime: being, as President Richard Nixon called him, "the most dangerous man in America" for his open encouragement to use mind-altering drugs.

Joanna grew up in the European world of rolling-in-dough socialites with too many Lear jets, too many Greek islands, and too much time on their manicured hands. But far from being pampered by wealth and social standing, Joanna spent her childhood isolated in a Paris hotel suite with a neurotic, self-absorbed mother, little-to-no parental care, and plenty of unsupervised time for the nightly visitations of the chauffer (read: rapist). She became a rebel—a rebel in the family (she was disinherited for this display), a rebel at boarding school, a rebel nomad, a rebel thinker—and when she heard about the anti-war/hippie phenomenon bursting California's seams, she headed across The Pond to join up.

Joanna met Timothy Leary in 1972 through her ex-boyfriend, gangster/book-agent Michel-Gustav Hauchard. Leary had escaped from the California Men's Colony and fled to Algeria along with another political prisoner, Black Panther Eldridge Cleaver, then moved on solo to Switzerland, and through it all Michel had been his chief supporter and guardian. Already, by age twenty-three, Joanna had distinguished herself with the much-heralded publication of *The Little Green Book* that clarified ecological concerns in a parody of Mao Tsé Tung's *The Little Red Book*, but that also, because of the wrath of the Chinese Legation in London, caused her to be pushed down the steps at the Asian embassy and nearly kidnapped in Bonn.

From the many stories Michel had told Leary about Joanna, the LSD guru was able to make his first penetrating—and pointedly seductive—observation during their initial encounter in a boisterous Swiss-German beer hall: "I have great admiration for a woman who can make a scandal and a statement at the same time"—and off they went in his 911 Porsche Targa, in flight through Europe to the rocking rhythms of the Rolling Stones and the Eagles; à la Hunter S. Thompson on acid, cocaine, espresso, Jack Daniels, French Bordeaux, Afghani hashish, and Gitanes; running out on Switzerland's finest hotels just before payment time; all the while talking up a storm on such topics as the (ever-so-tiresome) Wheel of Fortune and (much-preferred) Magic Theater, cosmic circuitry, Perfect Love, and outer-space colonies. "You are looking for a way out of the decadent aristocratic game, the limbo of Jet Set desperados," Leary told Joanna. "Your intelligence has always told you that there is some-thing more. I'll show you the way. We can really make the wheel spin, you and I, so that we spin off into other circuits. There's a whole lot of uni-verses out there, and every one of them is fascinating."

If he was a fugitive from U.S. authorities seeking to imprison him for "corrupting American youth" with his emblematic "Tune In, Turn On, Drop Out" message, she was on the adventure of her life.

But, as might be expected, the high of cosmic consciousness dissipated when the two came face-to-face with the tangle of trumped-up charges and Leary was re-captured in Afghanistan. Plus governmental secrets, media lies, twisted rumors, listening wires, guns, high-level meetings in D.C., low-level near-rapes in seedy hotels, and friends-turned-DEA-dupes—all overseen by the Nixon administration's drive to bring down the '60s Generation by turning their drug sage into the sacrificial lamb of Law and Order. As Joanna writes in her memoir *Tripping the Bardo with Timothy Leary*, "From the moment I awoke in the pink and yellow suite at the Beverly Hills Hotel the morning after Timothy had been returned to the United States after a cunning re-arrest by DEA agents in Afghanistan, to the day he was finally released from twenty-two federal and state prisons and rural jails and we broke up, I watched the Clear Light of the magical theater we had shared degenerate into a B-grade cops-and-robbers rerun."

Joanna and I became friends some twenty-five years later. One day during the early part of our friendship, she read me a story she had writ-ten for an alternative website about her very first LSD trip. In it she tells that while soaring free and high on acid, she discovered that all things are relative and relational. She was looking at a tree outside the window and began to see it as swirling through multiple realities and meanings. "When the three Harvard psychonauts—Ralph Metzner, Richard Alpert, and Timothy—stumbled upon the extraordinary psychological states that lysergic acid diethylamide unleashed," she told me, "they understood that the drug does not *produce* the transcendent state but instead acts as a chemical key to release the nervous system from perceiving *only* ordinary or consensus reality." Like a bird alighting on one branch then another and another, she explained, during this first trip she had become witness to the world from many different perspectives. Such an experience of relativity can be a liberating one for survivors of violence. The perpetrator might insist that his violation is the victim's fault, that he will hurt her again or even murder her if she tells, and if the experience lies outside the organism's ability to endure, it passes not into memory as any normal occurrence would, but rather escapes conscious notice behind the clanking doors of fragmentation and repression. Here in the darkness of not-knowing, it may turn on itself as self-blame, shame, or paralysis, as it had in Joanna's psyche. But now she realized that, unlike the mono version of events her perpetrator had drilled into her or her mother's unilateral but obviously absurd laws, she herself held a truth that nobody could touch. The epiphany came at the same time that quantum physics, psychodrama, and gestalt therapy—among other venues— were revealing the Rashomonic nature of reality, and thus Joanna launched her adventure to self-knowledge, her liberation from the past, and her motivation to become whole.

Future Primitive grew out of this inner journey. In 2006 she had the idea to initiate a series of interviews with thinkers and activists in the field of consciousness whom she believed constituted a necessary force in the race for survival of the Earth. The name she came up with originated in "a vision of the future rooted in a respectful understanding of the past." In her own words, "Future Primitive is a podcasting website that presents intimate conversations with authors, visionaries and innovators from around the world."

She started with some of the people she had met or heard about from her Timothy Leary days and went on to speak with Daniel Pinchbeck, author of *Breaking Open the Head: A Psychedelic Journey into the Heart of Contemporary Shamanism*; John Lash, exponent of the power of myth to shape not only the life of an individual but history itself; shaman-initiated anthropologists Barbara and Dennis Tedlock; poet, author, and activist Margaret Randall, who had been denied her U.S. passport for her support of post-revolutionary Cuba; animist philosopher David Abram; and president of the International Psychohistorical Association Lloyd deMause.

Our second venture into fledgling movie-making sprang out of a December 2009 dinner party at the home of Joey Fuller and Sarah Baldwin on the occasion of a visit by Sarah's father. Ian Baldwin hailed from Vermont and the family fund backing Joanna's Future Primitive website. One of the brains behind Vermont's effort to secede from the United States, he had given me a walking tour of Montpelier during their 2008 congress on independence at the Statehouse. Sarah was dedicated to her work as a photographic curator and, following in Stephanie Mills' footsteps, had made a public choice to forego motherhood. I had met Joey at a bookstore on Cerrillos Road in Santa Fe, and he had impressed me not only for his literary acumen and generosity of spirit, but also because, in his ratty-jeans/suit-jacket style, he appeared his generation's replica of a 1970s love of mine who had also worked in a bookstore in jeans and a suit jacket.

After dinner and a few bottles of wine to warm us from the icy snowfall outside, we decided to make a movie. We agreed on a theme I had seen on a Mexican telenovela: the parents of a young woman have chosen the "correct" husband for her. But this guy is one royal geek—and the man she truly loves is socially unacceptable. On Mexican TV the issue was class: the poor reject is a mere gardener, while the geek boasts a law practice. We chose parts. Joanna became the mother and Ian the father. Sarah would be the young woman, José Luis the geek, and Joey the unpardonable yet passion-stirring cast-off. We had five minutes of battery time left on someone's cell phone so the movie would be just that long, and with no preparation whatsoever, we launched.

One thing about the improvisational approach is that if one actor spontaneously inserts a detail, it stands as reality and everyone must go with it. Joanna and Ian started right off blaring accents that pinned them to some undesignated but clearly nineteenth-century "Old Country." José Luis was so awkward as the geek that his hands sweated, and Joey's entrance—in a billowing muslin shirt, with a foot-and-a-half-long pepper grinder stuffed down one leg of his pants—waxed dramatic as he professed that he was but a "lad from the provinces" with one glaring defect: he had been brought into this world boasting a penis that was a foot-and-a-half long. A group brawl ensued when, with but fifteen seconds of battery left, all suddenly granted that Sarah should marry Joey—and Joanna, her elfish spirit streaming through the mother character, popped her face in front of the camera and winked: "All's Well That Ends Well."

Harcourt-Smith (right) with Cuban-Chilean singer Consuelo Luz, Santa Fe, New Mexico, 2017. Photo credit and courtesy of Chellis Glendinning.

IX. FROM HIROSHIMA TO CHERNOBYL: THE ANTI-NUCLEAR MOVEMENT

The release of atomic power has changed everything
save our way of thinking.

—ALBERT EINSTEIN

PHYSICS WAS HAVING ITS way with us humans in ways more sinister than expanded consciousness and psychological insight: it lay at the very foundation of nuclear weapons and nuclear power plants.

The jarring coincidence of the terrifying Three Mile Island accident on March 28, 1979, with the release of the film *The China Syndrome* flung the door open to a bevy of anti-nuclear activists. Of course the reckless, anti-Soviet name-calling bubbling from the Hollywood-honed, melodramatic mouth of President Ronald Reagan and his announcement of enhanced weapons systems like Star Wars and the Cruise Missile played their part, as did the inevitable disintegration of four decades of mass psychological denial about the possibility of planetary demolition. I can say that when I walked out of that movie theater in San Francisco, I had the unsettling sensation that my life focus had just done an about-face.

There was no debate: I launched myself to the other side of the collective numbing that had gripped the population since the end of World War II, straight into an endeavor that would take over my every breath for the next thirteen years.

As others did the same, an energetic anti-nuclear uprising erupted, and the precariousness of life on Earth became stunningly evident: in one brief moment *the whole thing could blow*. At the time the United States had some 23,368 weapons ready to launch from missiles in silos, nuclear submarines, etc., enough to wipe out all life on the planet dozens of times over; while the designated enemy the Soviet Union boasted even more: 30,062.

A key to consciousness raising was the weekend symposium that Physicians for Social Responsibility was offering: a traveling Chautauqua in cities around the country, including in San Francisco, where Marc Kasky and I lived, sandwiched precariously between Livermore National Laboratory and a fleet of Soviet nuclear subs offshore in the Pacific Ocean. Founded in 1961, PSR's assemblage of doctors, public health officials, and ex-military generals had made its first mark by documenting the presence in children's teeth of the highly radioactive strontium-90 emitted during U.S. nuclear testing. This discovery led to the Limited Nuclear Test Ban treaty of 1963, signed by the U.S., the Soviet Union, and the United Kingdom, effectively ending atmospheric nuclear testing. By 1980 PSR had taken on the issue of health dangers again through a conference called "The Medical Consequences of Nuclear Weapons and Nuclear Power."

Marc and I sat in the dark of the auditorium riveted to our seats. Australia-born Harvard physician Helen Caldicott dubbed the excess of nuclear weapons in the world a "medical issue" and explained the process by which radiation breaks down cell unity in the human body. Physician/cell biologist John Gofman, who had worked for the Manhattan Project to build the bombs dropped on Hiroshima and Nagasaki, scared us to the bone with scientific facts about the relationship between radiation-induced chromosomal abnormalities and cancer. We saw early government films taken during above-ground nuclear testing in Nevada to determine the immediate impact of explosion, and we studied slides showing the distance that fallout can travel from the epicenter of a blast. Former Rear Admiral Gene LeRocque, who after leaving the military had founded the Center for Defense Information, regaled us with facts, figures, and his now-radicalized perspective on war; he summed up his post-Navy perspective: "I hate it when they say, 'He gave his life for his country.' They [soldiers] don't die from the honor and glory of their country. We *kill* them." Psychiatrist Jerome Frank of Johns Hopkins University laid bare the psychology of power-mongering conflict. Harvard law professor Roger Fisher inflicted hope as he presented the principles of successful conflict resolution in a world on the brink of universal suicide.

It was a stellar line-up; we left worried, afraid, and ready to detonate into activism like a couple of exploding novae.

Parallel awakenings were happening everywhere in the U.S. New groups to bring the mainstream consciousness up-to-date and build a movement were birthed: Mental Health Professionals for Social Responsibility, National Campaign to Stop the MX, Clam Shell Alliance, and on. Already established organizations like American Field Service Committee, Clergy and Laity Concerned, War Resisters League,

With its tiny boats, the Bay Area Peace Navy blocks the Cruise-Missile-toting USS Missouri from entering the San Francisco Bay, 1984. Photo credit: Bob Heifetz. Licensed under Creative Commons. Originally published in the now-defunct *It's About Times* of the now-defunct Abalone Alliance, November–December 1984, in an article titled "San Francisco Bids for Battleship Task Force."

Greenpeace, and Women Strike for Peace were inundated with new members. The same occurred in Germany, England, Japan, Australia, the Philippines, France, etc., where vibrant movements were sustained by such groups as European Nuclear Disarmament, Friends of the Earth International, International Physicians for the Prevention of Nuclear War, and Pax Christi International, as well as by actions like the women's encampment outside the Royal Air Force base at Greenham Common in England, whose goal was to catalyze the decommissioning of its on-site weapons.

On 12 June, 1982, one million people demonstrated in New York City's Central Park against nuclear weapons. Spurred on by Ronald Reagan's brash threats to the "Evil Empire," coupled with scary new technologies like the neutron bomb and the MX missile, it was at the time the largest anti-war demonstration in history. In July I ran into Steve Ladd at a protest in front of San Francisco's municipal building. He was working at War Resister's League and had been in New York City. He said it was the most astounding experience of his life to march with so many like-minded dissenters. For the International Day of Nuclear

A prayer circle before an action by the Abalone Alliance in protest of the Diablo Canyon Nuclear Power Plant. The AA was organized by affinity groups and used non-violent tactics—public education, civil disobedience at the plant site, marches, picketing the offices of the electric company. Photo credit: Jessica Collette. Licensed under Creative Commons. Originally published in the now-defunct newspaper *It's About Times* of the now-defunct Abalone Alliance, December 1981–January 1982.

Disarmament on 20 June 1983, protests were held worldwide, including at 50 locations across the U.S. In 1986, in the Great Peace March, hundreds of people walked all the way across the continent from Los Angeles to Washington D.C. In the 1980s and 90s, there were frequent protests and peace camps near the test site, the "Nevada Desert Experience;" these were often led by local indigenous groups like the Shoshone.

Just as each of us felt alone and afraid in stark awareness that we and everything we cherished could be blown to oblivion at any moment, so in our worldwide movement we also found ourselves in the embrace of the solidarity of a different sort of cloud—one with less fire and more life-giving air, that of spiritual connection.

DANIEL AND PATRICIA ELLSBERG: THE WHISTLEBLOWERS
(1931-), (1938-)

Every nuclear bomb is an Auschwitz waiting to happen.
—P.M.E., 1983

You needn't think there is nothing you can do. You can tell the truth.
—D.E., 1984

Dan and Patricia taking a break from the Pentagon Papers trial, 1973. Photo credit: Betty Baird. Courtesy of Patricia Ellsberg.

Patricia and Dan Ellsberg carved out an irreplaceable presence in the 1980s movement to end the possibility of nuclear war. That he—who had done so much to stop the Vietnam War by the leaking classified documents that later became *The Pentagon Papers* to reveal governmental dishonesty—stood among us gave an electrifying boost to morale. That she—a noted National Public Radio–affiliated journalist who had predated her husband in anti–Vietnam War action—was doing her part lent a sense of possibility.

And here they were in the San Francisco Bay Area—at demonstrations, rallies, planning meetings, trainings, and conferences—offering historical perspectives based on their experiences during the Vietnam debacle, inventing strategies on how to proceed, and putting their bodies on the line at strategic weapons-making locales like the Bay Area's Livermore National Laboratory. Patricia and Dan: if there was a force beneath the layers of insight and courage that fueled their actions, it was the power of morality. They were (and are) a political couple worthy of emulating.

Marc Kasky and I certainly tried to. I had plunged into the movement soon after Three Mile Island and the 1979 premiere of the film *The China Syndrome*. In December of that year, when we got together as a couple, he joined me without hesitation. We listened to Dan as he spoke from the podium in front of San Francisco's City Hall, goose bumps erupting across our skulls, calling upon the eager crowd to rise up in fervent protest. I met Patricia backstage at an anti-nuclear conference and was awed by her upbeat demeanor and nonchalant knack for public speaking. Marc and I even attended sit-ins and demos at Livermore dressed not in the standard raggy camping clothes of most of the protestors, but as Patricia and Dan did—in suits and shiny shoes, toting briefcases. Once a couple of undercover police officials dressed like Dan Aykroyd and John Belushi in *The Blues Brothers* pointed at us and in exasperation quipped just loud enough for us to hear, "Here come the celebrities." Their reference was obviously to Dan and Patricia.

A little history is in order: not many recall that U.S. involvement in Vietnam had been on an invisible rise since the first appearance of advisors in 1950. President Eisenhower had agreed to support the French in holding on to their Far East colony, and his administration sent updated military equipment, along with the necessary specialists who could teach its operation. After the Viet Minh whipped the Legionnaires back to Paris in 1954, 750 U.S. military experts arrived in South Vietnam to reorganize the anti-communist armed forces; 19 years later, in 1969, the number of U.S. "colleagues" had risen to 553,000.

Another little-known fact: the Air Force was already dropping the toxic herbicide Agent Orange onto terrain captured by the Vietcong as early as 1962; by 1971 when said program ended, 20,000 sorties had been flown, devastating five million acres of upland and mangrove forest, as well as 500,000 acres of crops. In 1964 the Gulf of Tonkin incident occurred off the coast of North Vietnam; the USS *Maddox* was conducting surveillance in international waters and mistook what were later called "freak" weather conditions for torpedo attacks. A panicked but uninformed Congress signed the Gulf of Tonkin Resolution—handing over power to the president to conduct military operations *without a legal declaration of war*. U.S. retaliation was launched, and by 1966 B-52 bombers were bombing North Vietnam outright. In 1969 President Nixon's clandestine bombing campaign of Cambodia began, and went on for fourteen months. The war was widening its range—and its use of Agent Orange.

Like ducks in a chronological row, Presidents Dwight Eisenhower, John Kennedy, Lyndon Johnson, and Richard Nixon all viewed the small-but-divided nation as a last stand for the clash between "democratic" military-industrialism and its archenemy, evil-eyed communism. Inside the U.S., leaders who came to oppose the war were being downed by sketchy characters toting high-powered rifles and handguns. As later revealed by theologian James Douglass in his 2010 book *JFK and the Unspeakable*, at the time of the Cuban Missile Crisis the President was nurturing a below-the-radar phone conversation with Nikita Khrushchev. Remarkably, each revealed to the other that he was at the mercy of his military establishment—and agreed that the arms race had to be stopped. At a 1963 speech at Washington University, Kennedy disclosed his evolving stance against the nuclear arms race, in favor of a nuclear test ban treaty and eventually full disarmament. Within months, he was shot dead. Martin Luther King, Jr. delivered his decisive 1967 speech against the war in Vietnam; in it he identified the U.S. as the "greatest purveyor of violence in the world." Soon thereafter he would call for mass draft evasion and what would prove to be a potent alliance between the civil rights and anti-war efforts. He was shot dead. And former Attorney General and popular candidate for president in 1968 Bobby Kennedy not only wanted to end the war but also favored racial equality. He was shot dead.

Just as the war was jacking up to a murderous pitch—just as U.S. sons, brothers, and husbands were returning home in body bags draped in red-white-and-blue—so the anti-war movement was exploding across the nation's campuses, streets, and city centers. The first Teach-In was held in 1965, at the University of Michigan; it was subsequently broadcast to more than one hundred campuses. That same year a Catholic pacifist became the earliest to burn his draft card, and the following year veterans of World Wars I and II and the Korean War set their discharge papers afire in protest. 1966 saw the Congress of Racial Equality reporting that the draft places "a heavy discriminatory burden on minority groups and the poor" and calling for withdrawal of all troops. In 1967 Stop the Draft Week occurred in eighteen cities, with some 15,000 to 18,000 young men burning or turning in their draft cards. Students and veteran peace activists conducted civil disobedience in front of army induction centers. Massive demonstrations, like ours in Oakland, sometimes involved outright street battle—with protestors in helmets wielding shields made of garbage can lids; law enforcement with clubs and tear gas. 1967 also saw the National Mobilization to End the War turning out 70,000 in Washington, D.C. for the March on the Pentagon. The eight-day upheaval at the Democratic Convention in Chicago in 1968 was marked by tens of thousands of protestors, many traveling across the continent to get there, against 14,000 National Guardsmen and innumerable thousands of police, who perpetrated 700 arrests, an excess of beatings, and the shooting death of seventeen-year-old Sioux Native Jerome Johnson.

Dan was a latecomer to all this. He entered in 1969, while Patricia had been in the streets of Washington marching since 1965. For their first date, she invited Dan to join a protest in D.C. He was working as an analyst at the Defense Department under Secretary Robert McNamara, and needless to say, she caught flack from her anti-war friends for going out with such a "traitor"; from his side he went on the march so he could be with her, but with trepidation for being caught on camera and revealed to his employers.

But Dan was not your average Pentagon wonk; he truly believed he could help stop the war as an insider, and toward that end he worked not just under McNamara as special assistant to Assistant Secretary of Defense John McNaughton, but earlier as a strategic analyst at the Rand Corporation focusing on the command and control of nuclear weapons. Later, in South Vietnam, he became a member of the State Department researching guerrilla strategies.

In 1969, guided by curiosity about those who were putting their bodies in the streets to protest the war, he attended a War Resisters League conference at Haverford College: WRL was of the wing of the anti-war effort informed by such historical figures as Mahatma Gandhi, Martin Luther King, Jr., Dorothy Day, and Peace Pilgrim. The event turned out to be a life-changer for Dan when he heard a speech by nonviolence advocate Randy Kehler. Randy stated that he would soon commit civil disobedience and that he was "very excited" to join his friends in prison! David Harris, Warren, Bob, John, Terry—all were already behind bars—and he spoke of how excited he was to be "invited to join them."

Dan wrote about this seminal moment in his 2002 book *Secrets: A Memoir of Vietnam and the Pentagon Papers*:

The whole audience was standing. They clapped and cheered for a long time.... I fell back into my seat, breathing hard, dizzy, swaying ... [and] then I began to sob silently, grimacing under the tears, shoulders shaking.... I got up—I was sitting in the very last row in the amphitheater— and made my way down the back corridor till I came to a men's room... . I staggered over to the wall and slid down to the tile floor. I began to sob convulsively, uncontrollably.... I had not been ready to hear what Randy had said. I had not been braced for it. When he mentioned his friends were in prison and remarked that he would soon be joining them, it had taken me several moments to grasp what he had just said. Then it was as if an ax had split my head, and my heart broke open.

It is to Kehler's loyalty to his country that Dan attributes his own dissemination of the 7,000-page, top-secret study of U.S. decision-making in Vietnam that became known as *The Pentagon Papers*—as well as his acceptance that, as a result, he might spend the bulk of the rest of his life in a federal prison. Patricia describes these times and events in a 2010 *Yoga Journal* essay:

During our first year of marriage, in 1971, my husband, Daniel Ellsberg, was indicted on 12 felony counts for espionage, theft, and conspiracy, which carried a possible sentence of 115 years in prison. His release of the Pentagon Papers (a 7,000-page set of top-secret documents that revealed how the U.S. Congress and the American public had been lied to about the Vietnam War) to the *New York Times* and 18 other newspapers resulted in a trial that lasted more than two years—and fortified our own deep commitment to the power of truth telling.

This period was one of the most intense, frightening, and meaningful times of my life. I was terrified that my husband would be physically harmed or sent to prison for the rest of his life. At the same time, he and I were gratified that we could use our access to the press to help stop what we felt was an unnecessary, immoral, and disastrous war. What is little known is that Daniel was inspired to release the truths in the Pentagon Papers in part by the example of Mahatma Gandhi and his concept of *satyagraha*. The literal translation of satyagraha is "holding to the truth," and Gandhi spoke of it as "truth force" or "soul force" or "love force."

The truth Gandhi referred to was the universal truth that we are all one. Through this recognition we can find a deep commitment to non-harming and nonviolence, and a willingness to sacrifice ourselves for the benefit of others. Gandhi inspired people to be willing to endure suffering as they participated in acts of nonviolent resistance, and to withdraw cooperation from people and institutions that deny the truth of our oneness by oppressing or harming others.

After spending two years in Vietnam while working in the State Department, Daniel was asked to write one of the volumes of the Pentagon Papers and then was given access to the whole 47-volume study. It documented how four presidents in a row, from Truman to Johnson,

May 11, 1973: U.S. vs. Russo and Ellsberg dismissed,
the greatest day of their lives. Courtesy of Dan Ellsberg.

deceived the public and Congress about our country's involvement in Vietnam, their aims, their strategies, and the costs and prospects for success or stalemate. After Daniel read the whole study, he felt that Americans needed to know the truth. Despite being aware that he risked spending the rest of his life in prison, he decided to reveal the top-secret study to the public.

Patricia Marx and Dan Ellsberg were born just a few years apart in the 1930s, she in 1938 in Philadelphia, he in 1931 in Detroit. Her parents were toy magnate Louis Marx and housewife Rene Saltzman Marx. A defining event in her young life occurred on the eve of her sixth birthday: her mother died of breast cancer. Patricia was overtaken by a grief she could not begin to understand—but the loss also catalyzed in her a sense of joy for simply being alive.

At home in upstate New York, she and siblings Barbara, Jacqueline, and Louis Jr. received encouragement to strive for excellence, which they all did. Patricia went on to Radcliffe College. Upon graduation in 1959, she became the host of "Patricia Marx Interviews," a nationally syndicated radio program at WNYC-FM featuring leading figures in the arts, politics, and sciences. Danny Kaye, George Balanchine, Günter Grass—they were among her guests. Patricia's unique and ground-breaking slant was to bridge the conventionally accepted fissure between spiritual and social issues, and as the conflict in Vietnam progressed, she invited more and more folks to talk about stopping the war: Michael Harrington, David Halberstam, Dick Gregory, and Theodore Sorenson.

Dan's parents were fundraiser Adele and civil engineer Harry Ellsberg, Ashkenazi Jews who converted to Christian Science. He grew up in Detroit where, reflecting the family's emphasis on the importance of education, he attended the Cranbrook School, later went to Harvard and, with a Woodrow Wilson Fellowship, the University of Cambridge in England. He graduated with a Ph.D. in economics from Harvard in 1962. A defining event in his youth was the day in 1946 when, his father at the wheel, his mother and sister died when the auto crashed into a wall. He was fifteen years old—and has spent the rest of his life dedicated to understanding and preventing disasters.

And now here the two were fighting against U.S. participation in a nuclear arms race even more out of control than it had been during the Vietnam War. Patricia was single-minded in her commitment—even as her belly ballooned out with he who would become her and Dan's son, Michael. Many believe that her effectiveness became more intense. Up on stage she was visibly reminding all of the presence of the next generation, and they were the ones who might not live to celebrate their bar mitzvahs or would inherit a world even more burdened by cancers, leukemia, still births, and genetic mutations from the radioactive cesium and plutonium of weapons-building/power-plant emissions. And there she was—behind the podium, at meetings—always stylish in a colored scarf, always beaming graceful compassion, always infusing others with hope based on the ability to take action.

Dan's devotion to the issue equaled hers. One time he and I were speakers at a college in San Francisco—he, scheduled to talk about the domestic and geo-politics of the arms race; I, on the psychological ramifications of living with the uncertainty the arms race imposed; both of us, on the value of acting to restore a future for humanity. The auditorium chosen for our presentation boasted some 200 chairs, all in perfect line-up, their metal frames shooting off the glint of the fluorescent tubes above. The allotted time came . . . and passed. No one showed up! We waited. One person meekly filed in and chose a seat somewhere in the middle of the emptiness. We waited a while more. A second, then a third entered and sat down. And that was it: a dismal, vacuous hall. Deflated, I was on the verge of calling it a day and going home. Dan turned and whispered: "How are we to know that these three are not the most crucial actors in stopping the arms race? We should go on as if the auditorium were packed with standing-room only."

That was Dan—he, after all, had thrown up a major barricade to the continuation of an entire war; and so we went on.

As grandfather to modern whistleblowers in the U.S., Dan became a public advocate for Julian Assange of WikiLeaks, Chelsea (formerly Bradley) Manning, a U.S. Army soldier assigned to Iraq, and State Department analyst Edward Snowden as they launched their twenty-first-century-style electronic challenges to the U.S.'s two-faced hegemony. As he said in a speech at the Freedom of the Press Foundation whose purpose was to announce Snowden as the newest board member, "[Snowden] is the quintessential American whistleblower, and a personal hero of mine. Leaks are the lifeblood of the republic and, for the first time, the American public has been given the chance to debate democratically the [National Security Agency's] mass surveillance programs. Accountability journalism can't be done without the courageous acts exemplified by Snowden, and we need more like him. . . ."

Getting into his eighties, Dan has not stopped his work for real democracy for one heartbeat. He has written several books, including the 2002 *Secrets* and *The Doomsday Machine: Confessions of a Nuclear War Planner* (2018). In his dedication in *Secrets,* he calls Patricia "the love of my life." She is fulfilling her affinity for the spiritual depth of life as a Buddhist meditation teacher, spiritual coach, and workshop leader with her sister, futurist Barbara Marx Hubbard. As she has written on her website describing the principle of the work, "After years of both exploring and teaching psychological and spiritual trainings, I believe each of us has within us a source of radiant love, wisdom, strength, and profound well-being. It is our birthright."

A political couple to emulate, indeed.

SUNSHINE APPLEBY:
DISOBEDIENCE IN A WET SUIT
(1944-)

I ask myself: how did I come to find myself
facing a machine gun pointed directly at me?
—S.A., LETTER TO CHELLIS GLENDINNING, 2015

I am sure that many people don't know what to do with Susan Upton, by her own choice known as Sunshine Appleby. Her parents certainly didn't; they locked her away in the loony bin for three years where—and I speak with certainty—she wowed the doctors with her intelligence, alertness, and imagination. And I hope that they all know now that their whacky patient became one of them: a registered nurse and certified massage therapist.

I myself can't be sure how I met Sunshine; she seemed always to be there. Maybe through our elder feminist-dyke friend, Sarah Davis, who lived in a painted Victorian in the Haight? Marc Kasky knew her from the Ecology Center. And then, there she was in the whirlwind of the anti-nuclear movement.

She was everywhere, and everywhere she stood out. Tall, peppery blonde-brown hair, slightly jutting front teeth—more concerned with doing the right thing than with caring about what people thought of her— she was usually dressed in a wrinkled shirt bought for twenty-five cents at Goodwill and tattered yoga pants. From her backpack arose little sacks of sunflower sprouts, hand-ground peanut butter slathered on thick slices of whole-wheat bread, and a glass jar of filtered water. I visited one of the slews of apartments she rented in San Francisco, a slightly below-ground affair, and learned that every single item that was brought into the kitchen met one of three fates: it was devoured; it was recycled into another use; or it was transmogrified into compost. The woman had a steel water filter and a Champion juicer, with nary a plastic bag in sight. Yes, Sunshine was a live-lightly freak with a predilection for raw foods. Her footprint, decades before the Ecological Footprint was even a glisten in the eye of its inventor, resembled that of a tire-sandaled Guatemalan peasant more than of a saddle-shoed white woman born into an East Coast upper-middle-class family.

But born into that family she was: the T. Graydon Uptons of Hartland Four Corners, Vermont and Washington, D.C. Through the years her father, T. Graydon, worked at the U.S. Treasury Department, the World Bank, and the Inter-American Development Bank. Her mother, Vassar-educated Ann Nash Upton, was a homemaker with four children. Early on, Susan had health problems that included panic attacks, ulcerative colitis, and insomnia, causing unbearable pain that without warning would bedevil her in any situation from shopping to riding the bus and would always cause her mother not concern, but embarrassment. Susan was also legally blind and wore thick glasses. Despite such impediments to her parents' stereotypical expectations, the still ever-promising Susan was the apple of their eye—that is, until they discovered that this daughter of theirs was her own person.

1963 was Sunshine's breakaway year. A recent high-school graduate, she crafted her own free-form summer: she went west, jumped a freight train from California to Colorado, and chased circles around her dream to be a poet like the Beatnik women who had, by a few short years, predated her. But when the maples and oaks swathed the hills of the eastern seaboard in cloaks of dazzling red and yellow, she returned to perform her familial duty, entering the exclusive women's Bennington College. All along she had thought of herself as a pacifist. But that first semester, after an incident in which she angrily pounded the roommate who had usurped her cot and pitched her clothes and books into the hallway, Sunshine locked herself in a bathroom stall for three days, "being unable to respond to anything but the question of how can I harbor two such radically different feelings at the same time: loving peace and having the ability to be a killer at the same time?" When the janitor unscrewed the hinges of the toilet door, Sunshine's mother checked her into a mental institution.

Although she rarely talks about her subsequent dedication to non-violent civil disobedience, she described what followed this enforced dark night of the soul in a personal letter to me as "a journey inward." Upon release, she took classes at George Washington University in D.C.

where, by a fluke of fate, she found herself in the middle of an anti-war protest; witnessed heavily armed police atop horses beating people with batons: was tear-gassed by helicopters and went totally blind for six weeks, during which time she lost her rental, her job, and her academic scholarship. Not to be daunted by disagreeable fortune, she took off for Mexico, where she witnessed the injustice of poverty, studied with Liberation Theology priests as well as with Ivan Illich, and was in Mexico City in 1968 when the historic massacre of protestors in Tlatelolco Square took place.

Out of curiosity she attended a community meeting for people interested in non-violent, faith-based activism; here she met pacifists Elizabeth McAllister and Philip Berrigan, two people who became life-catalyzers. In 1980 she returned to the nation's capital, this time certain of her purpose in the world. She moved into Jonah House where McAllister, Berrigan, and a bevy of nonviolent peace activists and priests lived. Here she began reading such subversive material as Dorothy Day, Peace Pilgrim, and Mahatma Gandhi, as well as everything she could get her hands on regarding nuclear weapons and U.S. participation in the arms race. Years later, on the seventieth anniversary of the bombing of Nagasaki, August 9, 2015, she wrote me a letter about her dedication to civil disobedience, a lifelong practice in which she had, as of 2016, racked up a whopping ninety-two arrests:

> The main thing that enabled me to act as I did was the general field I was hanging out in and the enormous pressure of the times. . . . Civil rights. Hundreds of ordinary citizens protesting the Vietnam War. Kent State when the U.S. government was shooting its own citizens. Millions marching in the streets protesting racial inequalities, the fervor of Martin Luther King. Living under martial law in D.C., where tanks rolled down the avenues, soldiers roamed the streets carrying machine guns, and no more than three people were allowed to gather publicly. . . . It was not one thing [that thrust me into activism], but rather the effect of the 100th snowflake when finally the branch bends.

Also by the 1980s, Sunshine had finished her education as an on-call nurse, and thus she was able to dip into and out of paid work, but her "portable profession"—traveling from Washington State to California to New Hampshire in order to protest—was her true calling. Early on she learned that the government does not give a hoot for its citizens; rather we are merely, in military terms, "collateral damage." And, without a monstrous income, she was able to live simply, cheaply, and communally wherever she was—sharing with her fellow activists both the emotional burden of existence under the constant threat of extinction and visions of creative strategies for a world at peace.

I visited Sunshine one afternoon in yet another basement apartment in San Francisco—as if in an underground air-raid shelter, she always seemed to be nesting below ground—and I noticed that a window opening to an air well could not be locked, leaving it blatantly ajar. The neighborhood was a dangerous one.

"Aren't you afraid?" I wondered. Her answer came like a sudden thunder crack on a sunny day.

"Listen. After you've been face-to-face with a nuclear submarine with nothing but a thin layer of rubber and a few feet of water between you and it," she replied, "little things like a man entering your apartment tend to fade."

Among her hundreds of acts of civil disobedience, most all of them directed at the U.S. military, perhaps the most dramatic was the aforementioned. It took place in 1982—in a wet suit. The adversary was a 560-foot-long (read: *nearly the length of two football fields)* Trident nuclear submarine that, after manufacture in Groton, Connecticut, was to be housed at the Navy base at Bangor, Washington. The vessel carried up to twenty-four intercontinental ballistic missiles, each of which had as many as eight independently targeted warheads, in all holding an explosive force of 300 kilotons of TNT—some twenty times the power of the bomb dropped on Hiroshima. In other words, according to climate-change activist Matt Dundas in his 2008 article "The Rise of Non-Violent Civil Disobedience: The Peace Blockade, Part 2," the port was slated to be "the service station of the world's deadliest weapons." The plan to oppose such had been hatched by theologian Jim Douglass while in jail from a different action, the idea being that small but fast-moving boats would deflect the ingress of this USS *Ohio* in a kind of water-based guerrilla resistance.

When the action was announced by the Ground Zero Center for Non-Violent Action, forty-six people signed on to participate, many admitting that they did so because they didn't have a choice: they knew that they could die in this battle, but it was necessary.

Execution presented several hurdles. One was timing; no one knew exactly when the ship would arrive. This problem was miraculously solved by movement contacts at the Panama Canal who would report when the USS *Ohio* passed through, and from there the trip up the coast would take a few days. Another challenge had to do with skills. The action would require the kind of technical ability and discipline normally associated with an army. Very quickly, for the arrival seemed imminent, Greenpeace offered a three-day training in which basic water safety was taught, as well as how to lift and lower nine one-person rowboats out of two larger boats in less than three minutes. A last challenge concerned support. Here the movement's success at building relationships with other sectors of society came to the fore. Simultaneous with the action, a 6,500-person rally protesting the stationing of the submarine took place on the S'Klallam Reservation, while twelve bishops and church executives from six denominations, along with their parishioners, held a prayer vigil on a boat in a nearby cove. Plus, the international press was standing by to film.

Between 2 and 3 a.m. on August 12, 1982, Ground Zero sentinels noted Coast Guard (CG) cutters moving about the bay like ants upset by a disturbance to their hill. The activists bolted awake, said their prayers, got into their wetsuits, and hurried down to the dock. Here the CG burst upon them brandishing M-16s, seizing boats, and hauling them away. In the scuffle a few boats got away and raced into the harbor.

Just then, like a monstrous water snake, the USS *Ohio* slithered into sight.

Dundas describes what happened next: "Video footage taken at the time shows protesters getting washed overboard by high-powered Coast Guard hoses," he writes. "The boats that got away from the initial Coast Guard onslaught tore toward the 'National Security Zone,' a 1000-yard perimeter around the submarine, a boundary that once crossed meant risking [a] ten-year prison sentence and $10,000 fine." Seventy-eight-year-old Ruth Youngdahl Nelson was riding in her son's tiny motorized rubber dinghy and a Coast Guard craft was hot and heavy in pursuit. Just as a Guardsman was about to hose the team into the sound, Dundas recalls, Ms. Nelson shouted, "Young man, *not* in my America!" Stunned, the Guardsman lowered his hose, and the resisters escaped for another run at the humongous submarine—only to be surrounded, captured, and arrested.

"With almost every Ground Zero boat at a halt," Dundas continues, "there was only one which succeeded in advancing all the way to the *Ohio*. A speedboat carrying Renee Krisco, Ed Turtle, and Sunshine Appleby circled the colossal beast while outrunning multiple Coast Guard boats and a helicopter. Surrounded by law enforcement, the boat got right up next to the *Ohio*."

As Sunshine describes the encounter in a letter:

We three, in a tiny rubber boat with a gas engine the size of a lawnmower, were able to block the path of the Trident, circle it, and jump into the water. I swam toward it; our driver Renee, a nun, guided the boat away from the Trident; while Turtle, a teacher, jumped out and swam away in an attempt to confuse the suddenly appearing-upon-the-scene helicopter and a large CG boat. The military men were yelling at me with sexual allegations—the C word—telling me what they were going to do to me if I didn't stop swimming toward the submarine. Meanwhile, I nearly blind and quite well-dressed in my wetsuit, red bathing cap, rubber booties, and rubber gloves—continued to dog-paddle towards the monstrous behemoth, black in colour and several football fields long. Inside my wetsuit I carried a loaf of bread to feed the soldiers bread, not bombs, and an arrest warrant signed by the attorney general because, under international treaties, the Trident is illegal: its load of some 200 nuclear weapons would not distinguish between noncombatants (read: women and children) and the armed soldiers resisting an attack.

I was on a mission.

However, with the helicopter coming closer to the water creating heavy waves and the boat of shouting soldiers getting louder, I turned onto my back, closed my eyes, and said "God help me." At that moment the Trident disappeared, the helicopter, the Coast Guard boat, the waves, the screaming voices: I entered a place/non-place of silence and peace that passed all understanding. I had the experience of being rocked in the arms of the Divine Mother. I felt a love really indescribable.

About twenty minutes later I "awoke" to the voices of my boat mates calling me to help them reconnect the gas line the CG had cut with a long boat hook. I looked around me and saw nothing but a vague outline of my boat mates in the mist. I noticed something was different but could not put my finger on it, a sense of peace. We held the gas line together manually and put-putted back to shore.

What I realized is that when we *feel from our gut* that there is nothing left to lose, no matter the personal consequences, the danger of nuclear war overshadows all of one's small concerns. I became free to act from my heart. As I was swimming towards the Trident, I felt only profound determination.

I think the action was a wake-up call for the U.S. military. The people on the CG boat came from the small town of Bangor, where the Trident was to be stationed. The protestors organizing the blockade came from that same small town. The two groups knew each other; their children attended the same schools, they saw each other in the market, at church, at the movies. They knew we were unarmed and peaceful: thus the reluctance to fire upon us. A modest but for me life-changing benefit of the action: I was healed of my irritable bowel syndrome and have never had an attack since.

By 2010 Sunshine was aware of the inner tension presented by life within the superpower with the greatest cache of nuclear weapons and the most rationalizations for detonating them. Plus, now that computers connecting law enforcement agencies could reveal her ineffable arrest record wherever she went, she felt that further use of civil disobedience would be ill-advised. She decided to move to New Zealand, a place she regarded as saner, healthier, and more ecological. She also decided to leave behind her role as an employed health professional and "move from the stress of nursing to the joy of authentic healing work." Although she did apply for and receive a New Zealand registered nurse license, she opened a massage therapy practice instead and relaunched her campaign for low-footprint, ecological living and the medicinal value of raw foods.

New Zealand did not turn out to be the eco paradise Sunshine had imagined; as she puts it, it was more like a "U.S.-in-training," with its agricultural industry spraying tons of pesticides, genetic-engineering firms releasing altered organisms, coal mining and hydraulic fracking causing water pollution. Disappointed, she wrote to me, wondering if she should come to South America. At age seventy-one, though, after a life chock-full of jail cells and basement apartments, Sunshine decided to stop moving around; the nomadic protestor bought a small, sunlit house in Takaka/Golden Bay. There, amid straight-spine saguaro cacti and spreading silver fern, she continues with her massage work, promotion of healthy diet—plus *legal* protest against the use of pesticides.

KOZMICK LADYE:
THE RENT IS DUE ON THE PLANET
(1930-1992)

There are no coincidences, and the meter is ticking
until contract renewal. Dealer's choice time is
approaching, and ignorance of the Big Laws will soon
be no excuse.
—K.L., TO A *SAN FRANCISCO EXAMINER* REPORTER, 1980S

Every social movement attracts its social philosophers, some of them what might be called "street eccentrics"—and Kozmick Ladye was just this in the anti-nuclear movement of the 1980s. She cut one colorful figure in San Francisco, each day draping her wan body in grimy second-hand clothes that presented her as a rainbow flitting up Haight Street. Red! Orange! Yellow! Green! Blue! Indigo! Violet! She was the best-known Street Eccentric in the City by the Bay, famed for the cosmological political rants she would insist on delivering in any welcoming, semi-welcoming, or outright hostile environ.

One such place was my goodbye party. After 20 years of living in the Bay Area, I was on the verge of moving to New Mexico. The year was 1986, at the height of the anti-nuclear movement. It's not a move I ever

Mural Remembering American Anarchism at Bound Together Books, San Francisco. Kozmick Ladye (last row, fifth from left) along with Albert and Lucy Parsons, Sacco and Vanzetti, Alexander Berkman, and Ricardo Flores Magón. Artist: Susan Greene, 1995. Photo credit: Marvin Collins. Courtesy of Susan Greene.

would have come up with myself. I considered San Francisco/Berkeley to be the Center of the Universe; Marc Kasky and I had been together for seven good years; and at thirty-nine I was cresting into a leadership role as a political activist. No, I would never have entertained notions of changing location. But my doctor had been following my persistent fatigue and low immunity, tracked it to an allergy to microorganisms that thrive in wet, mold-ridden places, and recommended I live in the desert.

My goodbye party was a royal send-off. I invited just about everybody I could think of who had been important to me—from my dear Aunt Sue Miller of Walnut Creek to lesbian-feminist writers, ecology freaks, peace activists, fellow writers from the *San Francisco Bay Guardian,* and these new, forbidden comrades from the Soviet Consulate on Green Street. Somehow, though, Kozmick Ladye had slipped my mind. But not hers. She showed up at the door invitation-less, and red-faced from my faux pas, I asked her in.

A few moments for testimonials were planned. This was to include voices from all aspects of the movements I had had the good fortune to be part of: homeopath Dana Ullman from the holistic health movement; Aunt Sue, who described me as I was in childhood; and Marc Kasky, who spoke of our work together in the anti-nuclear movement. Needless to say, although she was not on the roster, Kozmick Ladye *had* to speak. Or, better put, it would have been as unthinkable as the atomic bomb that she would *not* speak.

The thing about her is that she somehow found out about and attended every single meeting that corresponded to her interests—in the 1970s, ecology get-togethers, in the '80s, anti-nuclear sessions. She appeared in her rainbow garb at events as varied as Commonwealth Club lectures, Grateful Dead concerts, and anti-weapons demonstrations at Lawrence Livermore Laboratory. When the moment arrived for input, comments, or questions, she would eagerly wave her hand in the air, and truth be told, the majority of group facilitators resisted calling on her. Why? Because she lived on a different level of existence than the rest of us. She spoke of... well... cosmic things that gave substance to the very definition of the phrase "Far Out." And she was as serious as we were about stopping the war and shutting down the weapons labs. Just from her own special angle.

So, needless to repeat, Kozmick Ladye insisted on speaking.

I don't know what kind of chile pepper was stuffed up my ass, because at first I said "no," explaining that we had a schedule to keep to. (*"WHAAAA*?!" my loudest inner voice balked. "A *schedule* to keep to? It's *a party* for Chrissake!") Kozmick Ladye proudly stepped to the microphone and the audience, most of whom had used eye-rolling to endure her rants in the past, went ballistic with hilarity, roaring at her witty metaphors and poetic imagery.

"I'm a messenger, a catalyst, a space-time traveler, a true cosmic character," she called out. "I'm a self-fulfilling prophesy, here to raise your consciousness. It's time. *WAKE UP! THE RENT IS DUE ON THE PLANET!*"

And then I saw it. Truly appreciated for perhaps the first time in her career as the Paul Revere, or Thomas Banyaca, of Extra-Planetary Blowback, she could not contain her own enjoyment of this precious moment. A sly smile erupted on her face, and the crowd exploded into even louder hoots.

Kozmick Ladye was born Janet Kramer in 1930 near Boston. A surprise to many: before coming to San Francisco, she held a job as a Congressional aide in Washington, earned an M.A. in social work, and worked in a suicide prevention center. Then, in the early 1970s, she moved to the Bay Area and dropped acid. It was a definitive trip, complete with revelation, and she began to send her now-famous "rainbow letters" to hundreds of journalists, dignitaries, and elected officials. The public rants soon followed.

When Kozmick Ladye finally took leave of planet Earth, at age sixty-two in 1992, the *San Francisco Chronicle* ran the longest obituary with the largest photo I had ever seen on those pages. The woman was an icon of the anti-nuclear movement—and a veritable San Francisco treasure.

X. LONG LIVE NED LUDD!
TECHNOLOGY CRITICISM

*If we are to prevent megatechnics from further
controlling and deforming every aspect of human
culture, we shall be able to do so only with the aid of a
radically different model derived directly, not from
machines, but from living organisms and ecosystems.*

—LEWIS MUMFORD, *THE PENTAGON OF POWER,* 1970

THE NINETEENTH-CENTURY LUDDITES, LABORERS who took
up hammers against the industrial revolution's assault on small-scale/
sustainable/sovereign communities, inspired a crop of late-twenti-
eth-century technology critics. As did the insights of Second Wave schol-
ar-activists Lewis Mumford and Jacques Ellul, who wrote piercingly
forceful analyses of mass technology's role in devolving societies during
the first half of the 1900s. We neo-Luddites came next; we are the ones
who grew up ensconced in/defined by late-industrial technics and technique, the ones with eyes honed to see society itself as Mumford's
Mega-Machine and Ellul's Technological Bluff. Our generation then was

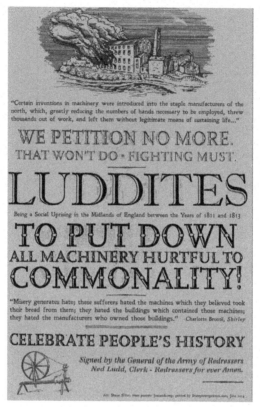

Luddite Poster, 2014. Photo credit: Dorian Foto. Artist: Shaun Slifer.
Courtesy of JustSeeds, Pittsburgh, Pennsylvania.

witness to what *Dark Mountain* magazine's Tom Smith calls "hyper-technological modernity at the cusp of the digital age" with its supercomputers, genetic engineering, wireless control and communications, nano-technologies, and robotics: the ultimate encasement in the mores and politics of techno-domination.

Needless to say, we were not always popular. Au contraire, we were after all challenging the sacred notion of Progress.

But devoted, yes, this we were.

One of the principal questions of the effort was "Where Did Humans Go Wrong?" and despite the perpetual limitations of mere words to grasp The Whole of Things, we were able to illustrate various twists and turns along the way and make stabs at finding an origin. Or at least a thickening of the trend toward the mechanization/digitalization of all aspects of life that we see today. Sigmund Freud, of course, saw the onslaught of civilization as the illness that caused the human psyche to repress and adjust via complex compartmentalization of consciousness. Paul Shepard explored the changes in child-rearing, and thus in human psychology, that accompanied animal and plant domestication some 10,000 years ago, while John Zerzan looked to the creation of symbolic thought and the division of labor as the start of the downward spiral. Kirkpatrick Sale pointed to the change 70,000-plus years ago from scavenging to active hunting, as the launch of the urge to dominate. I wrote about the Neolithic as a definitive period of formation of modern social and psychological ills. Many—from the academics we studied to our independent peers and colleagues—pointed to the devastating effects of the industrial revolution. Jerry Mander was busy identifying the ways in which specific technologies (television) and those that were to come (supercomputers and genetic engineering) would affect human society, while Langdon Winner showed how government facilitates the development and dissemination of mass technology. And we all took solace from Luddite-leaning poets along the way—from Shelley and Wordsworth to Robinson Jeffers and Mary Oliver—who explored the inexplicable/unspeakable "progression" of human existence.

In the mid-1990s our Megatechnology gathering dubbed itself the Jacques Ellul Society. Ellul had been a French philosopher/sociologist/ lay theologian who in the mid-twentieth century, at the very height of popular enthusiasm for technological "progress," elucidated the deception of said development, calling it myth and propaganda. He authored fifty-eight books and more than a thousand articles, the dominant theme being the threat to independent thought, human freedom, and religion catalyzed by modern mass technology. Among his most influential books is *The Technological Society*. Walking in Ellul's footsteps, our organization brought together us neo-Luddites—from Wendell Berry to Vandana Shiva—to discuss the socio-politics of mass technology, to launch a magazine called *Techné*, and to invent approaches to challenging the God-like position of technology in the techno-civilization that was killing the planet.

W.H. "PING" FERRY: TECHNOLOGY AS SYSTEM
(1910–1995)

*The decision to shoot for the moon ... can be recognized
as a long-range W.P.A. for the electronics and missile
industries.*

—W.H.F., "THE DILEMMAS OF ABUNDANCE," 1961

Ping Ferry was Lewis Mumford's colleague and long-time pal. He viewed mass, mechanized society as a systemic, technologically-enhanced catastrophe and waxed skeptical at every new offering foisted upon its eager but bewildered consumers.

I know. He told me so after my "Notes toward a Neo-Luddite Manifesto" appeared in the *Utne Reader* in 1990. I had heard his voice in interviews on National Public Radio on such subjects as the threat of nuclear war, the dangers of mass technology, and the injustice of racial inequality. I also knew about the family fund he administered along with wife Carol Bernstein Ferry, from the coffers of which they gave away millions to worthy individuals and social-change projects. But it never occurred to me that one day I would actually *know* this stellar individual. And yet here he was, materialized before my eyes in a few cogent paragraphs of crudely typed words on a small slip of stationery. He wanted me to understand that, at heart, the problem was not a single endangering technology—it could never be just a Dalkon Shield IUD or an asbestos pipe sleeve—it was the whole shebang together as a complete ecology, thrusting its dysfunctional methods and values into normality like a bulldozer mowing over a family farm.

A correspondence between Scarsdale and Chimayó was launched—his letters always typed on his hokey old typewriter—and I learned that Ping was not only a friend of Mumford, but of just about every person of influence of the mid-twentieth century. While teaching at the Choate School, he had shepherded Joseph Jr. and John F. Kennedy through Latin and English; he had done PR for Sidney Hillman of the CIO Political Action Committee; he had worked with Henry Ford II at the Ford Foundation and knew John D. Rockefeller at Rockefeller; he was a comrade of Victor

Navasky of *The Nation*, as well as Richard Barnet and Marcus Raskin of the progressive think tank Institute for Policy Studies. After working with University of Chicago president Robert Hutchins at Ford's Fund for the Republic, Ping helped Hutchins found the Center for the Study of Democratic Institutions in Santa Barbara, California; he was a friend and supporter of E.P. Thompson; John Kenneth Galbraith, Robert McNamara, Tom Hayden, Robert Oppenheimer, and was a colleague of the Berrigan brothers. An especially treasured soul mate was Trappist monk Thomas Merton, with whom he shared questioning dialogues about the direction the world was taking and how to respond with both effectiveness and spiritual presence.

As our friendship developed, Ping regaled me with packages containing novels that had recently impressed him, and through our letters we discussed the atomic bomb, his writings about poverty while at the Santa Barbara think tank, poems by Merton he had taken the time to retype, and the theories I was conjuring about western civilization suffering from post-traumatic stress. One day in the mid-'90s, after giving a speech at a conference on the very subject upon which our friendship was founded—the *systemic* nature of the technological onslaught—I decided to mail a cassette tape of said presentation Scarsdale-way. To my astonishment he mailed it back, unopened, explaining that he had not and would not listen to it; he had allowed this whole new generation of techno-gadgets, like the cassette player that would be required to play the tape, to pass him by—and was quite satisfied with his choice.

Wilbur H. Ferry was born in Detroit in 1910 to Fay and Hugh Ferry. His mother was a homemaker, while father Hugh started out as a worker at the Packard Motor Company factory and worked his way up to become president/chairman of the board. Both were conservative Catholics, and according to biographer James Arthur Ward, author of *Ferrytale: The Career of W.H. "Ping" Ferry,* Ping's life choices were marked by rebellion against his father's heavy hand in foisting corporate values of obedience, regimentation, and social climbing upon him.

After high school Ping went to Dartmouth College, where he played football and became what he termed a loner. After graduation in 1932, his lack of direction took the forms of drinking, aimless roaming, and numerous bouts in jail. He had something of a smattering of jobs. He taught prep school, worked a craps table in Havana, was a reporter at eight different newspapers, and did public relations for Eastern Airlines. Through a post–World War II job at PR firm Earl Newson and Company serving the Ford Motor Company's fledgling foundation, he landed upon his true calling: he gave money away to organizations dedicated to resisting the legal and economic privilege by which U.S. corporations maintain power, as well as those touting unique ideas about how to bring equality to American society.

What followed was his and Hutchins' launching of Ford's Fund for the Republic. It became a House Un-American Activities target when they hired a couple of known Communists and funded a study defending Hollywood screenwriters blacklisted for questionable affiliations. Under IRS surveillance and the threat of losing tax-exempt status, the fund morphed into the independent Center for the Study of Democratic Institutions, and Ping stepped into the dual roles of said institute's vice president and a vocal agitator for nuclear disarmament, regulation of technological dissemination, racial justice, and true democracy. He fell in love with Carol Bernstein in 1971. He obtained a divorce from his first wife, and he and Carol married in 1973. It was a fortuitous match for social movements: using the millions she had inherited from her former husband, independent stockbroker David Bernstein, the newlyweds continued her left-leaning DJB Foundation as the eccentric, no-strings-attached donating institution it had become known as.

During this exploration Ping's originality and outspokenness ripened into full form; he came to embody exactly what he liked to call himself: "The Town Crank." And surely, he was. An avowed peacenik, at the start of World War II he attempted to dodge the draft with a 4-F status; in the heat of the McCarthy years he worked with Al Capp to launch an anti-conservative cartoon; he chimed in against the death penalty; much agonized by escalating violence between the races, he vociferously called for resolution of the problem via physical separation of the races; during the Vietnam War he refused to pay taxes. To circumvent a nuclear war he proposed that the U.S. and USSR exchange a host of school children and before pushing the button, each country's leaders would have to manually murder the young ones. In the '80s he embarked upon a tour of U.S. enemies that included Moscow and Havana; and he dared to challenge the notion of "progress" by inserting a radical analysis of technology into the national zeitgeist.

In 1964 Ping sent a memorandum to U.S. President Lyndon B. Johnson and other government figures called *The Triple Revolution: An Appraisal of the Major U.S. Crises and Proposals for Action.* He had invited a group of thirty-four intellectuals, including Linus Pauling, Irving Howe, Gerard Piel, Bayard Rustin, Tom Hayden, and Norman Thomas, to put together the document, and after its publication, it became a runaway seller and college courses were created to discuss its fundamental points. The group prophetically identified three interrelated technological, foreign-policy, and racial crises:

* *A Cybernetic Revolution,* in which computers were creating "a system of almost unlimited productive capacity which requires progressively less human labor;"
* *A Weaponry Revolution,* in which nuclear weapons capable of incinerating civilization had (or so the experts proclaimed) "eliminated war as a method for resolving international conflict;"
* *A Human Rights Revolution,* in which people worldwide, in particular people of color, were arising to demand equal rights.

Regarding technology, Ping presented his perspective that rampant cybernation was the guilty party fueling the other two developments, and convinced by his analysis, the assemblage ventured a bold prediction: technological development without governmental regulation and economic redistribution efforts would result in unspeakable inequality, eventually relegating the poor and people of color to a permanent underclass—which is precisely what has come about. The document recommended a guaranteed annual income above the poverty line instead of the current "patchwork of welfare measures." It also proclaimed that only an outlawing of war coupled with complete nuclear disarmament could free the human race from its current state of terrorization and liberate national resources for needed housing and food production.

The first time I actually came face-to-face with my esteemed pen pal was at an in-house symposium called "Technology for the Common Good" that he had instigated at the Institute for Policy Studies in Washington, D.C. The year was 1991—twenty-seven years after he and his peers had drafted their memorandum. Our 1991 gathering included political economist Gar Alperovitz, lawyer/consumer advocate Ralph Nader, conversion specialist Joel Yudken, political scientist/nuclear engineer Richard Sclove, author/filmmaker Saul Landau, and others; like the 1964 meeting, it was made up of just about all men—albeit all men I had long admired. Unsettled at being one of only two female presenters, I was relieved to see that dear friend Kirkpatrick Sale was in attendance at the Friday night cocktail party. After delivering some audacious remarks about how the "new" philosophy of postmodernism was in fact just fresh linguistic dressing for tired, old liberal/capitalist modernism, he introduced me to Ping. At eighty-one, my correspondent from Scarsdale was a dapper soul of the down-to-earth variety. Decked out in a tweed jacket with patched elbows and a bow tie, he put me at ease with his warmth. I later found out that not only had Ping prompted the event by pushing the folks at IPS to ask the tougher questions about technology; he had funded it.

Afterward, executive director Michael Shuman and research fellow Julia Sweig took on the compilation of a book garnered from conference presentations, *Technology for the Common Good*. Beginning with a quote from Erich Fromm—"That millions of people share the same forms of mental pathology does not make these people sane"—I contributed an essay about addiction to technology. The pay was to be $1000 for each essay but, to my surprise, two separate checks showed up in New Mexico for a total of $2000. My suspicion was that Ping had purposefully instructed the institute to pay me twice.

After a 1994 workshop Jerry Mander, Okanagan writer Jeannette Armstrong, John Mohawk of the Iroquois Confederacy, and I conducted in upstate New York, Kirk picked John and me up for a stay-over at the house he and wife editor Faith Sale had built in Cold Spring. It was deep summer, the maples and elms as dense with foliage as they had been before the colonists arrived four centuries before. Kirk's garden was in full glory—zucchini, tomatoes, lettuce, carrots, onions—and the swimming pool, fed by the aforementioned frigid fountainhead, lay in the yard awaiting only the hardiest of aquanauts.

One night Ping and Carol arrived for dinner and afterward drove me to their place in Scarsdale. Here I was given a room in the old part of the house that, with its 1920s bathroom fixtures and white ceramic tile, dark furniture, and chenille bedspreads, reminded me of my grandmother's house in Cleveland Heights. In the morning I got a glimpse of the infamous multiple-car garage that had been refashioned into one giant room in which Ping and his office comrades answered requests for grants. One unique thing about DJB's philanthropic method was that, rather than donate money into perpetuity as other foundations did, thus guarding their assets, they were making an end run toward *giving it all away*. Instead of giving large amounts to humongous organizations, an action they believed only caused infighting, they gave smaller amounts to grassroots groups like Agape Foundation and Los Alamos Study Group. Another quirky feature was that they demanded absolutely *no* final report regarding use of monies or success of project. Plus, they volunteered donations to groups that had never even asked for them. Ping referred to himself as "a non-infrastructured philanthropoid."

On Day Number Two Ping proposed that we drive through the New York countryside to the town of Amenia to pay our respects to Sophie Mumford. Her husband, the infamous Lewis Mumford, had recently passed on at age ninety-four. Lewis Mumford was one of those thinkers who had influenced my work in both style and content. Not only was he a multidisciplinary independent scholar who in a formal sense worked outside of academia—as I, Kirkpatrick Sale, Stephanie Mills, Susan Griffin, and others emulated—but he also so brilliantly applied metaphors like Megamachine to the reigning templates behind contemporary civilization. And he wrote with passion, so much so that while reading his work, I would be so full of emotion I would have to put the book down and just *breathe*. His twenty-six volumes covered topics from architectural history, urbanization, war, history going back to the Paleolithic, regionalism, and technology criticism, and they included *Technics and Civilization, The City in History,* and *The Pentagon of Power.* Mumford ended up with invitations to speak and lecture at Harvard University, the University of California, Berkeley, and Stanford. He also became a beacon of intellectual prowess, insight, and inspiration for my generation's radical thinkers.

We set out in Ping's big American automobile, the eighty-plus-year old commanding the wheel. Scarsdale's suburban feel quickly gave way to a landscape of winding two-lane roads through tall trees and cornfields. We passed through Millbrook, and he pointed out the farmhouse where Timothy Leary, Richard Alpert, and Ralph Metzner had done research (on themselves) on the effects of LSD on human consciousness (theirs). And we lunched in a small-town restaurant festooned with ruffled curtains and braided rugs.

Upon arriving in Amenia, we walked through the hedges to the wooden door of the Mumford domicile. I quivered with anticipation: here this marvelous Ping Ferry had brought me all the way to the home of the thinker who had influenced my life's work more than any other. Although riddled with health problems, Sophie was gracious, alert, and, in her eighties, embarking upon what she described as the start of her own writing career after so many decades in the shadowlands of her husband's. We sipped Lipton tea and chatted for a spell and then . . . she pointed me towards Lewis's writing room. I rose from the stuffed chair and edged towards it with the sense of numinosity that one usually reserves for the approach to a great cathedral.

The floor was made of planks. There was no rug, and the room was almost empty. At the far wall, under a dappling of light from a clearstory window, stood a writing table, a wooden chair, a vintage black typewriter, plus some clipboards, pencils, and erasers. Everything was exactly as it had been the last day he had worked there. His corduroy jacket was still hanging from a nail on the inside of the door.

A final gift from Ping came my way as I was packing to leave for New York City, where I was to stop in on fellow-Clevelander/feminist-ceremonialist Donna Henes: Ping generously offered me complimentary lodging at the Yale Club across the street from Grand Central Station.

Aside from all the influential people he knew and all the activists, thinkers, and artists he helped; aside from his vast intelligence, penetrating insights into the nature of society, and wild ideas about solving problems—it seemed to me that Ping's greatest attribute was kindness. As journalist/publisher Victor Navasky put it, it was "the impossible example he set for the rest of us."

JERRY MANDER: FIREBRAND ADMAN
(1936-)

I became a rebel through advertising.

—J.M., "NACHO CONSULTS JERRY MANDER,"
NACHO CHRONICLE, 2010.

Dear reader: you have to understand that, unlike today when the world is fractured into an infinity of venues for gathering knowledge, in the 1970s and '80s a single book could ripple through a generation just as fast as a new Bob Dylan album had in the '60s. Was it Jerry Mander's *Four Arguments for the Elimination of Television* (1977) that accomplished that feat? Or his *In the Absence of the Sacred* (1991)? I can't be sure, but both startled the reading public into new ways of thinking; one man in Australia even ordered 25,000 copies of *Four Arguments* to distribute for free.

Jerry certainly blew my mind. Although *Four Arguments* focused on a single technology, it gave me the intellectual tools to deconstruct any technical system. *In the Absence* pitted mass technological civilization against its chief and chosen historical rival, indigenous cultures and self-sustaining communities. Both themes became centerpieces of my life's work.

I met Jerry in 1977 at a tap-dance performance given by his wife's friends, Anne Kent Rush and Nina Winter. Ever since the UC Berkeley's Pacific Film Archive had run the entirety of Fred Astaire and Ginger Rogers' films, we feminists were agog about tap dancing à la the 1930s. My class recital—which took place on Broadway Avenue in Oakland, but was decidedly off-off-off Broadway—found me in the back-back-back row of tapping aspirants, hoping to the Goddess that no one could see me. Hell with the routine, which I could *not* do, my most pressing goal was to be in the same location on stage as the rest of the class.

But Kent and Nina, now *they* could Ball-and-Chain!

I did have a minor role in Kent's event, though. This was to read my comical essay "The Magical Goddess" about the female figures of '30s Hollywood musicals, with an emphasis on Ginger Rogers' spicy talents and the mandala-shaped forms in Busby Berkeley's extravaganzas. After the show, Jerry rushed up to express his enthusiasm. At forty-one, he boasted a bush of white curls that flared out in all directions from his head. I later realized that his zeal stemmed from the fact that our way of thinking was similar: we both drew associations between normally disparate, unassociated phenomena, and we both aimed to dig to the deeper meaning of their juxtaposition.

The friendship blossomed to the aroma of ground coffee beans and the earnest tenor of Italian opera singers in the cafés of North Beach. Malvina's, The Trieste, The Puccini. He was living on the steepest street in the city, Filbert, with his wife Ani and their two sons, where he was the braver-than-brave participant in the flowering of feminist themes regarding woman-man equality and, when the scandalous book *Open Marriage* came out, an accomplice in the experiment of honesty apropos sexual relationships outside of marriage.

Jerry was also working at Public Media Center, where he continued his original occupation as an advertising executive, although no longer in the profit-making interest of Rainier Ale, Rover cars, and *Scientific American* magazine, but rather for progressive issues like preventing the building of dams in the Grand Canyon, saving the whales from extinction, and stopping the supersonic transport project. All the while, he seemed always to be writing a book, somewhat tortuously, he himself admitted, as he refused to stop until he found *just* the right way to say something; he delivered *In the Absence of the Sacred* eleven years after Sierra Club Books' due date! On the upside, just as computers were entering the author business, he was ever so proud of the fact that he typed on a 1930s Underwood Standard like the ones hard-boiled reporters in black-and-white films had used to bang out the news.

I saw that typewriter. I was visiting him at the house he and Ani bought in Bolinas, the seaside enclave north of San Francisco where such beat/hip luminaries as Ponderosa Pine, Joanne Kyger, and Richard Brautigan penned poetry, grew pot, handcrafted artifacts, refused a U.S. zip code, and fought the state of California over the spraying of health-threatening pesticides on the nearby highway. The house was on stilts overlooking the endless expanse of the Pacific Ocean, and just across the bushes from that of punk rocker Hughie Lewis. It was calm there. We made a dinner of brown rice and vegetables and, in the commanding presence of the Underwood, talked about guidelines he had garnered from his advertising days for researching and writing books. Like "Don't use footnotes; put everything in the text" and "The best titles startle." I also became privy to Jerry's secret for budget hair control: he would get the raging bush cut extremely short and for six months let it grow and grow—until it acquired a substantive unmanageability, then he would cut it all off again.

In Bolinas Jerry was introduced to a concept called "bioregionalism." Echoing the regionalism of Lewis Mumford's day but adding the factors of watershed and ecology, it advocated breaking down Turtle Island/ North America into ecologically defined zones for reestablishing sustainable communities— à la Ernest "Chick" Callenbach's *Ecotopia*. I too was grappling with such ideas, and once, stymied by the daunting task of rupturing the nation-state's totality, I asked Jerry, "How big is a bioregion?" He thought for some time—it was a fresh concept for him as well—and finally said, "As big as you can walk across." His one-liners, all of which I still recall and have lived by, clearly sprang from the same fount of talent that fueled his success as an adman.

Jerry was raised in Yonkers, New York, a neighborhood that in the 1930s and '40s was still largely rural. He grew up being revolted by the influx of mammoth shopping malls, sprawling parking lots, and cookie-cutter houses in the post–World War II microbial bloom of American suburbia.

Social awareness was also passed to him by his parents, Harry and Eva Mander—he from Poland, she from Romania. Like other immigrants, they worked feverishly to lift the family out of poverty. Jerry wrote about their challenges in *Four Arguments*:

My parents carried the immigrants' fears. Security was their primary value: all else was secondary. Both of them had escaped pogroms in Eastern Europe. My father's career had followed the path familiar to so many New York immigrants. Lower East Side. Scant schooling. Street hustling. Hard work at anything to keep life together. Early marriage. Struggling out of poverty.

Curiously, success came to him during the Depression. He founded what later became Harry Mander and Company, a small service business to the garment industry, manufacturing pipings, waist bands, pocketing and collar canvas.

Jerry grew up the beneficiary of his father's successes—and inside a rapidly changing American society. His earliest goal was extraordinarily American: to be a professional golfer. He earned a B.S. degree from the Wharton School at the University of Pennsylvania and an M.S. in international economics from Columbia—and went into advertising. He explains his turn away from commercial marketing toward promoting progressive causes as a change of consciousness due to the grossly manipulative nature of the business.

Jerry in (uncommon) professional mode, hair flying in all directions as always. Courtesy of Jerry Mander.

I wonder if growing up in a family at the margins of a society, poles apart from what they had previously known, has something to do with Jerry's ability to see beyond the details and capture the underlying theme and structure of a system. Surely Eva and Harry spoke about the contrast between how things were done in the United States and how things had been in Eastern Europe, thus nurturing in their son insight into what lies below the surface. Jerry went on to write, co-write, or co-edit eight books, each of which cuts through ideological myth and promotion to analyze mass technological society, the corporate economy, militarism, or capitalism.

In 1978, after *Four Arguments* came out, he and Diana Dillaway of *Mother Jones*' Foundation for National Progress put together a discussion to explore the use of technology to further mass political systems, "Technology: Over the Invisible Line?" Socialist Murray Bookchin, Native American rights activist Oren Lyons (Seneca/Onondaga/Iroquois Confederacy), ecologist Stephanie Mills, recovery-of-the-commons activist Lee Swenson, among others, holed up on the Mills College campus, presenting papers showing technology's role in politics and battling it out between ecological and socialist perceptions.

A decade later, this seminal gathering was followed by what became the Megatechnology and Development conferences and finally the Jacques Ellul Society. The original get-together took place at philanthropist Doug Tompkins' house in North Beach in 1988. It was the first time that many of us had laid eyes upon our peers whose books and movies we had long admired, the instigators of a post-Luddite, post-Mumford/Ellul critique of technological civilization. Godfrey Reggio, who had made the *Koyanaskatsi* film, was there on the grass patio. There was poet/farmer Wendell Berry, feminist Susan Griffin, sociologist Jeremy Rifkin, author/filmmaker Helena Norberg-Hodge, and ecologist David Suzuki. In a tense moment over cocktails, Kirkpatrick Sale took the opportunity to apologize to Langdon Winner for a review he had written in the *New York Times* critical of Winner's groundbreaking *Autonomous Technology: Technics as a Theme in Political Thought*. Kirk's criticism in such a respected newspaper had effectively squashed whatever potential popularity the book might have had. To our relief and amazement,

Langdon replied with a smile and bravely stated that he himself had written things for which he was later sorry.

The group met throughout the '90s, always happy to be together and, as Stephanie penned in *Turning against Technology*, "never feeling so sane." In 1996, at the last of our Ellul meetings, Jerry was already knee-deep into warning about the economic system being foisted through neoliberal trade treaties like the North American Free Trade Agreement and the General Agreement on Tariffs and Trade, the latter of which spawned the World Trade Organization. During a break he told me, "I'm getting into this anti-corporation movement because I'm in a position to do something about it, and I have to follow this opportunity." I took the comment in; it made sense—yet I didn't fully understand its place in relation to our technology focus. I now wonder if it wasn't an apology for his approaching departure from our work as head-on critics of technological society.

The International Forum on Globalization had been born in 1994, spawning a separate and larger cadre of activists and thinkers. For reasons of not alienating potential campaigners in that movement, many of whom embraced cell phones and computers without question, Jerry set aside the more edgy issue of technology's impacts and turned his attention to corporate globalization, organizing educational forums in the U.S., Canada, South America, and Europe. His anthology, *The Case against the Global Economy*, put together with Edward Goldsmith, came out in 1996, three years before the first major anti-globalization uprising. In those times he also worked as executive director of Doug Tompkins's venue for philanthropy, the Foundation for Deep Ecology.

In celebrating Jerry's life, I have grown aware that behind that shock of white hair and laid-back North Beach/Bolinas veneer swelters one firebrand of a thinker and mover-and-shaker: in all these years he hasn't stopped working for a more just and sustainable world. Arriving at the ripe age of eighty—and using the knowledge he gained through both an education in international economics and participation in the anti-globalization movement, as well as that special twist of mind that is all and only his—he penned *The Capitalist Papers: Fatal Flaws of an Obsolete System*, then re-energized the original neo-Luddite group with a forum in New York City to critique the Bold New World of Technology.

When I think of Jerry, I am drawn to a golden day at the San Francisco Bay's edge where sight-seekers walk among sea lions and runners take off to sprint the beach out to Fort Point. The era was late '80s, and Jerry confided in me his desire to write a book about his male friends, some of whom dated back to Yonkers and with whom he still shared a men's group. "My next book will be about their friendship," he stated with certainty. I was startled by this turn toward the personal, yet too, I thought, such a project would present the perfect opportunity to express psychoanalyst Erik Erikson's latter-stage–of-life task of reviewing one's life and in the process clarifying meaning and wrapping things up.

Between then and now, a world gone awry in the wake of corporatization got in the way of fulfilling that spark. But now, after a lifetime of "advertising" collective issues, maybe he'll write that book and, dear reader, you will get to witness another side of his considerable humanity.

STEPHANIE MILLS: A LIFE OF THE MIND
(1948-)

*There comes a point at which the fabric of the planetary
ecosystem is so shredded that the whole thing folds and
we're all dining on jellyfish.*
—S.M., QUOTED IN *MY NORTH*, APRIL 18, 2011

Stephanie Mills gives one the sense that goodness is safe and sound inside the human heart. She combines the qualities of humility, honesty, and intelligence with a rare ability to feel at ease smack-dab in the muck and mire of things that don't fit together. She also, notably, boasts an uncommon talent: she can speak and write in deadpan Chaucerian English.

I had heard of Stephanie for years: she made the headlines of both the *San Francisco Chronicle* and the *Oakland Tribune* in 1969. The commencement speech she gave at Mills College was a scandalous address entitled "The Future Is a Cruel Hoax," called by the *New York Times*

Steph leans against a found tire at Lake Mead, California, 2011.
Photo credit: Richard Register. Courtesy of Stephanie Mills.

"perhaps the most anguished . . . of the year's crop of valedictory speeches." Its topic was the social/ecological instability that would result from the imminent state of overpopulation á la Anne and Paul Ehrlich and her subsequent decision to not bring children into this world. In true Mills literary form, she later called her stance "the ecofeminist version of burning a draft card."

Steph went on to the plum job of contributor and later assistant editor at *Whole Earth Catalog/CoEvolution Quarterly* where, aside from writing articles on ecological themes, she battled it out with editor Stewart Brand about what became his fixation on the splendors of interplanetary travel, space colonies, and the computerization of humanity. It was the 1970s, the decade moon roofs, nuclear power plants, and credit cards came into common use; yet already she was questioning technology.

After graduation, Stephanie also served as editor for *Earth Times*'s brief four-part issuance into the emerging environmental movement, a job she sadly left because of the all-too-common lack of synchronicity between enthusiasm and bottom-line figures. In the late '70s she became editor of Friends of the Earth's *Not Man Apart,* a job she was asked to leave because she had breached acceptable limits by writing editorials

that proposed an environmental-justice perspective. Not all environmentalists, it turned out, wanted to be reminded of the racism festering
at the South African locale of the World Wilderness Congress.

Wherever she was working, Steph always found time to write. Books
to follow reflected her autodidactic, craftsmanlike leap into the field of
ecology: *Epicurean Simplicity* on simple living, a Thoreau-inspired collection of essays called *Tough Little Beauties, In Service of the Wild* on
ecological restoration, and *On Gandhi's Path*, about radical, communi-
ty-minded economist Bob Swann.

I finally met Stephanie at the 1988 Bioregional Congress in Kerrville,
Texas. Sixty-some women had gathered under a circus tent apart from
the men folk, and we took turns introducing ourselves. Still recovering from a divorce and a near-death car accident, both of which had
demanded her innermost resources for survival, Stephanie spoke of
the joys of leading a Life of the Mind. Hers was unlike any other
check-in.

We reconvened at the Megatechnology and Jacques Ellul conferences initially pulled together by Jerry Mander and Helena Norberg-Hodge, starting in 1989 and running through 1996. In rooms filled
with some thirty accomplished intellectuals and activists, it was often
hard to get a word in edgewise. Here was Wendell Berry breaking the
ice—and causing raucous hilarity—by proclaiming, "I'm a Neo-Luddite!"; Beth Burrows presenting the facts on what at that point was still
the "coming" disaster of genetic engineering; Jerry warning of the "new
technologies" that would include GMOs, nanotechnology, super computers, satellites, and weapons of mass destruction that we could not
yet imagine; Vandana Shiva enlightening us about the grievous
socio-economic effects of "free trade" as it was foisted on India in the
1700s; John Mohawk of the Onondaga Nation reminding us of the social
structures of indigenous communities that held out hope for an ecological use of technology; biologist Martha Crouch regaling us with how
she left university teaching as a protest against the academy's cooptation by bio-engineering corporations; Godfrey Reggio telling us that
the problem was the system as a whole that was causing us not merely
to use destructive technologies, but to *live* them. That first meeting

took place in the '80s, and since then all the grievous predictions, one by one, have come true.

Through it all, Steph radiated an aura of dignity. When she chimed in, she added her humble ironic twists that set everyone at ease, and in the end she was chosen to edit the content of our discussions toward a book called *Turning Away from Technology*.

Given that we both aimed to live as off-the-grid as possible, she more rigorously than I, we began to correspond in the old-fashioned way, by hand-inked epistle. And so it was through some twenty-plus years of letters that I came to love Stephanie.

Typically, she would start each with a description of the birds visiting her plot of "woodburb" in upstate Michigan, the coolness of the lake in summer, the color of the leaves as they fluttered in the autumn wind. "It's good to be home in the oyster-shell gray and chalk-white world," she scratched on a postcard upon returning to Michigan after a year and a half of tending her father as he died. "Snowing, snowing, but gently. A soft pure blanket. It's cold-teens by day. The emerald ash borer's depredations mean that most of the firewood available is dead ash; quick to burn (if dry, which

A pile of Stephanie's letters, 2014–15. Photo credit: Dorian Foto, Sucre, Bolivia. Courtesy of Chellis Glendinning.

mine isn't) and low on BTUs. Got 2 little winter survival plight shaping up here as I try to re-inhabit my post-Dad, post-Scottsdale life."

Or this on a September day in 2014: "I'm out on my back deck for it's a balmy sweet Fall day, with sunshine and a splendor of gold and green light streaming through the changing sugar maple leaves. It's not too late in the year for there to be a mosquito sussing out the prospects for a meal of my blood. Crickets are trilling. Red squirrels and chipmunks are dashing about, getting their winter supplies together. A hawk is leering, a crow carving, a blue jay is yelling. And the truck traffic goes by on the road."

In every letter Steph's kindness showed through. At a time when she knew that I was residing in the shadow of Job, she eloquently penned: "I picture you so dashing and full of attention and conviction and surprise, moving through excitements and past obstacles and into deeper understanding of your new milieu [in Bolivia]. . . . I hope that the moments of contrast when you contend with doubt, loneliness, and suffering, as every human must, are few and mercifully brief."

Always attention was given to the distressing state of the planet, which she tended to capture with punchy metaphors. "It's comforting to be with the flowers, to greet them as beloved," she wrote. "I want to enjoy biodiversity while it still exists." And on dramatic upheavals of weather, like hurricanes: "Instant Mumbai on the Atlantic seaboard. Could it be a perfect opportunity to stop and reconsider the whole project of modernity?"

And true to her dedication to a Life of the Mind, she would report on what book she was devouring, which predictably was of the ilk of *Crime and Punishment, Homage to Catalonia, Paradise Lost,* or *War and Peace.* Then, occasionally and with no small smattering of guilt, she would veer in the direction of "detective novels set in 1st-century A.C. Rome, spy novels set in Europe during WWII, and swashbuckling, intricate intrigues set in Scotland in the sixteenth century."

This attention to the written word began early. Steph was born an only child in lushly green, palm-tree-studded Berkeley, California, and grew up in arid, saguaro-festooned Phoenix, Arizona. Her parents, Robert Mills, a mechanical engineer who sold specialty castings to the hard-rock mining industry, and Edith Mills, a homemaker, were inveterate readers and correspondents. They were also fluent speakers of both the Queen's and colloquial English. They poured attention onto their only child, nurturing her curiosity, helping her to build a library, and engendering her independence. She attended both prep school at Windsor Hall Preparatory School and public school at North Phoenix High School.

Writing for publication began in high school. As early as 1970 she was posing the question "Whatever Happened to Ecology?" as a query into why the radical egalitarianism of ecology as a stencil for action had been left to men in three-piece-suits. The question was as much a metaphor for human action as is was about the living tissue of Gaia. The book she wrote in the mid-'80s, of the same name, was an integration of the Ehrlichs' research regarding the impacts of overpopulation/development on the planet with a chronicle of her evolution as an eco-political thinker. Written with her emblematic self-effacing humor, the book features a gallop through the nascent environmental movement of the 1970s-'80s, including encounters and friendships with advertising innovator Howard Gossage, author Jerry Mander, environmentalist David Brower, save-the-whales activist Joan McIntyre, environmentalist Ponderosa Pine, bioregionalist Peter Berg, feminist Starhawk, and a host of other activists of note—just as it explores political conundrums such as the practice of abortion, anthropocentrism, and Inside-the-Beltway reform versus Never-Say-Die radical action versus Walk-the-Talk/Do-It-Yourself sustainable withdrawal from the system. Always it reveals Steph's irrepressible inclination to say and write what she sees and wishes others would see—no matter the repercussions for future employability.

One of the last times Steph and I clinked cups of Lapsang Souchong was at the 1995 Learning Alliance conference "Technology and Its Discontents" in New York City. Along with Kirkpatrick Sale, Steph and I were on the verge of performing our *Interview with a Luddite* play and feeling rather giddy. Who knew that it was all to end? Who understood that the global economy's preference for the privatization of the world's riches would soon suck dry the monies available to our heresies? Or could predict that our most loyal funder, Doug Tompkins, would decide that a more direct use of his capital to save the planet's ecology would be to buy up wild lands in Patagonia? We still believed that the luxury of yearly get-togethers to discuss pressing issues involving technology, the planet, and social movements would go on as it always had.

In her letters Steph sometimes refers to the sense she has of being a pariah at dinner parties: she feels compelled to challenge people's belief in the future by regaling them with the state of a planet on the edge of collapse. The compulsion lets loose its Gorgonian locks due to the fact that she keeps up with the details: the daily animal extinctions, unbridled deforestation and desertification, the ever-widening breakdown of entire ecosystems. Not to mention the held-together-by-toothpicks financial markets, the ongoing wars, nuclear buildup, and social breakdown, the grim prospects of Peak Oil, and the equally grim impacts of barraging living beings with electromagnetic radiation. I am reminded of a *Sylvia* cartoon by feminist Nicole Hollander in which our wry and cynical protagonist is sitting at the neighborhood bar regaling her cohort about the perils of nuclear war when the other retorts: "Sylvia, don't make yourself unpopular."

Perhaps by way of karmic justice, Steph was invited to be a fellow of the Post Carbon Institute. Early on in this endeavor she traveled to California to chow down a weekend's worth of dinners with Peak Oil expert Richard Heinberg, sustainability activist Gloria Flora, botanist Wes Jackson, photographer Zenobia Barlow, and other systems thinkers, analysts, and policy makers whose knowledge and distress equaled her

A small portion of Stephanie's immense library.
Photo credit and courtesy of Whitney Smith.

own. The 2010 retreat was held at the Brower Center in Berkeley for the purpose of clarifying the institute's mission, strategizing about communicating to the public, and sharing Steph's over-the-edge vision of the precipice that humanity currently straddles; in the presence of such like-minded peers, Steph was able to feel sane again.

Back in Michigan, she has become involved in the effort to de-globalize/ re-localize by creating a money system generated via direct trade and earned hours of service. "Who knows what's going to become of the U.S. economy," she told an interviewer in 2011. "It's too large a system to manage intelligently and for the common good, whereas at the local level the feedback loops are shorter." The work involves initiating a home-grown currency, called Bay Bucks, in the Grand Traverse bioregion as a way to encourage local relationships, sustainability, and investment. "If we got a deflationary depression and cash got scarce, there would still be people with skills, people producing goods . . . and that's why there were hundreds of local currencies in the U.S. during the Depression."

In regards to her preoccupation with the environment, Steph wrote in one letter that the next mission was not just the task of reintroducing ourselves into the natural world; it was to face the reality of nature's galloping demise and to create honorable ways to live in/with this unspeakable tragedy. Like everyone else who has attempted the challenge, Steph hasn't mastered an entirely adequate response. One would have to inquire then: whatever happened to ecology?

She certainly has never stopped asking

THEODORE ROSZAK: VOICE FOR THE EARTH
(1933–2011)

Repression of the ecological unconscious is the deepest root of the collusive madness in industrial society; open access to the ecological unconscious is the path to sanity.

—T.R., *THE VOICE OF THE EARTH*, 1992

I first spoke to Ted Roszak as he was sitting on an old wooden school chair backstage, gathering his thoughts for the presentation he was about to deliver at an anti-nuclear conference. It was some time in the 1980s, and in his early fifties he was tall, lanky, and possessing a decidedly pointed chin. Also handsome. Gathering my courage, as the man was well-known, I approached and heaped praise upon him for what I naively referred to as "your book." He looked up at me quizzically and asked, "*Which* book?"

It was true; at that point, Ted was the author of some ten tomes, including *Person/Planet: The Creative Disintegration of Industrial Society; The Cult of Information*, about the negative impacts of computers; and perhaps his most popular, *The Making of a Counter Culture*, in which he linked the explosion of political/cultural movements among the '60s generation to the sterility and soullessness of modern society. Of his 1972 *Where the Wasteland Ends: Politics and Transcendence in Postindustrial Society, New York Times* reviewer Anatole Broyard wrote that it was "nothing less than a State of the Union Message on the condition of the human soul." Before his delve into the healing offered via merging psychology with ecology, the central theme in these early books tended toward sociological critique of technological society; his description of himself was "a leading spokesman for anti-science and . . . a Neo-Luddite crusader," while journalist G. Pascal Zachary of *The Wall Street Journal* dubbed him "the godfather of the neo-Luddite movement."

I remember little of that particular anti-nuclear conference, as we activists attended so many such events, but I cannot forget that, bristling with conviction, Ted stood behind the podium and proclaimed that, regarding nuclear weapons, we would win because we were "Dead to Right." And that's how he was: squarely confronting the somber labyrinths to highlight the possibilities. To his way of thinking, examination of the deeper historical, societal, and psychological patterns offered a key to transformation. Such scrutiny led him to be outspoken in his opposition to technological civilization as a whole and unabashedly open to other ways of living and thinking. He seemed always to be in a process of exploration of the unknown and a state of wonder at what he found there. Once, after Okanagan writer Jeannette Armstrong had delivered one of the stories of her people—a lengthy yet simple tale that involved all kinds of animals, their problems, their solutions, their trickster humor—Ted said that he had not had such an intellectual workout in years.

Born in Chicago at the height of the Depression, the man who was to become a social philosopher grew up Catholic and working class. After World War II the family moved to Los Angeles, where he graduated from high school. Then, upon earning his B.A. in history at the University of California, Los Angeles, and Ph.D. in English history from Princeton, he taught at Stanford, the University of British Columbia, and San Francisco State, finally settling in at California State University/East Bay, where he stayed for thirty-five years. He married Betty Greenwald, a painter highlighting spiritual themes and an author in her own right, whose emphasis on the non-rational provided great inspiration to Ted. Joyfully, they had their daughter Kathryn in 1960. She has gone on to become a dancer, choreographer, and writer—like her parents, breaking through cultural walls with creativity.

In all, Ted wrote or edited fourteen non-fiction books, including the 1969 *Masculine/Feminine: Readings in Sexual Mythology and the Liberation of Women,* which he put together with Betty, presaging the feminist uprising that was about to erupt. Six of his novels were published (with four more yet to come), and he was twice nominated for the National Book Award. He also received a Guggenheim Fellowship. One of his fiction pieces is the cult classic *Flicker.* Another was written in the mid-'90s during our efforts to bring neo-Luddism into the world. *The Memoirs of Elizabeth Frankenstein* is narrated not by Victor, as in Mary Shelley's version, but by his half-sister and soon-to-be wife Elizabeth. Ted's approach was to bring to light, this time from a woman's point of view, the conflict between rationalism and romanticism, between the rampant search for scientific fact and primordial wisdom, between destruction of nature via "progress" and preservation of ancient cultures based in the natural world. His intention was to draw attention to the oppression of women and their likewise suppressed knowledge of nature's power.

For all his accomplishments, Ted was a remarkably humble soul. He was the gentlest of introverts and seemingly a tad less at ease in the everyday material world than in that of ideas and anima. One stand-out memory occurred at a psychology symposium in a hotel in San Francisco. I was on the panel, he in the audience. In preparation for the writing of *My Name Is Chellis and I'm in Recovery from Western Civilization*, I was toying with theories about the contemporary social conundrum and psychological disorders being structured by the Neolithic era's slow lunge away from nature-identified cultures toward the human/nature rupture that domestication initiated. Ted sat cross-legged on a chair with his eyes closed, consciously attending to my words with every cell of his body.

He had a special interest in the subject: he himself was exploring theories regarding the human-nature relationship that would soon lay the ground for a new academic discipline he called ecopsychology. *The Voice of the Earth* came out in 1992. As Worldwatch Institute's Lester Brown has commented, the book is "nothing less than a psychoanalysis of civilization." Contemporary technological culture psychotically disconnects from the planetary, Ted pointed out. Drawing on the works of Carl Jung and Sigmund Freud, as well as on the Gaia hypothesis, he proposed the existence of an "ecological unconscious" in each of us, a living imprint of evolution capable of linking us synergistically to our original environment, the natural world. But this awareness has been repressed by the demands for adaptation to dysfunctional, mechanistic mass society. And so follows the concept of joining ecology with psychology. Ted rooted his notion of a reclamation of the innate self with references to tribal animism, systems theory, ecofeminism, and deep ecology; he proposed psychic restoration via communion with wilderness, shamanistic exploration, nature mysticism, natural healing techniques, and creative expression.

And in *The Voice of the Earth* he makes another of his daring statements: that the great question of our times is not what we humans might do about our ailing planet as we so industriously gag the life out of her; it is rather *what she will do with us!* He was always doing that sort of thing, turning things upside down so that we could—and would—see the human condition in a fresh light. He also had an eye for organizing. As a result of his attention to the research I presented at the San Francisco conference, he invited me to the first ecopsych seminar at Esalen Institute in 1992, where I was given the opportunity to know him a little bit better.

That knowing was enhanced when I saw him at a dinner held after a weekend meeting of the Jacques Ellul Society. We met high up in the Berkeley hills just as the rays of the sun began to vanish behind the Golden Gate Bridge. The bay was sparkling like a meadow of diamonds and the electric lights of San Francisco were just beginning their nightly glitter show. He told me he was writing about aging. What on Earth for? I naively thought, as I was in my be-young-forever mid-forties. But he said that now that he and Betty were getting older—with the eighty million Baby Boomers he had championed earlier in his career soon to follow suit—it was time to refurbish the place of old people in American society. From a visionary perspective, of course. He saw the chance for the '60s generation to put the finishing touches on its chosen mission of changing society for the better. *America the Wise* came out in 1998, *The Making of an Elder Culture* in 2009. In these offerings Ted encouraged a needed adjustment, from commercialized, future-obsessed Youth Culture toward the revaluing of the resources of those who have known life for a long time, like elders in indigenous cultures.

Dear Ted Roszak gave up his long journey through life on July 5, 2011. Needless to say, he was writing up until the day he died. According to Betty, he had suffered from liver cancer. The passing of this stellar example of what a human being can be came as a tremendous loss to us all, and yet, if we are to learn from his talent for unearthing possibility in the midst of unanswered questions, confusion, and despair, loss might be transformed into gratitude for his contributions to life.

KIRKPATRICK SALE: LUDDITE SECESSIONIST
(1937-)

Progress is the myth that assures us that full-speed-ahead is never wrong. Ecology is the discipline that teaches us that it is disaster.

—K.S., "FIVE FACETS OF A MYTH," *RESURGENCE*, ISSUE 192, JANUARY/FEBRUARY 1999

Sitting in the French Roast at 6th Avenue and 11th and looking ever so au courant in my black ripstop jumpsuit, I glanced up. Amid the throngs crossing the street in lockstep to the WALK signal strutted a... *whaaat?* ... an eighteenth-century highwayman in billowing cloth shirt, lace-up boots, and commanding black cape—with (needless to say) not so much as one New Yorker batting an eye. *KIRK!*

I traveled all the way across New Mexico to West Texas to the 1988 Bioregional Congress for the sole purpose of meeting Kirkpatrick Sale. I had read his sharp political commentaries in *The Nation,* where he was a regular contributor, and his column "Letter from America" in the British rag *Resurgence,* and I was aware he was a historian who had written books on subjects such as Students for a Democratic Society, small-is-beautiful community, and bioregionalism. Who was to know that he would become one of my all-time favorite people?

The Congress had just hosted the annual speak-for-those-who-cannot-speak-for-themselves assembly in which people dressed as sea lions, redwood trees, condors, and leopards presented their concerns regarding survival. The spotted owls were hobbling away, stray feathers aflutter in the air, and I made my move. I was traveling with my gorilla companion Roosevelt, and I invited Kirk to go on a canoe trip with us down the Guadalupe River. (Roosevelt is a life-sized stuffed animal created by toy entrepreneur/peace-movement philanthropist Henry Dakin and modeled on Koko, the gorilla who communicated by sign language; Roose has been my companion since 1987.) Perhaps the invitation would seem a bit strange to such an erudite New York scholar, I posited, slightly mortified; on the other hand, this scholar had just willingly attended an event populated by talking animals and trees.... Without a flinch Kirk accepted, and the three of us were soon paddling, slapping branches out of the way so Roosevelt would not be unnecessarily catapulted into the waves, and laughing up a storm.

From then on we were thrown together at Jerry Mander's Megatechnology meetings, conferences where we would share the podium, and whenever one or the other was working near the other's home ground. I loved him because he was brilliant and thoughtful. I loved him because he was passionate. I loved him because he was honest, so easily sharing the intimate details of his life. I loved him because, for some reason or other, he reminded me of a character in a Dickens novel; all he needed to complete the picture was a velvet waistcoat.

And he was daring, always daring.

Kirk grew up in Cayuga Heights, a village outside of Ithaca, New York, in the heart of the Finger Lakes. His parents were Helen, a housewife and bookstore owner, and William, a professor of English at Cornell University. The village set the stage for Kirk's social philosophies and attitudes; it was rural, it was human scale, it was rooted in family farming and practices of over-the-back-fence communalism. From the start Kirk harbored a mistrust of the complex world outside and its supposition of authority over all.

In the 1950s he studied English and history at nearby Cornell, where, as editor of the *Cornell Daily Sun*, he led the emerging protests of the Beat era alongside roommate Richard Farina, who became a noted Greenwich Village writer and folk singer. Kirk's early employment included working in periodicals such as *New Leader*, which had been founded by Eugene Debs and Norman Thomas, and the *New York Times Magazine*. His hangout was the infamous White Horse Tavern, where he drank Arf 'n Arf alongside Farina, poet Tod Perry, and his eventual wife, editor Faith Apfelbaum, while crooning along with folk singers the Clancy Brothers and Tommy Makem in the back room.

As a historian, Kirk took on social issues from the perspective of events and trends through time. His first book, published in 1972, was *The Land and People of Ghana*. According to political commentator Jack Hunter, his second book, *SDS*, "is still considered one of the best sources on the youth activist organization that helped define 1960s radicalism." Two radical thinkers were seminal for Kirk's later work. One was social/architectural scholar and inventor of the concept of Society-as-Machine, Lewis Mumford. The two corresponded for years, and finally in 1989 he and W. H. "Ping" Ferry drove up to Mumford's farm house in Amenia, New York, and shortly after that Kirk had the unhappy task of writing an obituary for the master in *The Nation*.

And then there was Leopold Kohr, who had said, "if something's wrong, it's too big" and had coined the phrase "small is beautiful." He became

Kirk's dear friend in 1978, and his book *The Breakdown of Nations* became a decisive work for Kirk's intellectual and political development. The two met first at his apartment in Greenwich Village and many times thereafter in London, and Kirk invited his mentor to speak at the E.F. Schumacher Society in Massachusetts. Kohr humorously explained to his eager audience that he couldn't see or hear anymore—so all that was left for him was to talk. He brought the house down with his lecture on the wisdom of small-is-beautiful, and Kirk went on to elaborate on the same themes: decentralism, bioregionalism, anti-empire, and technology criticism.

Following in the footsteps of his mentors—both independent scholars—Kirk wrote *The Conquest of Paradise* about what could only be called Columbus' crash landing, ecologically speaking, in the Americas. *Rebels against the Future: The Luddites and Their War on the Industrial Revolution* followed, delineating the missing details of the nineteenth-century anti-machine uprising while showing the similarities between their struggle to stop the Industrial Revolution's demolition of sustainable community and today's onslaught by computer, satellite, and bioengineering technologies. *After Eden: The Evolution of Human Domination* demonstrated a heretical crossover into that realm of human curiosity called archaeology. In it, he bears witness to a planet-wide volcano that occurred 70,000 years ago and shows how the age-old method of scavenging meat was forced by subsequent climate change and ecological disaster to mutate into active hunting. The change, according to Kirk, initiated the human split from the natural world with its attendant alienation, chronic fear, and compensation via the drive to dominate.

His topics of concern are broad and expansive, just as they always bring the reader back to basic valuing of community, nature, and sustainability.

In the 1990s cell phones, computers, communications satellites, and wireless waves began to restructure people's means of living, thinking, and relating. I admit to being shocked, as if by a stun gun, at how fast and completely this brave new world overtook the planet and all its creatures. With unprecedented efficiency it came to define not just the global economy and a historically unheard-of supremacy by transnational corporations, a rising gap between the ultra-rich and the ultra-poor, desperate migration, extinctions, ecological coherence, and human health—but our every thought, feeling, action, and interaction. In 1996, simultaneous with the influx of the onslaught of these "new technologies," our little Jacques Ellul Society bit the dust. (Another organization of the same name but unrelated was later founded in France.) I was mute: I could find no words to speak of the topsy-turvy nature of what was unfolding. As a conscious strategy, Jerry Mander had stopped presenting his systemic analysis of technology so he wouldn't alienate the young cell-phone-computer devotees of his newly chosen focus, the anti-globalization movement. I tried calling Langdon Winner at Rensselaer Polytechnic, and all I got was an alien machine taking digital messages. Kirk had been stirred enough by the politics of secession that he founded an institute to support those who favored breakaway from the United States.

At the same time I had the sense that *now* more than ever our criticism of mass technological society was needed. Stephanie Mills and Kirk joined me in a three-way conversation called "Three Luddites Talking" that was published in *Counterpunch*. Paradoxically we opted for the easiest way to accomplish the work between Michigan, New York, and New Mexico: passing a growing document from one to the other via email.

The get-together, as it were, sparked some of the most lucid, eloquent, and mature thinking on the parts of Kirk and Steph. We covered the onslaught of the technologies then grasping a hold of humanity, the origins of the technological runaway, the qualities of a value-based systemic analysis, the history of criticism including our own, and how we each saw the world today. At one point we were discussing why the Ellul group had fallen apart. Steph had spoken about the loss of funding, while I had offered internal-dynamics reasons—at which Kirk exuded a blast like a stern north wind. "I doubt that gossiping and backstabbing brought us down," he piped. "The movement *petered out*—and I think that's the right phrase, for it doesn't exist as a movement today—for reasons much larger than our funding, our foibles, or our follies. It ended because we lost. *The other side WON!*"

And that was Kirk. Honest, forthright, and so clear in his perceptions that you couldn't help but be affected by them.

After decades of looking at mass techno-civilization, human-scale sustainable community, and rebel revolts—and so as not to let the phasing out of our movement get him down—Kirk took a turn toward the make-it-happen wing of bioregionalism: secession. According to his calculations, some 150 separatist movements are alive in the world today—with twenty-five in North America, eight in South America, thirty in Africa, thirty in Europe, twenty-seven in Asia, ten in the Pacific Rim. Quebec. Scotland. Tibet. Sicilia. Palestine. The Mapuche Nation. Cataluña. Wales. Venice. Kashmir. In the U.S.: the states of Vermont, South Carolina, Hawaii, Texas, Louisiana, Oregon, and Alaska, the indigenous Nation of the Lakota, northern California, Puerto Rico, five counties in Maryland, eight in Colorado, etc.

In 2004 he and economist Thomas Naylor founded the Middlebury Institute to "create a movement that will place secession on the national agenda, encourage secessionist organizations, develop communication among existing and future secessionist groups, and create a body of scholarship to examine and promote the ideas and principles of secessionism." Kirk's First North American Secessionist Convention in 2006 brought together forty advocates ranging from indigenous activists and bioregionalists to libertarians and Christian conservatives who together issued a statement of principles called the Burlington Declaration. His second convention, in 2007, received worldwide media attention. A guiding principle of secession movements is respect for the politics, and sovereignty, of each governing entity, which is, of course, a legal code of international relations in the world today. The 2007 convention was criticized by the Southern Poverty Law Center, because its co-host, the League of the South, was a "racist hate group."

I was a speaker at the Second Vermont Republic Congress that took place the week before the third Middlebury convention in 2008. It brought together Vermont's green-left-progressive bioregionalists with a representative from the Alaska Independence Party, which had just been the focus of national media attention for the fact that the husband of ultra-right, vice-presidential candidate Sarah Palin was a member.

As a progressive myself, but one who lived in a land-based, sovereignty-minded New Mexican village and had long since integrated its politics

of autonomy into my thinking, I was touched by AIP chairwoman Lynette
Clark's response to a question posed by Green journalist/professor Rob
Williams of Vermont: "Why are Alaskans pro-gun and pro-privatiza-
tion?" She explained that people in Alaska wear guns for security because
they live in territories harboring dangerous animals like bears and
wolves. (In fact, she confessed, that moment in Vermont was the first
time in ages she was *not* packing her 45-caliber, and she sensed that
something was missing from her body!) Clark went on to regale us with
a story to explain the rationale behind privatization. If a winter storm
rages and everybody is snowed in, why be paralyzed for two weeks before
the state sends bulldozers to clear the road? Why not just pitch in and
hire old Claude in the village to plow them? He could do it right away.
She also explained that in her community, only the rare individual uses
the U.S. dollar; everyone else trades. Fish for blankets. Fur pelts for snow
boots. And if she needs to pay money for taxes or buy something down
in the city, she goes into the hills, digs up some gold, and uses that. In
some enlightening ways the "right-wing" lady from Alaska was the environmental-justice advocate's, the primitive anarchist's, and the bioregionalist's dream-come-true.

As an eighteenth-century highwayman let loose on Manhattan's streets,
Kirk was true to form, playing the part even before stepping onto the
stage. Flaunting his cape, he swished up to my table at the French Roast.
"Shall we take a cab to the theee-*au*-ter?" he proposed in a voice deeper
and more enunciated than his usual.

Yes, we were to put on a play. *Interview with a Luddite* was to be Friday
night's fare at the Learning Alliance's "Technology and Its Discontents"
conference. Earlier that same year—1995—the mail-bombing Ted
"Unabomber" Kaczynski had thrust the subject into the national zeitgeist with the publication of his anti-industrial treatise in the *New York
Times* and *Washington Post*. Kirk's *Rebels Against the Future* had come
out, and what amounted to a history book about an uprising in nineteenth-century England—the Luddite rebellion—was suddenly garnering
more attention than, Unabomber-less, it otherwise would have.

The conference would feature ourselves, climate-change activist Bill
McKibben, Langdon Winner, and Stephanie Mills. When Steph arrived

at Kirk's basement apartment on 11th Street, we decided she would be in the play too. Only the day before had Kirk and I even conjured up the plot. Now, with but one day before the show and possessing neither script nor set, we put our heads together.

A modern-day Luddite (me), we decided, would go to a psychiatrist (Stephanie) concerning her distress that the publishing industry now required her to submit her writing from a computer. The doctor would recommend that she sleep on it, and she would flop down on the consulting couch. From dream state would enter the original Luddite from 1811, Lancashire, England (Kirk). First he would regale her with the conditions and history of his times. Then curiosity would overtake him; he would ask the modern-day Luddite about her times and struggles. "Did we make an impact?" he would press. "Did we lay the ground for an easier time for you?" After she would tell him about the twentieth century, she would awaken only to find her nineteenth-century companion still present–and at laying eyes upon his first computer in the office of the psychiatrist, he would take his hammer and, as in days of yore, smash the machine.

Given that I was about to appear in a theater performance before a New York audience for which there was no real script and which had had no rehearsal, I was inappropriately composed. Maybe it was like the time during an anti-war protest when the Berkeley police with their batons, mace cans, and rage were running amok at my heels, and my mind unexpectedly switched to a delightful English garden amid daisies, roses, and white trellises, with me leaping in the slowest of slow motion across the trimmed green grass.

The play went–dare I say it?–smashingly. Kirk was like a Shakespearean actor, blending detailed knowledge of the Luddite rebellion with ample flourishes of cape and stamping of boot. Stephanie's rendition of the thoughtful but uptight Dr. Erdkof was so true to life one would think she should have been a psychiatrist. Afterward Emerson Blake, editor of *Orion* ecology magazine, said to me, "Amazing. You *memorized* that whole script!"

A few weeks later the *Village Voice* ran a cartoon making fun of us for being foolhardy in challenging modern technology, and *New York* magazine published "Die, Computer, Die" cynically trashing Kirkpatrick's book--and featuring a snide reference reeking of urban superiority to the "mud hut" (read: passive-solar adobe house) that was my home in New Mexico.

And so it was for us neo-Luddites in the years leading up to the full-tilt boogey invasion/assault by technological innovation, a berserk run that would reorganize humanity and take all of life's creatures with it on a rampage toward demise.

It's no wonder Kirk turned his attention to a more hopeful (and human-scale) politics of secession from the empire called the United States.

XI. THE SECESSIONISTS

Whenever something is wrong, something *is too big.*

—LEOPOLD KOHR, *THE BREAKDOWN OF NATIONS*, 1957

"FREE VERMONT" signs at 4th of July parade, with reference to campaign of secessionist Dennis Steele for governor, 2010.
Photo credit and courtesy of Rob Williams.

OF ALL THE EFFORTS to propose secession from the United States of America in the 2000s—whether rooted in Realpolitik or in fantasy visions, whether morally-fueled or inspired by practicality—it is said that Vermont, Texas, Alaska, and the bioregion Cascadia (northern California/southern Oregon) claim the most chance of success.

To those U.S. nationalists who so easily laugh off the prospect as unthinkable, outright silly, or constitutionally impossible, secessionists have been quick to identify the urge to self-rule and small-is-governable as the emergent politics of today's world. At its 1945 launch the nascent United Nations registered fifty-one nations in the world, which grew rapidly to today's 193, a number sure to rise as movements thrive in Scotland, Cataluña, Kashmir, Tibet, Wales, Portugal, Sicily, Palestine, Quebec, Venice; also among indigenous peoples who seek their stolen land and sovereignty, and on. According to secessionist/historian Kirkpatrick Sale of the Middlebury Institute, some twenty-five movements are active within the U.S. alone, while others simmer toward boiling in Europe and Asia. He estimates that, of those in the U.S., maybe ten are dead serious and some 150 more are in various stages of development. "The *feelings* for separatism exist everywhere across the globe as nationalism proves to have been a mistake," he wrote me on September 9, 2016, "but the power still remains with the centralists and statists and will for a while longer, I'm afraid. But it *will* come crumbling down."

The Vermont effort is of particular interest because its roots echo a unique history of rebel self-reliance dating back to the arrival of Europeans on North American soil. In the mid-1700s Ethan Allen's Green Mountain Boys fought off empire-minded British and French encroachers from both east and north, while delegates from twenty-eight towns declared independence from France's expanding colony of Quebec and the Brits' growing territories of New Hampshire and New York. Upon proclaiming success and Vermont as its own separate realm, the first acts as an autonomous republic were to abolish slavery and extend voting rights beyond the elite category of property-owning men. The Green Mountain state has expressed its unique bent towards do-it-yourself autonomy ever since. For instance, after the flood disaster of 1927, U.S. President Calvin Coolidge offered federal aid; Vermont Governor John Weeks quipped, "Vermont will take care of its own." And so it is no surprise that, as the U.S. mutated from the "land of the free" into the world's most gluttonous and militarized imperium, Vermonters would slam their rubber muck boots down on their sovereign ground and shout, "NO!"

In the global context of zeal for decolonization/liberation and small-is-beautiful governance that has arisen since World War II, Vermont did not stand alone. But its first serious reemergence since the Vermont Republic of 1777–91 may have come as a surprise. The banner years for resuscitation were mid-decade in the 2000s. Rallies, parades, theater performances, and conventions were held. The Second Vermont Republic was founded. Yak farmer/University of Vermont journalism professor Rob Williams started the newspaper *Vermont Commons* and webmaster Dennis Steele a radio station. The books *Secession: How Vermont and All the Other States Can Save Themselves from the Empire* and *Vermont Manifesto*, both by Duke University economics professor Thomas Naylor, laid out the moral reasons for leaving the U.S. and the moral/economic/social/ political/ psychological benefits of small nations. A learned yet passionate article penned by University of Vermont professor Frank Bryan and artist/ publisher Ian Baldwin appeared in the *Washington Post*. Kirkpatrick Sale launched the Middlebury Institute to coordinate and support the secession movements existing in the U.S. Pro-secession candidates ran for public office. The university's Center for Rural Studies did a poll and found that thirteen percent of eligible voters in Vermont favored secession. Statesman George Kennan and historian John Kenneth Galbraith gave the thumbs up. National Public Radio, *New York Times, Huffington Post, Washington Post, Los Angeles Times,* Associated Press, *Utne Reader, Fourth World Reader,* Fox News, *The O'Reilly Factor,* as well as international newspapers and radio stations—all did features on the effort; Thomas Naylor even appeared in one article wrapped in the newly conceived Second Vermont Republic flag.

Although I was a New Mexico resident, in 2007 I was blessed with an invitation to join the advisory council of said republic. I also began to write for *Vermont Commons,* the community newspaper that blends sustainable practices like sheep-raising and wind-solar-compost energy-production methods with the politics of autonomy. I did this with the

Jim Hogue as Ethan Allen, who fought for Vermont independence
in the 1700s, during parade for Second Vermont Republic, 2003.
Photo credit and courtesy of Rob Williams.

promise that, upon attaining independence, I would be among the first
"from elsewhere" to receive a passport.

But this fervent round lost its wind when Barak Obama became president and the resulting outburst of passionate hope was followed by a
debilitating malaise, heightened when the untested president ironically
accepted the Noble Peace Prize while conducting two wars in the Middle
East. After 2016, though, under the even more alarming shadow of U.S.
racist, right-wing populist movements and a loudmouth, emotionally
unbalanced president recklessly fingering the nuclear button, Vermont's
contemporary Green Mountain men/women re-arise.

IAN BALDWIN: GREEN MOUNTAIN BOY
(1938–)

*I myself will never return to Empire again. Never again
will I accept its psychological embrace or be bound by
its dreams of a narcissistic behemoth.*

—I.B., "SECESSION: WHY I SUPPORT A SECOND VERMONT
REPUBLIC," *VERMONT COMMONS*, 2008

Joanna Harcourt-Smith told me about Ian Baldwin. He was a true caballero, a gentleman, she said. Amiable, intelligent, honest, and caring, he's
the sort of man anybody would want to befriend. She forgot to say that

he was particularly fine-looking, but then, this I could see for myself. Bushy eyebrows framing a chiseled face, strong straight nose, kind hazel-green eyes.

I first laid eyes on Ian at the Second Statewide Convention on Vermont Independence in Montpelier in November of 2008. It amazed me that the Second Vermont Republic folks had secured the capital's Statehouse for their rebel congress, but there we were—all 300 of us gathered in the light-filled Representatives Hall, raring to participate in the fate of Vermont democracy. It's a huge round room boasting shiny wood chairs and desks amphitheater-style, each arranged so that every legislator has a clear view of the speaker's pulpit, all reeking of history. On the wall above said podium hangs a piece of that history: a lookalike of the celebrated painting of George Washington, originally by portraitist Gilbert Stuart. Rescued from a fire in 1857 that destroyed the old granite Greek Revival building, the 1836 replica by George Gassner was re-hung in the rebuilt House chamber.

Sandwiched in between historian Kirkpatrick Sale's speech on the depth and breadth of the current global movement toward secession and yak farmer/journalism professor Rob Williams's lecture on the inter-twining of food/energy sustainability with the political task of establish-ing an independent country, Ian invited me to accompany him on a tour of Montpelier's State Street. I was thrilled. We walked down the stone steps of the Statehouse and turned around to take a look at the building: a majestic Renaissance Revival structure crowned by a fifty-seven-foot high dome sheathed in copper and coated with the purest twenty-three-carat gold leaf. From atop the dome the goddess of agriculture, Ceres, reached into the Vermont blue.

It was a typical Saturday in small-town New England, what with the weekend's customary sense of release stirring the populace just as dowdy ladies scurried about to finish their shopping. The buildings on State Street are pretty much historic, the years of their construction dating to the early 1800s. The Queen-Anne-style Edward Dewey house. The mid-Victorian Department of Personnel building. A host of stately brick houses from the 1820s. The Gothic granite Episcopal Church. Although a "flatlander"/newcomer to the Green Mountain state, Ian knew the sto-ries about each and regaled me with their inevitable quirkiness.

When we arrived back at the Statehouse, he noticed a parked truck of unknown ownership. Its meter had ticked beyond its last paid-for minute—a sitting duck for a fine—and he unselfconsciously dropped a coin into the machine.

The Second Vermont Republic was the brain child of Thomas Naylor; he was the one to call the early meetings together and to pen both *Secession: How Vermont and All the Other States Can Save Themselves from the Empire* and *Vermont Manifesto*. But, in fact, the impulse to self-reliance and independence goes back to the eighteenth-century reality that Vermont was *never* one of the original thirteen colonies, not to mention a shared urge throughout New England to take leave of the fast-militarizing nation-state during the War of 1812.

Ian and his wife Margo moved from New York City to make their home in the Green Mountain State in 1982 where, two years later, they launched their ecology-minded publishing house Chelsea Green Publishers. Their first success was an English-language edition of French novelist Jean Giono's ecological fable *The Man Who Planted Trees*. It was superbly illustrated by the wood engraver Michael McCurdy. Other books followed: Helen Nearing's *Loving and Leaving the Good Life, Beyond the Limits*, a twenty-year update by Donella Meadows, Dennis Meadows, and Jørgen Randers of the 1972 international bestseller *The Limits to Growth*; and Athena and Bill Steen's *The Straw Bale House*—all together establishing the company's reputation as a publisher of books on sustainable living.

The events of September 11, 2001, jarred Ian to the marrow. First off, he doubted that the official narratives describing the attacks—he would call them "cover-ups"—were true; the investigating commission had left out some revealing details about explosions and subsequent fires inside a building not even touched by the attacking planes. Then there was the intact and mysteriously incriminating passport of one of the Twin Towers hijackers discovered in the debris of that same building. Many believe it was planted. Ian was alarmed again when the Patriot Act was conjured up and passed into law so quickly after the attacks, as if it were already written and ready to put an immediate clamp on U.S. citizen rights. He had already participated in the anti–Vietnam War movement, but now was awakening to an even starker sense that he could no longer abide by his country's conduct. "By the time the Iraq 'shock and awe' invasion began," he has written, "I was profoundly alienated from my own country."

In January of 2003, knowing the Iraq assault was a done deal, Ian thought hard about seceding—as a party of one. Another option, that of becoming an ex-patriot, was hard for him to imagine. He thought of his mother, who was nearly ninety years old: her ancestors had arrived from England almost 400 years earlier. Plus, the notion of leaving his children and grandchildren clawed at his heart. Then a friend, writer Tim Matson, mentioned a meeting being hosted by Thomas Naylor.

"It's about secession," Matson said.

"Secession?"

The idea was profoundly novel, and with it Ian suddenly felt a sense of possibility. And so, in March of 2003, he drove with Matson to socialist historian Murray Bookchin's Institute for Social Ecology to discuss the idea of Vermont's secession from the United States. Ian was raring to learn how to build a movement to free Vermont from the clutches of a country addicted to war: a true independence movement.

Book by Ron Miller and Rob Williams describing the many reasons for a Second Vermont Republic. Courtesy of the *Vermont Independent*.

He was already a committed decentralist. He had read E. F. Schumacher's "Buddhist Economics" in the late 1960s and befriended the author in the early '70s. He also knew Bob Swan, the founder of the U.S. community land trust movement. In 1980, two years after Schumacher's death, former Jain monk Satish Kumar invited Ian to start an E.F. Schumacher Society in the U.S., following the example Kumar himself had set by founding England's Schumacher Society. Ian then joined with Bob Swann, historian Kirkpatrick Sale, ecologist David Ehrenfeld, and John McClaughry of the public policy think tank Ethan Allen Institute—and the Schumacher Society (U.S.A.) was launched.

But Ian had never before connected an economics of small-scale to a *politics* of small-scale—and, lo and behold! politics lay at the heart of the secessionist movement Naylor was proposing. Through the work of building this new movement, he not only met Naylor—but also Kirkpatrick Sale, Rob Williams, author/radio host Carolyn Baker, scholar/political scientist Frank Bryan, the actors and musicians of the notorious Bread and Puppet Theater, and a host of other enthusiasts who wanted out of the moral monstrosity of the U.S. empire. Along with Williams, Ian proceeded to launch the movement's newspaper *Vermont Commons* and with Bryan wrote a seminal essay for the *Washington Post*, "The Once and Future Republic of Vermont."

This mover n' shaker was born in New York City on a snowy day in December of 1938, first of the four sons of executive recruiter Ian "Mike" Baldwin, a staunch conservative Republican, and librarian Rose Weld Baldwin. He wrote in an autobiographical sketch that by age two, he had "lived a full life." As a toddler he had fallen into a pond where he lay face down, helpless and blacked out until, many minutes later, his frantic mother found him—just in time to save his life. Three months later, he became inexplicably ill and landed in a hospital, where he was traumatized by a mysterious treatment involving the administration of liquid medicines colored ruby, amber, lapis lazuli, cobalt, and purple. He recalls looking out the window of his room and feeling "an existential aloneness, abject, and a bitter defeat," not to mention a terror of doctors and medical treatments that lasted for years afterward.

In her study of the origins of creativity *Notebooks of the Mind*, linguist

Vera John-Steiner has linked childhood illness and trauma with a proclivity to perceive the world in imaginative terms. Free-wheeling, rebellious, and drawn to poetry and painting, Ian has indeed led the life of the artist. He wrote poetry and edited the literary journal at St. Paul's School in New Hampshire, and went on to Columbia College in New York, where he wrote for the *Columbia Review*. Much to his parents' dismay, an untamable wanderlust overtook the undergrad after two years of university. He headed out just as the Beats were doing—by the seat of his old, tattered Levi's. He traveled by motorcycle, diesel-belching bus, freighter, single-prop plane, Jeep, and on foot to New Orleans, Chiapas, Guatemala City, and finally Mexico City. But the trip didn't completely satisfy Ian's soul, so, just as his fellow students were kicking up the autumn leaves in Washington Square at the start of his senior year, he made preparations for a second expedition—this one around the world. The year was 1960, and by January of 1961 he was on his way to Hong Kong, Bangkok, Angkor Wat, Cambodia; Burma, Calcutta, Kabul, Iran, Israel, Greece, Genoa, Italy; and then across the Atlantic back to New York. Through it all he was often without funds, begging food, even stealing some, and sleeping in doorways.

To his parents' relief, upon return he got down to work to complete degrees in English Literature and Oriental Studies, and his first post-graduation job presented itself: college traveler for the publisher Holt, Rinehart and Winston. The opportunity turned out to be prophetic: in one way or another his life would revolve around publishing. In a later job at the Institute for World Order, he oversaw an international publishing program that brought together many of the thinkers who could shed light on pursuits of peace, economic well-being, social justice, and ecological balance from multinational, regional, and transnational viewpoints. Traveling from country to country to recruit writers and publishers for the book series that would result, he met with such intellectual luminaries as Carl Friedrich von Weizsäcker, Johan Galtung, Saul Mendlovits, George Lackey, Richard Falk, and Elise and Kenneth Boulding.

A stand-out quality about Ian is his knack for befriending creative people. In Calcutta, before he even graduated from Columbia, he had already sought out and taken afternoon tea with filmmaker Satyajit Ray, whose masterpiece *The Apu Trilogy* had captivated him in New York City. Through the years, his circle of honored friends came to include Helena Norberg-Hodge, David Ehrenfeld, Lynn Margolis, Amory Lovins, Helen Nearing, John Lash, Michael Ruppert, Naomi Wolf, and Joanna Harcourt-Smith. Not to mention the fine folks of Vermont seeking to secede from, as Rob Williams puts it, the "Un*tied* States of America."

His own creativity has taken many shapes. Obviously he is a master at business planning, as seen by his work with Margo to successfully navigate their Vermont publishing house through hard financial times to national recognition. He began oil painting in 1995 and studied lithography at the Rufino Tamayo Studio in Oaxaca, Mexico. Back home, he and brother Michael bought etching and lithography presses for the start-up of Two Rivers Printmaking Studio in Vermont. But the sudden onset of insulin-dependent type 1 diabetes interrupted his plans to help run the newborn studio.

I was fortunate enough to spend more time with Ian when he visited his daughter Sarah in Santa Fe, New Mexico. It was Christmas of 2009, and after a few bottles of wine, and feeling well bolstered against the icy night, we danced about the living room in free-form style and then, loosened up, we performed an improvisational theater piece that we filmed with a cell phone. In it, a completely off-the-cuff Ian excelled as the Old Country/traditional-values father of a daughter who longed to marry a most socially inappropriate man.

With the election of Barak Obama, Vermont's secession movement gradually lost steam: a black liberal American was promising "hope and change," and many Vermonters were dazzled by the symbolism, believed the rhetoric—and lost interest in recreating their community as a separate country. Then, eight hyper-war-ridden years later, with the 2016 presidential election over, Ian and his secessionist colleagues saw a door fly open for resuscitating the Vermont secessionist effort. In the primaries Vermont Senator Bernie Sanders had given Hillary Clinton a run for her money as the outspoken socialist/progressive contender, but needless to say he didn't capture the nomination; just as in 1968 when Hubert Humphrey stole the nomination from Eugene McCarthy, the old Democratic Party Machine made the same sorry mistake yet again. And besides, according to the secessionists, the U.S. system was so immoral and corrupt, it was beyond Band-Aid remediation. As we all know too well, Donald "You're Fired" Trump, the flaming and wealthy corporate-right-winger, surprised the world—YIKES!

In a state unusually given to town meetings, experimental schools, local farmers markets, homemade goat cheese, yak raising, pottery making, herb-dyed yarns and weaving—in essence, cultural and political autonomy—Ian asks: will Vermont's tradition of economic self-sufficiency and history of fierce independence give birth to an independent republic one more time? Needless to say, empires do not fade away of their own accord—but, whatever is in the cards for the Green Mountain bioregion, Ian Baldwin will play a role in it.

XI. THE LANDSCAPE OF FREEDOM: PEOPLE-OF-COLOR ENVIRONMENTALISM

*We, People of Color ... do hereby reestablish our
spiritual interdependence to the sacredness of
our Mother Earth; we respect and celebrate each
of our cultures, languages and beliefs about the natural
world and our roles in healing ourselves:
to insure environmental justice; to promote economic
alternatives which would contribute to
the development of environmentally safe livelihoods;
and to secure our political, economic and cultural
liberation that has been denied for over 500 years
of colonization and oppression, resulting in
the poisoning of our communities and land
and the genocide of our peoples, do affirm and
adopt these Principles of Environmental Justice.*

—"PRINCIPLES OF ENVIRONMENTAL JUSTICE,"
FIRST NATIONAL PEOPLE OF COLOR ENVIRONMENTAL LEADER-
SHIP SUMMIT, WASHINGTON D.C., OCTOBER 1991

Environmental Justice, a popular poster in the EJ movement by artist Ricardo Levins Morales, 2006. Courtesy of Ricardo Levins Morales.

THE STRUGGLES OF AFRICAN Americans, Latinos, Pacific Islanders, Native American peoples, and Asians took on a fresh slant and a new language in the late 1980s. Influenced by the environmental awareness spread largely by white, middle-class, urban activists since the early '70s, seasoned and upcoming justice workers began to link issues such as low-paying jobs, police violence, breakdown of culture, deteriorating health, and drug addiction with the purposeful exploitation of their lands, labor, and resources for contaminating mining and manufacturing, toxic dumping, and chemical pollution. In fact the movement had been in gestation since the Civil Rights Act of 1964 outlawed all discrimination on the basis of race, color, and national origin. In 1969 the California Rural Legal Assistance filed suit on behalf of six migrant workers—the first of its kind—which resulted in the banning of the pesticide DDT. Robert Bullard's seminal *Dumping in Dixie* came out in 1990. The First National People of Color Environmental Leadership Summit soon followed—just as locally focused groups like Citizens for Environmental Justice in Georgia, Indigenous Environmental Network of Minnesota, Appalachia Ohio's Rural Action, and the Deep South Center for Environmental Justice were being launched.

Ironbound residents in Newark, New Jersey, June 1, 1984, in opposition to the construction of a dioxin-emitting garbage incinerator. Photo credit and courtesy of Ironbound Community Corporation.

In 2016—in one of the most exciting actions to ignite participation— the Standing Rock Sioux spearheaded a protest of a petroleum pipeline that would cross from Canada through to the U.S. South, all along the way endangering ecologies, water systems, and public health. The Sioux called themselves "Water Protectors"; their dramatic encampment, boasting tepees, horses, drum circles, and flags from supporting tribes the world over, quickly became symbolic of key environmental-justice themes while drawing thousands of Native and non-Native activists to join in nonviolent resistance with them.

CARL ANTHONY:
FINANCIAL NETS, NOT DRIFT NETS
(1939–)

Why is it that white people find it easier to think like a mountain than like a person of color?

—C.A., "ENVIRONMENTALISM AND THE MYSTIQUE OF WHITENESS," *SUN MAGAZINE*, AUGUST 1995

Carl and I stepped onto the stage at Fort Mason's Cowell Theater. The year was 1997, and the place was packed. SRO, as they say. "The Landscape of Freedom" had been promoted by Earth Island Institute as a public conversation between an unusual duo: an Anglo environmentalist living in a land-based Latino community and an urban African American environmental-justice pioneer who was president of a white conservation-minded organization. The event promised to shake things up. Typically the enviro/enviro-justice clash was between urban whites who favored strict preservation of uninhabited wilderness and people of color who fought for defense of their lands, rights, and cultures.

For me the purpose of the presentation lay slightly off the beaten track of Save-the-Planet versus Save-the-People. I aimed to share the exploratory telephone conversations between Berkeley and New Mexico that Carl and I enjoyed every Saturday morning. In one hour we were capable of covering topics such as the nature of domination, the psychological repercussions of "rolling" traumatization via institutional injustice, Marxism in the contemporary world, and the phenomenology of oppression. It was this intimacy and thoughtfulness that I sought to replicate. But, once on stage, we faced an unforeseen obstacle. As quantum physicists are wont to point out, a scene and the particles inhabiting it inevitably change with the addition of an observer. We were seated facing the audience, not each other, and the massive presence before us caused us to taint our customary ease with an edge of performance.

But still, I would have to say: we pulled it off.

We introduced ourselves in the manner we had learned from Jeannette Armstrong of the Okanagan tribe in British Columbia—by speaking to the question of who we are according to our lineages and our ancestors' relationships to the natural world. I offered: "Our challenge is to remember who we are—despite all the brokenness, despite all the paradoxes, despite all the ways we cannot remember or haven't been told. . . . What does it mean to talk about ourselves in [this] way that, in [contemporary] society, was never taught?"

To the hilarity of the audience, Carl started by paraphrasing a quote from Malcolm X: "If you put the cat in the oven and the cat had kittens in the oven, you wouldn't call them biscuits." He went deeper. Talking about ourselves in this way "means learning the language of my insides, learning the places of pain that I have not had the courage to think about," he said. "It means understanding that all of us are the end product of life on the planet. We are connected to the amoeba, we are connected to the rainforest, to the horses and the cows and the lobsters. . . . If we're going to move toward being human beings, it's about time we understand who we are. . . . We talk about the Whole Earth. [The task is] to make each activity, each event, each encounter, each piece of work whole. This goes against everything we have been taught. . . ."

He then turned to me. "One of the things I've learned from you, Chellis," he said, "is that we need to practice making time and making space just to have emptiness in it—[which is] very much related to healing the earth, because in our frantic going to-and-fro to get things done, we create a great deal of damage. By slowing down, we can improve both the quality of our lives and increase the harmony in our communities and in our relationship to the planet."

Carl asked me about the emotional harm perpetrated by growing up in a place like Hunter's Point (a ghetto in San Francisco). "We grew up, developed, we *evolved* in the natural world," I answered, "because there was nothing else but the natural world until recently. [Being in nature] is not a luxury: there are developmental stages that *require* being in relationship with the sky and the rush of forest branches in wind and the change of the climate and the falling of rain."

For Carl this thought brought up an "image of cattle who are in a harness and kept in a harness their whole lives without freedom to graze. . . . The frightening thing in my mind is that a society that puts the animals into a harness is also doing the same thing to itself," he said. "So the more boxed-in we become . . . *the less we have the capacity to be free.* . . . I particularly want to pick up on the incarceration of young African American males at an astronomic rate. Many feel that's, well, that's just them, they're mostly criminals. . . . But one of the ways racism works: it screens reality." Offering a path toward healing, he proposed that we make connections between all the issues that affect us, implying that single-issue politics can be part of a process toward integrating the many viewpoints. "It seems to me the task is to find the thread that connects," he said." We cannot afford an environmental movement that sees [other] issues as disconnected."

I took a dare. I spoke about the possibility that, given the relentless assault on the planet's resources, life on Earth could go down the tubes. "When I think about the possibility that we may not make it," I offered, "the most important thing I can do is to stand in alignment with Creation so that, if indeed we go down, there [would be] at least some people still in alignment.... The odd thing is that I bring no less passion to this task than I did when in 1968 I was passing under Sather Gate [on the UC Berkeley campus] and I declared with all my youthful hubris: 'We [activists from all the social and decolonization movements of the 1940s-'60s] are going to take over the world!'"

Carl always managed to pop out with an unpredictable insight. "The moment we are in right now reminds me of a moment that I cannot fail to recognize," he said. "It was a moment in the middle of the 1400s when a Portuguese ship went down the coast of Africa and pulled into a place where people were living and had been living quite sustainably for a long, long time.... There was no way for the people of West Africa to know what was in store for them.... I think we are at a similar place, and whenever I lose faith I think about those people who were in the holds of those ships packed like sardines, going across an ocean in chains, unable to stand up, and I measure my struggle against their struggle."

At the end of our presentation, Earth Island Institute's founder/former Sierra Club president David Brower stood up and announced that he whole-heartedly agreed with the tenets of the environmental-justice movement. But the reality was that while Earth Island Institute had sponsored our event, in the day-to-day practices that lay outside the sphere of Brower's input, the administration did not actually support environmental-justice politics. For example, the white urban environmentalists of Santa Fe's Forest Guardians were attempting to impede community survival traditions in the forests of northern New Mexico—and if we were to look at the situation in a systemic way, push them out of long-informed sustainability and into the global economy. Using lawsuits as their primary tools of attack, they sought to regulate who would hold the ticket to enter the woods (photographers, tourists, and hikers, according to them) while forbidding local Latinos from practicing hunting, gathering, firewood collection, and small-scale tree cutting. In 1997

Forest Guardians came out with a full-page ad in the *New York Times,* *Washington Post,* and *Santa Fe New Mexican* soliciting funds in favor of what they called "ZERO CUT"; Earth Island had signed on. Clearly, from their offices above Broadway in San Francisco, they didn't understand sustainable logging as different from blatant clear-cutting, and they did not remember that, back in the 1980s, it had been these poor, rural Latinos who had forced the transnational/industrial logging corporation Duke City Lumber out of the mountains.

Earth Islanders had also traveled north to Washington State to crush the efforts of the Makah tribe to save their vanishing culture—for some 2000 years based on the language, craft, and products of whale hunting. Due to the removal of the gray whale from the Species Extinction List, the U.S. government and International Whaling Commission allowed the tribe to do a one-time/one-whale hunt in 1999. It would be the first time they would be permitted to do so in more than seventy years. Paddling into the Neah Bay in handmade cedar canoes with the intent of taking a whale, they had their yew-wood harpoons tipped with mussel shells and a retrofitted World War I gun they designed for a quick and compassionate death. But, together with enviros from the Pacific Northwest and animal-rights activists, folks from Earth Island Institute upset the aboriginal canoes with metal speedboats lunging toward their delicate craft, thrashing the water like a blender to scare off whales, and shouting "MURDERERS!"

According to Carl, on a daily basis at Earth Island, they faced the same lack of understanding, despite the fact that Carl's environmental justice project Urban Habitat was one of the organization's most prized projects precisely because it was for-by-of people of color and that Carl himself was the institute's president.

Carl Anthony got into his work as an environmental justice activist through a curious route. He was the child of housepainter/ship fitter/farmer Louis Anthony and homemaker Mildred Anthony. An attentive son of Philadelphia's history of quality urban planning and an activist in the civil rights movement of the 1950s–'60s, he sought to blend a politics of freedom for people of color with that of the emerging community-design movement. His goal: to contribute to community planning so that low-income people and people of color could benefit from better layout of their living spaces. In 1963 he joined with "Father of Participatory Architecture" and member of the cohort of Lewis Mumford, Karl Linn, to convert vacant lands in East Coast inner cities into public spaces. By 1965 Carl was launching what became known as "neighborhood commons" through the Neighborhood Commons Project in Harlem. He received his degree in architecture from Columbia University in 1969.

In the early '70s many African Americans were looking for their roots, history, and identity by traveling to Africa. Carl's rendition of the journey was to study the traditional architecture of indigenous Africans. During the adventure, he was particularly impressed with the houses and arrangement of communities of the Dogon tribe of Mali, who he suspected were his direct ancestors. Here the homes were built of adobe, painted with animals and geometric designs using plant-mineral pigments, decorated with earthen sculpture, and set in a close-knit formation among men's granaries and meeting quarters, women's granaries and menstrual houses. When the inhabitant of a house died, that person's home was not taken over by another; it was allowed to sink back to the sand floor of the desert.

Upon his return, he landed a job teaching architecture at the University of California, Berkeley. Here he began to recruit African American and Latino students. He also pushed the newly developing field into virgin terrain when in 1976 he articulated his perspective in a paper called "The Big House and the Slave Quarter: Prelude to New World Architecture." In this essay he demonstrated that the exploitation of a controlled slave population made possible the development of industrial agriculture. When the university prohibited him from introducing the material, the by-now professor up for tenure quit and took a leap: he invited Asians, Latinos, Native Americans, and other African Americans to join him in fostering projects to address the neglect and injustices rampant in communities of color. The new project was called Urban Habitat, and under its auspices, with environmental attorney Luke Cole of the California Rural Assistance Foundation, he founded the groundbreaking, award-winning journal *Race, Poverty and the Environment.*

Carl leading regional equity climate-justice demonstration, Oakland, 2012.
Photo credit and courtesy of Paloma Pavel.

I met Carl in the early 1990s. I was working with the indigenous people of the Southwest I had joined at the 1992 World Uranium Forum in Austria. This historic gathering, organized by filmmaker Claus Biegert of Germany, brought together indigenous peoples from all parts of the world to construct a record of the multiple ways that nuclear development was destroying the health and cohesion of indigenous communities. When we returned to New Mexico, we began to organize small-scale educational gatherings of the same style; we also worked to change tribal policies regarding cleanup of uranium mines and federal compensations to families of deceased miners. Always eager to expand his comprehension of environmental-justice issues, Carl accepted my invitation to come to Laguna Pueblo high above the desert—overlooking the then-defunct Jack Pile uranium mine—where we were putting on a conference attended by Navajo, Laguna Pueblo, and Acoma Pueblo miners and activists.

At six-foot one, Carl was a towering presence among the far shorter locals. I thoroughly enjoyed introducing him according to people and place, relations and ecology, history and responsibility to nature. "The person we are about to hear from boasts bloodlines from the Dogon and Shanti in Africa, Scots, from French Huguenots, Cherokee, and Seminole," I explained. "The way I see it, *he's related to everyone in this room!*" Chuckles burst like popcorn from the audience. How preposterous was

THAT! Standing high above the podium like an architectural marvel of the modernist period, Carl flowed right into the good humor—and went on to construct a picture of the global environmental justice movement that gave everyone a feeling of solidarity with people they had never met but who now seemed like long-lost brothers and sisters.

Carl's second trip to New Mexico was for a conference in Albuquerque about the social, cultural, psychological, and health repercussions of the loss of tribal sovereignty. Aboriginals from as far north as Alaska and as far south as Chile traveled to Albuquerque to present their reports. Carl was hot to connect with the Florida Seminole/Muscogee contingent. They were the breakaway group who had *not* agreed to accept welfare payouts and cans of condensed milk in exchange for government-controlled domestication in Oklahoma; they refused to sign a peace treaty with the U.S. Now, 155 years after that conquest, they still lived in their chickee villages in the Everglades and still practiced hunting, fishing, and gathering—albeit precariously, for, as the years went by, both developers' Drain-the-Everglades mentality and the sale of plots to private owners were reducing their land base.

Round about the late 1960s, these few who still held to their culture decided that young Bobby Billie would learn to speak English so that he could relate to the increasingly encroaching outer world. The same went for his younger brother, Danny Billie. When it came time to travel the distance to attend the sovereignty conference, Bobby got a driver's license and rented a van, and the group set out to traverse the American South to Albuquerque. Notable in their journey was that, aside from gas and bathroom stops, they did not get out of the van for the full thirty-hour drive: as they traveled through the lands of other indigenous peoples, it would have been irreverent to set foot upon their terrains without invitation.

The most comprehensive presentation I have ever witnessed at a conference was delivered by this group: Bobby, his mother, and Danny. Each had five minutes to communicate the tribe's experience of the devastation wrought by loss of sovereignty. There was a set of questions they had been given to guide their presentations, but no other tribal members who had spoken had actually followed the proposed order of inquiry.

Florida schools had taught Bobby the art of following instructions, and his presentation in English went down the list like that of a Ph.D. student taking orals. "Only a handful of native speakers remain in our tribe," he said. "Less and less animals populate the Everglades." "Our traditional ceremonial grounds have been bought up by newcomers who prohibit our entry."

Next up came Bobby's mother. She delivered her testimony in the Muscogee language of the Independent Traditional Seminole, and while not understanding a word, we in the audience had the remarkable opportunity to hear the rhythmic poetry of their land and soul.

Finally, the microphone was passed to Danny. He too had learned English, but soon into his talk he broke down into the universal language of emotion: he began to sob. He cried for a full minute as we in the audience gagged back our own tears. Then he stopped and said he could not go on. Narrator Chili Yazzie of the Diné/Navajo Nation told him he had four minutes left and he should indeed go on—whereupon Danny turned to the microphone and *sobbed aloud for four more minutes.*

Carl was astonished. Quivering with anticipation, he approached his newfound people, telling them that Seminole blood flowed just below his black skin. They were astonished too—and thrilled. Indeed the Black Seminoles had been important figures in their history as a tribe, fighting against the U.S. Army with courage and pluck. A bond was formed that would lead to Carl's assistance with psychological and social problems stemming from the encounter with the outer world—and, for him, the sense that he had unearthed a crucial link to his own identity.

After a shakeup emanating from the ongoing lack of consciousness about environmental-justice issues, Carl left Earth Island Institute. Urban Habitat left. I had been on the Board of Advisors and, guided by Carl, I too left—as did a small cadre of members, advisors, and groups. He went on to a position with the Ford Foundation as director of the Sustainable Metropolitan Communities Initiative, and as a Senior Fellow he received a stipend to write the book he had long envisioned: *The Earth, the City, and the Hidden Narrative of Race.* It was published in 2017.

ARNOLDO GARCIA:
BREATHING FOR JUSTICE
(1952-)

I breathe in rain
I breathe out green
I breathe in steps
I breathe out journeys
I breathe in wind
I breathe out sky
I breathe in laughter
I breathe out happiness
I breathe in chaotic talking
I breathe out community
I breathe in her
I breathe out poetry
I breathe in daughters and sons
I breathe out hope
I breathe in forests
I breathe out shadows
I breathe in canyons
I breathe out wings
I breathe in rivers
I breathe out oceans
I breathe in words
I breathe out mountains
I breathe in sage
I breathe out clarity
I breathe in dust
I breathe out the bones of my peoples
I breathe in fire
I breathe out clouds
I breathe in a bird crashed on the window
I breathe out glass with wings
I breathe in ink

I breathe out veins
I breathe in Buddha
I breathe out Mexican

—A.G., "A MEDITATION ON BREATH"

Arnoldo Garcia. He was Carl Anthony's sidekick at Urban Habitat. His parents had been documented and undocumented Mexican farm workers in Texas, and he grew up moving from one broken-down, termite-ridden hovel to the next, from one crappy rural schoolhouse to another, from one irrigation ditch boasting parts of human bodies to the next. I met him in the casita of Carl's environmental-justice institute on the luscious grounds of San Francisco's historic military base, the Presidio. There he headed Urban Habitat's development and worked on an environmental health project in San Francisco's Hunter's Point.

Very soon we were thrown together when Carl decided that the two of them and I would facilitate a workshop at the 1997 International Forum on Globalization conference in Berkeley. "Cultures of Resistance," it was to be called. Your typical brouhaha with an IFG director came down when said personage wanted, at the last minute, to throw two other speakers into our session; it seemed impossible for him to comprehend that it wasn't just a matter of opening up a five-minute slot

Poetry reading at Chicana-owned Beso Maya Gallery, Oakland, 2015.
Photo credit: Lea Arellano. Courtesy of Arnoldo Garcia.

for another couple of talking heads. As there were already a plethora of on-stage speakers in the main auditorium, we had taken the word "workshop" to heart; we had created an event for attendees to *participate* in. In the end, we may have lost our bargaining power with that organization, but we had our way: we put on a session that blended themes of oppression and violence with urban ecology and political action—inviting all the good folk to be equal contributors.

Arnoldo Garcia. A man of reflection. A man of heart who pens poetry. A man who crisscrosses the continent to attend meetings like they were being held in his living room. A man with a distinct set of morals who lives his values, who shuns hierarchy and reaches for the goodness in human beings. A man who manifests like a Mexican serpent shapeshifting with the seasons until the magic startles others into awareness.

Arnoldo first saw the late-fall light of a South Texas day in 1958. His mother, Guadalupe, was a farm worker. By the time he was born, his grandmother Manuela, whose roots reached back to Michoacán and farther back to Palestine, had managed to launch ten of her twelve children across the border to the U.S. to work. Arnoldo knew nothing of his father.

As he described the situation in a 2013 letter to me: "I was born into a woman's family whose stewards were a *curandera* and an indigenous man who knew how to take care of the people, his community and family, and the land. This traditional grandmother of mine—seer, healer, and matriarch of matriarchs—was pissed off at [her daughter] Guadalupe for making a baby without going through the protocols of the matriarchal protection of the family. Grandfather José, though, he was calm, always, and he never condemned his daughter and then, when the time came, stepped in to take care of me. My grandmother did, too; and I became her soldier, her cadre for her bitterness, her plants, her stories, her dreams, her cooking, her music, and small joys of having survived pandemics and pan-demons that hurt and almost wiped out her family."

When he was but three years old, Arnoldo crossed the expanse of the country two times: once from Texas to Michigan accompanied by his mother who was going north to join her lover, the second time from Michigan to Texas—in a car teeming with strangers and children who bullied him, with zero comprehension of what or why. A child by himself back

The family, preparing to depart the Pacific Northwest after the harvest, 1950s. Photo: Gilberto García Ochoa. Courtesy of Arnoldo García.

in Texas, he made it through two years of "forced solitude," picking cotton, grapes, strawberries, raspberries, apricots, cherries, and sugar beet; he learned to prune, irrigate, and prop plants so they would grow stronger. He was also doused in chemical pesticides while working in the fields and when tractors passed boasting massive fans to blow toxics onto everything in sight.

One day a 1957 Chevy pulled up to the strangers' dilapidated house—and out of it popped his grandmother and his two brother-uncles Rafael and Gilbert to take him back to the warmth of the family of his origins. "The rush of feelings and joy—what I felt that moment I still feel and makes me cry." And as he reports: "When I see photos of us, I can see that we were really poor. But the poverty was not ours. . . . We were rich in culture, in community, in spiritual ways, in how sharing what we had multiplied and kept us and others going."

Arnoldo was sent to school wherever the family found themselves. He began organizing in the fifth grade when the Latino movement was at its inception. From his "'60s Generation" brother-uncles Gilberto and Gustavo, who were eight and ten years older than he, he learned to organize classmates into picket lines, do political theater, and write poetry. He also received tips on talking to girls, drinking beer, and playing guitar.

Then, two fortuitous events shaped his will and ability to create a different future: 1.) practically everyone in his grandparents' family was a musician; of the two who weren't, one was a poet who recited epic and traditional Mexican poems, the other an enthusiast for bands, musicians, and vinyl; and 2.) one day while Arnoldo was working in a field of mint, a group of Latino activists from the university showed up and asked if anyone had finished high school. Arnoldo had—and was immediately whisked to Seattle and registered at the University of Washington, where he received grants and loans and worked as a janitor as he took classes.

And he organized. He was elected president of the Movimiento Estudiantil Latino de Aztlán/Seattle (MEChA); he joined the Centro de Acción Social Autonoma-Hermandad General de Trabajadores, which started as a local self-help center providing legal services to undocumented workers and became a national organization rooted in a working-class politic. He also formed a cultural group called Grupo Armar to play music at cafés, picket lines, marches, and fundraisers for Central American solidarity organizations; and he launched the zine *CeAtl* for Latino poetry, art, and stories. The magazine also crafted and gave away Che Guevara letterhead in sepia-colored ink boasting the famous quote: *"Let me say at the risk of seeming ridiculous, that the true revolutionary is guided by great sentiments of love."*

In 1984 Arnoldo moved to Oakland, California, with his partner and two daughters. (A son would be born later.) Finally, in 1988, he landed a minimum-wage job in organizing at the National Network for Immigrant and Refugee Rights. "Here at NNIRR," he wrote me, "I was central to shifting the work towards a deeper understanding and practice of human rights and deep justice. NNIRR allowed me to combine my life experiences, which are rooted in a community bisected by a militarized, now neoliberal, border and, specifically, my experiences growing up in a mixed indigenous family that, with some of the root connections either severed or deeply wounded, made for a strangeness that few understand. This is what happens when two individuals form a family rooted in a woman from a Palestinian family immersed in Mexican healing traditions and a man from an indigenous people that was never defeated or subjugated neither by Aztecs nor by Spaniards, but that finally succumbed to capitalist development, becoming itinerant agricultural workers that laid and built the railways from the innards of Mexico to carry away Mexico's resources, including her native plant intelligence carriers and labor."

A swirl of demanding work followed, including at Urban Habitat, at the U.S. Environmental Protection Agency's National Environmental Justice Council, and once again at NNIRR. A highlight of the latter was assembling a sixty-five-person delegation of organizers representing migrant workers, women, refugees, youth, and lesbian, gay, transsexual, bisexual, queer groups at the 2001 U.N. Conference against Racism in South Africa. He left the group in 2011 because he was feeling called to address the gun violence that was erupting in his Oakland barrio. He wrote me about this unexpected decision to pursue a new path of activism. "All our senses, our air, waters, land, waves, and spaces are under assault. Privatizations and deprivations, private and deprived ownership of everything. In the neighborhood one of my family members narrowly escaped being shot with a rifle. Seven teens have been killed by other teens, all in a twenty-five-block radius of my home. (Governor) Schwarzenegger and the California Assembly passed a budget that will strangle our public schools and push youth over a precipice of hopelessness and violence. My political daily work with immigrants doesn't make sense in this upside-down world, and my own hands are soiled from having worked in industrial agriculture, poisoned, losing my senses."

He was hired as a restorative justice coordinator by a public school in Oakland's Fruitvale District. The job entailed both counseling students on their immediate problems and developing strategies to move schools from the old punitive system to new ones that could foster change. Peer groups were launched to discuss race, conflict, violence, and inclusivity; power-over hierarchies like that between teachers and students were challenged; broken relationships resuscitated; and communities based in caring encouraged. It was important work, but by his own analysis, if transformation happened at all, it was as slow as a turtle on a dry, sandy beach.

In 2007 Arnoldo and I decided to put on a poetry reading in New Mexico. An organization called SOMOS—Society for the Muse of the Southwest—was arranging its summer series of readings. Plus, I was working with Mexican *indocumentados* who had arrived in Chimayó, and he who became *mi compadre* Raúl of a post-revolution *ejido* in

Sinaloa, was eager to talk with someone who knew the ins and outs of the immigrant predicament.

Arnoldo flew to New Mexico on a Thursday. He was so exhausted from his grueling schedule in Oakland that he slept for twelve hours on a futon on the floor of my office, and then we set about to create our presentation. We would go back and forth between his voice and mine. He would add back up with his García guitar. We would not break the mood by announcing whose work was whose; they would blend together into a single wave. Come Friday, Arnoldo, Raúl, and I crammed into my 1977 Honda Civic that lowrider artist Lowlow Medina had airbrushed with Emilio Zapata festooning one door, Frida Kahlo the other, and Subcomandante Marcos the hood. All the way up the river canyon to Taos, the two men talked earnestly about immigrant rights, and at one point a pickup truck filled with Mexicans flew by honking and throwing the thumbs-up for this unexpected appearance on a U.S. highway of the icons of their country.

The reading was to be held in a new location. In the past it had always been at a funky Bohemian café that boasted paintings by local artists, as well as the actual espresso machine from Café Trieste of San Francisco's North Beach. Now our presentation was to be held in an art gallery, and I am not exaggerating when I say that I was rendered *boquiabierta*/aghast when I saw the place. It was upscale. It had glass doors and slippery, blonde wood floors; it was illuminated by the latest in track lighting. Not only did Raúl's black eyes dart from side to side with awkwardness from the moment he stepped through the glass, he also had to sit next to an abstract painting that—for all his perilous border crossings and all the seat-belt-factory and septic-tank-cleaning jobs he had held—cost more than he would make in a lifetime.

Arnoldo's eyes opened as wide as the big sky above the mesa. When I told him we would read for SOMOS, he had thought I meant the Santa Fe immigrant rights organization Somos un Pueblo Unido! As he tuned the García, he leaned into my ear. "We are going to reveal our secrets tonight," he whispered, "but it's OK because these people won't even hear them." And so he strummed and we read—my poems about the starkness of a Mexican cot relocated to a pueblo in northern New Mexico, about Anglo racism against *norteño* Latinos, plus a portion of my opera on the *encuentro* between local Chicanos and Mexican immigrants; Arnoldo's focused on love between revolutionaries, ancestors and descendants, roots in land, and migration.

Upon his return to California, Arnoldo began to pen letters brimming with insight about the state of the world. "Every revolution has kept us farther away from the natural world and our roots," he wrote. "And the Earth herself will always have the last say. I remember a speaker at the International Survival Gathering in the Black Hills saying that for America to live, Europe had to die. Too few of us understood the metaphor."

"We can write, we can breathe," he noted in a 2015 email, "even if it is using dirty ink and contaminated air, air contaminated with burning crosses and burnt corpses. The horizons are red from the pollution caused by putting our deep ancestors in our gas tanks.... The revolution is here to become welcoming, open, supportive, loving and god forbid, community and commune, poetry and poets, Indians with their land under their feet . . ." And of his sense of self he wrote, so very distinct from the sorry world around him: "Staying alive and being different is our revolution. Our life has nothing to do with the U.S."

IKEY DE VARGAS: KICK-ASS NORTEÑO
(1946-)

Most of us went there [Vietnam] believing what the government told us, that what we were doing over there was good and necessary. Most of us came back knowing that if they were lying to us over there, they were lying to us here.

—I.D.V. QUOTED IN KAY MATTHEWS'
CULTURE CLASH, 2015

Ikey De Vargas' life has never had much to do with the United States. The going ethic in the 1980s–'90s world of Norteño New Mexico was to be skeptical of anything—person, product, process—"not from here." I met him in the environmental-justice wing of the Latino movement when he was up to his blazing-blue eyeballs in conflict with some folks not from here: a bunch of white, urban environmentalists from an organization called Forest Guardians who were attacking the right of Norteños to use the forests in the sustainable ways that they had practiced since the 1600s.

At heart, the conflict was a clash between concepts of wilderness. The locals eschewed the European separation of human from nature, survived in their "inhabited wilderness" by hunting, fishing, gathering herbs and twigs for their brooms, and cutting the too-dense thickets for firewood; whereas the urban enviros were fighting for Earth's fast dwindling "lung capacity" and insisting that only conservationist hikers, campers, tourists, and photographers should enter. The battle was archetypal for its times: rights of land-based people to the terrains traditionally stewarded by them versus preservation of what little wilds are left on the planet. It was between conflicting ideas of political entities: community-based land grants/commons versus national forest "owned" by all U.S. citizens. And it was between conflicting notions of survival: sustainability in nature versus protection of wilderness. The tactics are what thrust the issues into the public eye through the headlines of the *Santa Fe New Mexican,* plus in the villages of northern New Mexico via Kay Matthews and Mark Schiller's superb community newspaper *La Jicarita News.*

In 1990 Forest Guardians won an injunction in Federal District Court to halt both the gathering of dead and fallen wood and any kind of logging throughout the Southwest Region of the U.S. Forest Service. The area included millions of acres of public lands in New Mexico and Arizona. The goal was to halt all use of wood by claiming that the habitat of the Mexican spotted owl was at stake. The Norteños insisted that said owl had in fact never been seen in the region, and the Forest Service agreed. The Norteños also understood that such a ruling would not only destroy their centuries-old, land-based cultures whose survival depended on the land grants allotted them in the 1700s; given the extreme poverty of the northern villages it would also diminish their immediate ability to live through winters and thrust them into the gross inequalities of the global cash economy, just like all other marginal peoples who have been assimilated into the dominant society.

In reaction to the lawsuit, Ikey and his comrades hung personalized effigies of individual environmentalists from trees in the Carson National Forest. They responded by dramatically showing up in the frigid mountain village of Truchas to distribute firewood. It was an act that in reality was nothing but a symbolic gesture as the back of one pickup did not provide near enough for the entire village and, even for one family, not enough to last more than two or three weeks. Barbs went back and forth, usually landing in the headlines of newspapers, and there was no end in sight to the hostility generated.

Through it all Ikey was unflaggingly fierce. He had been in the Marine Corps in Vietnam. He described his unit as the elite who were assigned the most treacherous missions. When this group entered the mess tent, he said, the other soldiers stepped aside and let them have first crack at the food. Ikey brought back a furious case of post-traumatic stress whose topography included the outer realms of the human experience, and so he felt no limits as to how he should fight the enviros. They, on the other hand, were university educated, thought of themselves as rational, believed in U.S.-defined national forests, but in the end fell into their own version of outer limits: politics by personal attacks and self-serving rumors.

Fresh from having learned the politics of sovereignty from work with Navajo/Diné and Laguna Pueblo uranium miners, now living in the Norteño village of Chimayó, I was also on the advisory board of the urban-based Earth Island Institute of San Francisco. I decided to write an article addressed to "my people"—the white urban enviros. "A Letter to Environmentalists" went "viral" before anyone even had a computer: it was published in the *New Mexican, Albuquerque Journal, Santa Fe Reporter, Earth Island Journal*, and, as time went on, in books like Jake Kosek's *Understories: The Political Life of Forests in Northern New Mexico* and Kay Matthew's *Culture Clash: Environmental Politics in Northern New Mexico Forest Communities*. My naïve hope was to remind city activists of empire's historic takeover of land-based territories and the contemporary value of sustainable "off-the-grid" cultures that can survive in nature, neither destroying it nor stooping to join the global economy—naïve because I thought that an understanding of history might have an impact, even bring about a conversation. But no: Forest

Guardians' rejection of the essay was fixed and absolute; they rebuffed its every word, its every sentiment—including me.

And so I introduced myself to Ikey DeVargas.

Ikey is one gorgeous hunk of manhood. Part-Apache and part-Spanish, he is thin but muscular, boasts skin the color of an Anasazi pot, eyes like a summer pool in the Jemez, and an explosion of yellow-white hair. He is capable of both profound loyalty and volatile retort. He carries a hunting rifle in his rusting pickup, walks through the forest like a Tai Chi master, and picks trout out of the river with his bare hands. It was Linda Pedro of the Native American Church in Chimayó who pointed out to me that I had fallen in love with Ikey, and she was right. But that's not what we did together.

We did politics.

Ikey was always doing politics. He was in Vietnam when the 1967 shootout blew up at the Tierra Amarilla courthouse in an attempt to free local members of the Chicano movement's Alianza de Federales Mercedes; they had been jailed for demanding the return of the lands stolen from them by Anglo owners, often lawyers, and the U.S. government in its drive to acquire its public lands. With semi-automatic assault rifles the rebels overtook the police—shooting one in the lung, another in the cheek, battering a sheriff's deputy with a rifle butt, and taking two officers hostage. Ikey's friend Moises Morales was there, and so, upon his return from 'Nam, Ikey got the first-hand scoop. Afterward, Morales had been arrested for "stowing marijuana in his truck." Pro bono attorney Richard Rosenstock got the charge dismissed by revealing that the police had planted the contraband, and the controversy ended in a perjury conviction against the sheriff himself—plus, for Moises and Ikey, a lifelong friendship with Rosenstock.

Ikey returned from the war outraged at the government's violence against innocent land-based peasants in Southeast Asia. He was ready to fight for his own people's rights, in particular for the retrieval of the land grants the U.S. had usurped to create its national forests and against the multinational Duke City Lumber that was clear-cutting his beloved Carson forest.

Having plunged in hunting-boot deep, he founded a New Mexico branch of La Raza Unida and ran for the position of sheriff, as well as for county commission and state senate; forced Duke City out of the Vallecitos Federal Sustained Yield Unit; and sued the Forest Service to do their stated job of managing the land to benefit the communities.

When I met him, Ikey lived in a raggy trailer in Servilleta Plaza, at various times with dogs, cats, horses, chickens, his daughters, a pig named Isabel, and a blazing-red La Raza flag. Everywhere we went in the county—from Española to Tierra Amarilla—Norteños recognized him and enthusiastically called out his name. "IKEY! IKEY!"

One of the things I liked about him was his ideas: they were completely his own. They were not Marxist or anarchist or New Left or even urban Latino; they came from his observations of how things were and how they should be. I got to talk ideas with him on our road trips to the La Manga woods, during meetings at the Borracho Cabin where a donkey would stick its head through an open window to get a hee-haw in, at gatherings at the Oñate Center in Española marking the anniversary of the 1848 Treaty of Guadalupe (which supposedly bound the U.S. to a pledge that Norteños would keep their land grants), while lazily fishing on the La Madera River or listening to the Native group Apache Spirit's unique rendition of Latino songs.

"They have their heads in the clouds," he would say about the enviros in "Interview with Antonio 'Ike' DeVargas: Ten Years Later" in the December 2005 issue of *La Jicarita News*. "That group of people that attacks rural communities in the guise of environmentalism has no awareness about racism, class issues, poverty, and their consequences for rural communities.... It's a single-purpose agenda that fails to make any association with anything else going on in the world. They all want to be a John Muir and have a legacy." Unable to provide for his family and gripped by despair, one Norteño committed suicide, and the conservationists suffered a terrible fright one snowy morning when a pipe bomb packed with nails was found in their mailbox. And so it went—on and on and on for years.

Every June around the time of the summer solstice, Ikey and I would throw a fiesta at his trailer. The invitees formed a melting pot of locals from the forest villages, Latino activists from as far south as Albuquerque, and

Anglo supporters. All the food, except for store-bought beer and soft drinks, was from El Norte. Ikey would fish like mad that morning. I would bring wine made of capulín, others homegrown corn, lettuce, tomatoes, chile, and home-rolled tortillas. One year Ikey had suffered a head-on collision that demolished his vehicle and nearly his body. Traditionally, if a person has undergone an untoward event, you give him—not an ephemeral bouquet of flowers or a thin volume of literature. Hell no! You give him an animal to sustain him. Leonél Garcia from Chimayó gave Ikey his well-fed and at this point decidedly blimpish pig Isabel. And so the main course of the evening that year was a post-*matanza* Isabel straight from her underground crypt of coals, now laid out on a table covered in aluminum foil. As sad as I was to see our Chimayó pig turn into dinner, Izz was hands-down the best thing I had ever eaten.

That was one of the years that Urban Habitat's Carl Anthony came to New Mexico. He was headed to the Vallecitos Mountain Ranch where lawyer/meditation teacher Grove Burnett and community organizer Linda Velarde held week-long meditation retreats for activists. First came the party, though. Carl's presence was unforgettable. Norteños are generally short. (A local joke goes: Why are the people of the great pre-Colombian civilization at Chaco Canyon so short? The answer: so they can fit through the tiny, low-hung doors there.) On the other hand, Carl is tall and black. Those details made him stand out, plus his presence spoke of the fact that the struggle to protect the Latino right to continue their land-based cultural ways in the forest was not isolated. The Chinese community in San Francisco was fighting city health regulations to maintain their tradition of hanging animal carcasses in their butcher shops. When they tried to resuscitate their dying language and craft by harpooning a single whale, the Makah of the Pacific Northwest, who had received permission from the International Whaling Commission, endured environmentalists shrieking "MURDERERS!" and disrupting their canoes with motor-powered boats.

Yes, the people of northern New Mexico welcomed Carl Anthony to party with them.

Ikey hit pay dirt when his comrades from La Raza Unida were elected or hired to positions within the Rio Arriba County government. Former courthouse-raid radical Moises Morales was elected councilor, former Academia de la Nueva Raza writers Lorenzo Valdez and Estevan Arellano, county manager and director of the Oñate Center respectively—and risk-taker Ikey was named head of Risk Management. The job gave him a diverse schedule of travel and a steady income. It also put him on retirement track. But, just as Che Guevara had an inner compulsion to leave his desk job to return to battle, Ikey was a fighter and a man of the land: he went back to the forest. The battle against the enviros lasted until the mid-'90s when, upon appeal to the New Mexico and Arizona federal courts and the San Francisco appellate court, the original decision was reversed—awarding Norteños the right to proceed with a timber sale in the La Manga forest. But by then they were so burned out, broke, and scattered that they were unable to muster the energy, and internal battles among contenders had become so heated that no group could qualify for a contract. The final nail in the coffin was the 2001 Cerro Grande Fire in the woods surrounding the city of Los Alamos and the Los Alamos Scientific Laboratory that caused such devastation that all public entrance and activity was banned.

Ikey endured some untoward personal fortunes as well. A veterans hospital surgery was botched, and he has suffered health problems ever since. A kid waiting to go hunting in Ikey's trailer accidentally shot and killed a friend, and his son Antonio was slain in a drive-by shooting. Through it all and as always, he carries his wounds just as he maintains his buoyant spirit, sense of humor, and kick-ass attitude.

The man is a giant.

XIII. 500 YEARS:
NATIVE AMERICAN RIGHTS

Religion is for people who're afraid of going to hell.
Spirituality is for those who've already been there.

—VINE DELORIA JR. (YANKTON/NAKOTA BAND
OF THE SIOUX), *GOD IS RED*, 1973

ACROSS THE PLAINS AND up the salmon rivers, a new wind was blowing for Native American peoples. The arrival of 1992—500 years after the influx of Europeans into their lands—provided the perfect tool for bringing together indigenous peoples of North and South America to recognize their common experiences and disparate responses. I am amazed that, for all the funds the Spanish and U.S. governments poured into the España 500 campaign to celebrate Christopher Columbus's "discovery of the New World," Native people managed to eclipse the moment with not a penny in their pockets, but rather by meeting, networking, and speaking out. Because of this determination, not one commemoration was capable of taking place without, at least, a mention, if not an outright admission, of the disastrous effects of the Spanish conquest.

October, 11, 1992 in San Francisco. Photo credit: Bobby Castillo.
Courtesy of Confederated American Indian Movement.

The possibility of education opportunities off the rez gained by the up-and-coming generations also gave many the means to confront the system using its own tools. As Herman Agoyo (Okey Oweenge/San Juan Pueblo) put it, "Our weapons are no longer bows and arrows. Now we use briefcases." Plus, the increase in tribal revenues from Indian Gaming granted a new sense of pride, power, and possibility. Who can forget the boastful blockades of the sole highway leading thousands of buses and cars carrying workers to New Mexico's capital (read: statewide economic shut-down) made by Governor Jake Villarreal (Posuwaegeh/Pojoaque Pueblo)? Or the dramatic claim to sovereignty when Okey Owingeh/San Juan Pueblo was building its massive Okey Casino and Resort? State officials toting clipboards showed up to investigate if the buildings were up to New Mexico state code—and the tribal police threw them out! Who could have imagined the previously unthinkable construction of clinics, schools, and athletic facilities on Native lands? The repatriation of thousands of stolen indigenous remains, sacred objects, and cultural artifacts to the tribes where they belong? Or the resurgence of zeal among young people to resuscitate threatened traditions such as medicine ways, sacred ceremonies, ancient craft, time-honored foods, and sustainable farming?

LARRY EMERSON: *HATALII*/STORY CARRIER
(1951–2017)

The question is whether we revitalize and restore our
culture by restoring and regenerating the non-modern
realm still embedded in our language, ceremonies,
prayers, songs, and art.
—L.E. IN LLOYD LANCE LETT AND GREG CAJETE,
DINÉ CULTURE, DECOLONIZATION, AND THE POLITICS
OF HÓZHÓ, 2004

If I were challenged to say who are the people to most influence my thinking, without hesitation I would say Larry Emerson is on the shortest of short lists. Serious, deep, articulate, humble, enamored of ideas—all the perfect qualities of a significant intellectual—he appeared along with a coterie of Native peoples from tribes of North America at a three-day, invitation-only colloquium given by Fritjof Capra's Elmwood Institute. The year was 1991, the place Berkeley, California. Our goal was to explore how that which Fritjof was calling the "New Paradigm" mirrored indigenous philosophies and ways. Larry sat on one side of the circle among his fellow Native Americans, we European Americans clustered on the other—all twitching with a sense of unease about what we were about to embark upon; such intercultural exchanges were not common in those days. For that matter, neither were representation of indigenous issues in government, inclusion of Native folk in media reporting, or honoring of indigenous literature as an accomplished North American art form.

At first Jeannette Armstrong of the Okanagan in western Canada taught us about the Native American sense of personal and communal identity as shaped by one's people's roots in a specific terrain. In other words: where is your land and what is your inherited responsibility for it? She instructed us:

The way we talk about ourselves as Okanagan people is hard to replicate in English. Our word for human beings is difficult to say without talking about connection to the land.

My mother is a River Indian. She is Kettle Falls, which is the main confluence of the Columbia River system near Inchelieum. The Kettle River people are in charge of the fisheries in all of the northern parts of the Columbia River system in our territories. My great-grandfather was a salmon chief and caretaker of the river to the north.

My father's people are mountain people. They occupy what's called the northern part of the Okanagan proper around the part of British Columbia that is known as the Okanagan Valley. Their medicine comes from that spirit. . . .

We say, "This is my clan" or "This is my people." In this way you know my position, what my place is, what my specific responsibility for that specific location and geographic area is. That is how I introduce myself.

The Natives proceeded to introduce themselves, each in a similar manner focusing on land and community, and we learned that sitting among us were members of the Shoshone, Karuk, Na-Dené/Diné/Navajo, Yurak, and Okanagan peoples. Despite the fact that such a perspective was mirrored by our politics of the bioregional, we non-Natives then stumbled about in an attempt to repeat the challenge to do likewise given the loss of roots/memory/orientation perpetrated through the centuries of assimilation into the dominant society that our ancestors had endured. I will not forget Sierra Club Books editor Danny Moses' response, which he offered in a conscious attempt to sound ridiculous in comparison to the histories spoken from the other side of the circle. He said: "1495 Popham Avenue, a piece of New York City."

Larry was Na-Dené or Diné, otherwise known as Navajo. He hailed from a dry stretch of desert where he inhabited a house constructed of cast-off materials situated next to that of his parents in Tsé daa k'án/ Shiprock, New Mexico—just up the highway by three International-Scout hours from my home in Tesuque. He was tall with a pert Charlie-Chaplin moustache and a black ponytail feathering down his back. Despite the nervousness that caused him to continually clear his throat, he spoke from deep within his soul.

I vowed to get to know him.

After the Elmwood gathering, Larry and I took a long walk through the neighborhoods of Berkeley's Flatlands, talking and talking, beginning what became our perennial conversation about the similarities and differences between Native thinking and what those of us from the dominant society have struggled to create to replace western philosophies. After all the talk, I remember just two things that Larry said that day, both of which told me that I had much to learn from this mind and heart. One: as we were resting on a bench in the shade of a sprouting California bay tree, a song sparrow alighted on the sidewalk in front of us—just for a moment—and then it lifted off into the sky. Larry was speaking about the importance for humans to enter the natural world by understanding its manifestations as messages that are linked to our destinies. In the bird's fleeting presence, he inserted, "Like this tiny creature. This bird could be the one to tell us what we need to know right now."

Two: he said he had journeyed onto the nearby campus of my alma mater, the University of California, and looking over its Beaux-Arts/Greek-style buildings, porticos, and statues, as well as contemplating what alien ideas it promised to plant in a student's head, he decided he himself would *never* go there—and he most *certainly* would not send his son.

"My people," "we," "our way"—these are common words spoken by tribal and Pueblo members. Native American thinking starts with a solid grounding in both personal and community sovereignty, and from this foundation springs a host of assumptions. One of them is an undying emphasis not on the Me-First individualism insisted on by mass society, but rather on what is best for the community as a whole. Ergo, we get the battle cry of Oglala Lakota warriors willing to give their lives for the good of their people and culture, shouting "Today is a good day to die!" Ergo, we get the utter commitment to preserve indigenous ways and philosophies that blossoms again and again throughout the Native world—despite the dominant society's insistence that assimilation into modernism predominate, despite its doggedness on the subject-acts-on-object ideology that domineering projections require.

Another source of Native American grounding is the recognition that humans are members of the wider community of honeybees and churro sheep, of juniper ash and Indian paintbrush. Use of natural medicine follows. To the Diné illness is thought of as the manifestation of mental or physical upset brought on by a disruption of harmony—such as breaking a taboo, indecent conduct toward an animal, bad behavior during a ceremony, or contact with malignant entities like spirits, skin-walkers, or witches. Breaking a taboo is believed to be acting against the principles devised by the Holy People. The cure for such ruptures is the Blessing Way ceremony whose elaborate song cycles recount the Navajo creation story and teach an ethic of Walking in Beauty.

Larry was born in Tsé daa k'án/Shiprock, New Mexico. He once introduced himself saying, "My name is Larry Emerson, that is a colonized name and I have no idea what those two words mean except they come from boarding school." As he put it in Greg Cajete and Lloyd Lance Lett's *Diné Culture, Decolonization, and the Politics of Hózhó,* his true identity is something entirely different: "I am the Over Hanging Ledge Rock People born for the Water Flows Together People. My paternal grandfather's clan is Many Hogans People, and my maternal grandfather's clan is Towering House People. I am Diné."

Upbringing in the Emerson household was traditional—until, at age six, the U.S. government swooped in and carted him off to a Dutch Reform Church missionary school one hundred miles from home. In this alien environment, students slept in carefully watched dormitories and were forbidden to speak their native tongues or practice non-Christian customs. The teachers used physical violence—and sometimes sexual assault—as punishment. Such education was consciously designed to turn "savage" Native people into assimilated members of "civilization." Concurrent with the 1990s' arising of consciousness regarding injustices to Native American peoples, said schooling has now been dubbed "cultural genocide."

If Larry was to receive a more compelling awareness than what was being instilled at school, it was sparked by a coincidence. When he was eleven years old, an automobile tooled by on the dirt road heading west from Naat áanii Nééz. Cars meant white people; no Diné owned a vehicle. He walked up to the road, and there he found that the people in the car had dropped off a cardboard box full of books! He tucked it away under a tree for safe keeping—and began to devour the spate of volumes that had been so carefully chosen: James Baldwin, who taught him about New York City, racism, and homosexuality; social-studies and geography books that showed him a wide world beyond the Navajo (and once again gave focus to New York City). The planet, it turned out, was much bigger than he could have imagined.

Not long after, at age thirteen, Larry turned to alcohol. Given the historic robbing of collective tribal sovereignty by the U.S. government and subsequent defeat of cultural survival, the lack of economic opportunities offered to Natives sequestered on reservations, and the losses, disorientation, and physical attacks he had endured at boarding school, the choice is not unusual. Later, his psyche presented him with unremembered experiences of sexual violation that had been perpetrated by the "Christians," and explaining to me what had happened in the lunch line at a Native American conference, he told me that he had gone into conventional Western psychotherapy to recover from this trauma. "You have to use the cure of the culture that produced the illness you want to heal from," he said.

When I met Larry in 1991, he had long since taken the brave step to enter Alcoholics Anonymous for guidance in recovery. He had also finished undergraduate work at the University of New Mexico with an emphasis on Native American history and literature, and he had discovered in himself an attraction to healing. It was no surprise, then, that in the late '90s he embarked upon the arduous process to become a hatalii, which involves memorizing hours of story-songs in the complex Diné Bizaad, or Navajo language. Members of the dominant society translate the word "hatalii" to mean "medicine man," but Larry dislikes that word because of its multiple misuses by non-Natives and subsequent stereotyping. He prefers to say he is a "traditional knowledge scholar" or a "story carrier."

Although we did not know it at the time, this revered place in the Navajo world—and all that he has done since—was in gestation when I drove out to the reservation for a visit. As I pulled up in my rusted-out International Scout, I could see that the land was stark, blonde desert; stretching from horizon to horizon, the sky was as enormous as a cosmos; and the terrain was sliced in two by an ominous string of high-tension electrical wires carrying the technological fruits of nearby dams to western cities. The house boasted cast-off scraps of wood nailed together as if they were shingles on a Berkeley Maybeck, and in the lower reaches sat the round form of an adobe hogan, or sacred meeting space.

He had plans. He wanted to develop the land into a community healing center. To kick off this endeavor, he had invited some of his friends to a gathering that very afternoon in which *I* would talk about the thinking we of the dominant society were doing in critique of its unfettered development of technology. I was flabbergasted by the prospect. But, sitting in a circle inside the cool of the hogan, I did make a valiant, if crude, effort.

Afterward, he and I sat in his living room and looked at a book of photos taken by the famed non-Native photographer Edward Curtis, who in the early 1900s had traveled through the American West toting a Premo dry-plate camera and tripod to make portraits of Native Americans; he was just in time to capture them before thousands were murdered and the near-totality of their ways battered beyond recognition by U.S. conquest. There, in Larry's presence, I was revisiting these well-known images from the unique perspective offered by a rez-based glimpse, and he explained that indigenous people are not like these restrained stiff subjects who showed no joy or contentment; what was captured was the fright produced by the bizarre act of a white man making a photograph.

For me his insight was a revelation.

Another sprang from the friction between cultures that he knew so well. It concerned his first trip to a place that had become mythical for him ever since that box of books had appeared on the road: it was a trip to New York City. As the moment for departure neared, though, he was feeling no small modicum of terror: *this* would surely be a descent into the lunacy of the dominant society, with its racism against people precisely like him. He was in his twenties, wore a black leather jacket and his hair in a ponytail. He shared his apprehension with a friend and was given a piece of advice from a Native American perspective that renewed all confidence: "Hey man, struttin' down the street with your dark skin, your tough jacket, and your long hair—they're gonna be afraid of *you!*"

One day Larry spoke to me about the process by which one becomes a shaman. As a psychotherapist, I was also in gestation. More and more of my clients were survivors of traumatic experiences. As he spoke, my

breathing stopped: the progression he described was a mirror of a psy-
chodynamic procedure for recovering from traumatic stress.

"It starts with a breakage in one's soul," he said, "a childhood illness
or accident, an assault, a consciously created shattering event as produced in an initiation." He drew a circle. The trauma he was describing
was located at the start of the circle's flow on the lower left side. Then,
he explained as his pencil moved upward toward the arc stretching across
the top of the page, the person is challenged to heal the fractures that
have marked his/her psyche. The arc for this time of healing took up the
bulk of the circle's line; it was clearly a lengthy and arduous process
involving not only inner work but also help from the spirit world. "Then,
when that is accomplished," he continued, "one emerges with an ability
to venture into the other world to speak with the spirits and transmit
wisdom and advice for living." The shaman's job then becomes to serve
the community through this gift.

Larry seemed to have an inborn talent to commune with the spirit
world. I know because I witnessed him doing so when he came to visit
me in Tesuque. We were contemplating holding a second meeting of the
group that had gathered in 1991 in Berkeley. Walking the land surrounding my rented adobe, he sat down under a juniper tree and pointed to a
medicinal herb that was sprouting out of the sand. This very plant had
recently revealed itself in ceremony, he told me. Suddenly his awareness
shifted. It was as if he were looking inside rather than at the blue sky and
green branches that populated normal vision. His breathing slowed, his
eyes brimmed with tears. I sat in silence. After a few minutes, he returned
and reported that the juniper was the grandmother tree of the area, that
she has given her blessing to use the herb and also to hold our campout
in this patch of upland desert.

A surprise followed: Larry did indeed decide to attend a dominant-soci-
ety university. For some years he had been working with San Diego State
University's Carol Robinson-Zañartu in their joint creation, the Native
American Scholars and Collaborators Project, and she urged him to pursue a Ph.D. Swayed by her encouragement and positive attitude, in 1999
he packed up, drove to the coral-tree-studded hills overlooking the
Pacific Ocean—and enrolled in the counseling program at SDSU. One of

the most notable experiences occurred at the start of classes. Instead of being given conventional lectures and readings, his cohort of twenty-six students was ingeniously guided through a sharing/healing process. The group consisted of Asians, African Americans, gays, liberals, conservatives, and Native Americans, and the task was to express themselves in order to know themselves better and educate the others. During the process, Larry testified that he was confronted by his own biases and neglect of himself. Plus he learned how to locate himself as a Native American within U.S. society and to respect diversity.

After completing his master's degree in 2000, he continued on with formal instruction toward a Ph.D. in educational philosophy via a joint program at SDSU and Claremont Graduate University. Here he studied Michel Foucault, Paulo Freire, Edward Said—and from these readings was introduced to Eurocentric critical theories concerning deconstruction of power, pro-justice perception, and decolonization. Once again he was given the opportunity to clarify his thinking as a Diné. "I better learned *my* own lens by coming to understand *their* lens," he told me. And the two were distinct. Larry wrote a dissertation that was distinct as well; he did not use a linear western approach to accomplish his investigation; he did it by following Navajo principles. Dedicated to understanding "the dialectical nature of colonialism and decolonization," "Hozho Nahazdlii: Toward a Practice of Diné Decolonization" was published in 2003, and Larry continued as a sought-after consultant for Native American Scholars and Collaborators.

He also, at long last, launched his community healing center, which he dubbed Tsé daa k'án after the "ship rock" formation where, so many decades before, he had discovered the box of books that, in many ways, determined his life path. At the farm he used principles of permaculture to develop the desert sands into a green oasis—complete with bee hives, gardens, and compost bins—and hosted many a group of Native, European, and North American folks eager to learn about decolonization through traditional Diné ways that relink people to the natural world.

Larry became ill with stomach cancer in 2016, and for several months he did not get back to me regarding questions I had for completing this essay. I waited patiently, but in time I wondered why. Finally he contacted me, and after the shock of learning about the cancer, my first thought was—what with all the hatalii knowledge and wisdom he carries as songs and stories, what with his informed historical perspective and embodied vision for his people, what with his gentle nature and undying humility— it would be impossible to imagine this world, or the Diné Nation, without his crucial contributions.

We spoke via telephone. He was ebullient but cautious as he had received word that growth of the cancer had been miraculously halted. It had previously been defined as rampaging Stage 4—leaving him just one year to live. After a few chemo treatments, he told me, he had walked away from more of that kind of allopathic assault and turned to a strict regimen informed by natural approaches. These consisted of a regime of rest; vitamin and mineral supplements; pure oxygen treatment in a Hyperbaric Chamber; plus use of food as medicine—with an emphasis on Brussels sprouts, asparagus, kale, etc. "We should all be eating like this anyway," he said. And, of course, at the heart of his healing program lay Diné ceremony.

But alas! when he went to the clinic for his checkup the following month, he was told that the cancer had begun to spread again. When he did not get back to me, I suspected this and, as if suddenly viewing his life pass before my eyes, I understood better than ever, and was awed by, his profound contributions to his people and culture, as well as to non-Natives like all the students who visited his farm, read his dissertation, or sat in ceremony with him. I shall never forget the wisdom he shared, which was in essence a guide toward being a full human being—connected to and expressive of one's own talents as well as to community, place, the spirits, the stars, the Earth. Perhaps his greatest accomplishment was healing himself of unsavory life experiences generated by the political-power mongering of an expanding nation-state. It cannot be ignored that Larry heroically chose to live by his values, setting aside the Western mode of attacking the cancer with toxins, choosing instead to boost his body's own ability to heal. To make such a decision remains an uncertain choice, a plunge into the unknown. To make it he even set aside his own counsel to use the medicine created by the culture that caused the illness in the first place, and to the end he was true to his dedication to honor the natural world.

Sadly, Larry passed in mid-August 2017. His family came together at the farm in Shiprock. They buried him on the land next to his sister, who had also died of cancer, and a rainbow appeared in the immense sky above.

SUZAN SHOWN HARJO: BORN TO THE MORNING STAR
(1945-)

In the United States, there were more Native American human remains in museums and other repositories than there were living American Indian people.... Indian skeletons and body parts were exhibited and warehoused in the finest American museums and universities, and sold to the highest bidder.

—S.H., "IT BEGAN WITH A VISION IN A SACRED PLACE" IN *PAST, PRESENT, AND FUTURE CHALLENGES AT NMAI*, 2011

I can thank the year 1992 for introducing me to Suzan Harjo. The whole of Indian Country was abuzz for the unprecedented opportunity to confront the vehemence of the ill-conceived U.S./Spain campaign to celebrate the arrival of Christopher Columbus in the "New World." I attended as many Native American–sponsored events as I could. After one such happening at the Center for Contemporary Arts in Santa Fe, New Mexico, the standing-room-only crowd poured out of the auditorium and turned the lobby into a party. Perhaps because I was writing a book about the psychosocial dysfunctions that pervade the dominant society, some quick-thinking networker thought to introduce me to a sturdy, stylishly outfitted woman who turned out to be . . . the infamous Suzan Harjo. I didn't know it at the time, but she was a mover and shaker in The 1992 Alliance whose task was to counter this second Spanish invasion by promoting celebrations of tribes that have survived and mourning those that did not.

I had spent quite a bit of time contemplating if there existed any purpose in European Americans making apology to the Native American community. Suzan and I arranged to speak on the topic via phone as soon as she returned to Washington, D.C., where she worked through law, legislation, cultural exhibition, and the written word as an advocate for indigenous rights.

Why do I say "infamous"?

The answer is simple: Suzan is not just a forceful personality with an inquisitive intelligence but has distinguished herself in an abundance of endeavors during a generation when so many Native American women were struggling against the triple cruelty of being female, poor, and Indian. She was born in El Reno, Oklahoma, to homemaker Suzie Rozetta Eades (Tsistsistas/Cheyenne and Pawnee) and Freeland Edward Douglas (Hodulgee Muscogee/Creek), who was serving in the U.S. Army. She grew up in Beggs, Oklahoma, on her Muscogee grandmother's farm allotment, where, as she explained during a University of Nevada lecture in 2015, she was raised in "a family of fighters." "We were always being instructed on how to stand up against racism," she said, "and we were told we had to do it for all of us." Her idol was her kick-ass great-grandfather Chief Bull Bear, who in the nineteenth century had been leader of the Dog Men Society and a designer of treaties.

Mother Susie Rozetta Eades Douglas (Cheyenne and Pawnee) and Suzan in sunglasses, El Reno, Oklahoma, 1947. Courtesy of Suzan Harjo.

An unexpected opportunity arose when her father was assigned to a U.S. military base in Naples, Italy, and the family moved away from the socially repressive environment of Oklahoma. For five of her formative teen years—the very period when a budding mind is developing social ideas and sculpting a relationship to society—she had the opportunity to experience different worlds and cultures. To young Suzan, being in Europe felt like being an anthropologist: she "both fell in love with the subject and kept distance from it." And when she returned, she was astonished to discover that "the white kids knew *less* about their roots than I did."

Suzan launched a career as a theater actress, director, and producer in New York City alongside her first husband, artist/set designer John Shown. At age twenty-two she did what could only be described as "burst onto the scene": she and the man who would become her second husband, Frank Ray Harjo (Wotcoo Muscogee), coproduced the first Indian news program in the U.S., "Seeing Red," on New York's listener-sponsored WBAI-FM. The station boasted millions of devotees in a six-state area, plus was picked up by the Pacifica Network in San Francisco, Los Angeles, and Houston. She also directed WBAI's drama and literature department and rose to become the first woman to hold a top management position.

Just previous to her job there, a seminal event had taken place: she and her mother had visited the Museum of the American Indian in New York. There in a glass display case, her mother Suzie was shaken to the bone when she saw what she believed were clothes she herself had helped to make for her grandfather's burial. Also on display was a buckskin dress of a Cheyenne girl disfigured by a bullet hole over the place where her stomach had once been. Suzie was so outraged that she gave her daughter the task of getting these sacred items *out of the museum and back to the burial ceremonies they should have had*. And so began what became Suzan's life-long dedication to political action aimed at concrete results. The theme of repatriation became a passion for her that led to many successes, including the return of over one million acres of stolen lands and several sacred places to their first inhabitants. She also contributed to the conceptual design and wording of some of the most progressive federal laws of the twentieth century for the protection of Native American cultures: the 1978 American Indian Religious Freedom Act, the 1989 National Museum of the American Indian Act, the 1990 Native American Graves Protection and Repatriation Act, and the 1996 Executive Order on Indian Sacred Sites.

She was also a founder of the Smithsonian's National Museum of the American Indian. From 1967 until its opening forty years later, Suzan labored along with many others to secure laws and funding for, and to conceptualize and curate programs for, a museum that would accurately tell the story of Native Peoples and house in dignity recovered cultural materials from the Arctic Circle to Tierra del Fuego. Finally achieved in 2004, the museum is constructed in the exact spot where the original coalition envisioned it: on the National Mall facing the Capitol, as an inescapable reflection of the non-whitewashed history of the nation. Suzan was a founding trustee as well as curator/editor of the 2014 book and 2014-2018 exhibition *Nation to Nation: Treaties between the United States and American Indian Nations*.

Our first phone conversation lasted three hours. Suzan was an East Coast night owl, but fortunately for this morning person, in New Mexico the time was several hours earlier. Her studied assessment of possible benefits of European-American apology by both citizens and the U.S. government lasted thirty seconds; she felt it pointless and without concrete, or even psychological, value. The other two hours, fifty-nine minutes, and thirty seconds overflowed with stories of life experiences. She talked about personal incidents that demonstrated U.S. racism; her early career in theater and broadcasting; the Morning Star Foundation that she had started in 1984 in honor of Frank Harjo, who had passed on in 1982. Her ability to listen and feel compassion was boundless. I spoke about my Lakota blood brother who had been killed in Vietnam, current work with uranium miners at Kawiak/Laguna Pueblo and the Diné/Navajo Nation, and my mother's influence on me to become an activist.

That phone call was followed by countless more of the same duration and ilk. I learned that, for Suzan, the 1970–'80s had produced a whirlwind of activity as she broke into the D.C. political world, making lifelong connections that would lead to the achievement of crucial objectives. She worked as news director at the American Indian Press Association, as communications/legislative director and later executive director at the National Congress of American Indians, as legislative liaison at the Native American Rights Fund, and then as special assistant for Indian legislation for the Carter administration.

Also in those years Suzan became riled up about the use of "Indian" words and mascots as names for sports teams. An effort to deal with the problem had in fact been launched in the 1960s when the National Indian Youth Councils initiated a campaign to challenge stereotyping. Having grown up in Cleveland, I had been an enthusiastic fan of the Indians— their symbolic mascot was the cartoonish, toothy Chief Wahoo—so I knew that said-named teams were considered "normal" in baseball, as well as in football, ice hockey, and basketball. There were the Kansas City Chiefs, the Washington Redskins, the Chicago Blackhawks, the Florida Seminoles.

Given that the Native world suffers from so many emergency survival issues, to some, such naming seemed like a superficial issue. Suzan never saw it that way. Why? "Because it represents everything that's wrong in this world," she said at the Nevada lecture, "and getting rid of them represents hope, optimism, that change is happening, and that change is coming. . . . It's the same thing . . . as giving our children something to aspire to." She is always quick to explain that she never worked alone on the effort, joining with hundreds of fellow Natives including historian/ theologian Vine Deloria Jr. (Yankton/Nakota Standing Rock Sioux), painter Mateo Romero (Cochiti Pueblo), and social worker Amanda Blackhorse (Diné/Navajo). Needless to say, the struggle has lasted decades—this post-1960s wave began in 1992—and, as I write this, the struggle is not over. In 1999 Suzan endured death threats after both the U.S. Trademark Trial and Appeal Board and the Patent and Trademark Office announced rulings in favor of *Harjo et al. v. Pro Football Inc.* "I do not answer the phone even if I'm expecting a certain call at a certain time," she has explained. "We get a lot of hang-ups and some of those, I just assume now, are the death threats. . . . I don't want to hear people yelling at me even if they're not exactly threatening my life. . . . I had to get a restraining order against one stalker who had developed a hostile fixation against me."

The 1999 triumph turned out to be slippery, as the case soon lost on technicalities before federal district and appeals courts, and the U.S. Supreme Court declined to take it on. In 2006 a second case named *Black-horse et al v. Pro Football, Inc.* was initiated. Meanwhile Suzan and her colleagues have submitted *Harjo et al. Letters of Protest* to address the stack of new trademark applications.

Isn't this never-quite-finished quality a constant reality for those who confront the bluntness of established injustice? Sometimes the daring get to experience gratitude, though. In 2014 President Barak Obama honored Suzan with the highest tribute a U.S. civilian can receive: the Presidential Medal of Freedom. The traditional Tsistsistas chiefs also named her Vooheheva/Morning Star Woman, who fed the people with her gifts of squash, corn, beans, and tobacco.

Suzan came to Santa Fe again during the winter of 1992–3. I drove to the Pinguiltha/Picuris Pueblo-owned Hotel Santa Fe to pick her up. What then took place was a reunion of a couple of raring-to-go phone friends. She had traveled west for meetings regarding the long walk toward getting repatriation laws written, passed, and implemented, while holding back challenges to undo the laws altogether. In between her organizing work, we crammed in dinners and laughs, stories and confessions. On the last night, Suzan was ruffled by what had taken place immediately before I arrived to pick her up. Along with other Native Americans engaged in the effort, she had gone to the ultra-luxurious home of a man who fancied himself a "friend" to Indians. Here, with clueless self-satisfaction, he showed off a great cremation pot that he "owned"; then, dipping his fingers into its dark interior, he brought up remnants of its contents: *the blackened ashes of indigenous people's dead bodies.* Suzan was in shock. She was so gripped with revulsion that she couldn't even speak about what had happened.

After dinner, she and I sat shivering in my International Scout in the hotel's parking circle, but instead of revisiting the horror that lingered in her heart, she told me the story of The Padded Cat. Once a long time ago in New York City—she began her tale—ex-husband John Shown was decorating the Saks Fifth Avenue windows with human-sized stuffed animals and using the apartment she shared with husband Frank Harjo and their children as a sewing and staging area. The poor guy was in a panic: a reviewer and a photographer were due to show up at Saks any minute, and so he begged her to finish sewing a stuffed-animal feline, transport it to the store, and help with final touches on site. There was a problem: more than one impediment to fulfilling the request lay ahead. Suzan and Frank were expected at a Native American rights rally at the exact same time; the children needed to be picked up; and the taxi union was on the verge of a strike, and every cab in the city was filled to the brim with desperate riders.

Suzan and Frank made a plan. She would complete the work on the cat at the apartment and send a neighbor to the rally to drop off a drum she had promised, and then to Saks to deliver the stuffed animal, while Frank would join John to finish the window display. Sandwiched in between these critical tasks, there were also the regular but suddenly frenzied matters of picking up the children.

Reminiscent of a Preston Sturges madcap comedy, the young ones were successfully delivered to their various activities, the window displays were finished, and the neighbor dispatched... eeee-gads! the drum ended up at the photo shoot, while the cat attended its first political rally! Afterwards, a frazzled Suzan and Frank—with enormous feline in tow— were trying to hail a cab. At the sight of the three, passing strangers laughed uproariously, and Frank quipped: "Most days are ordinary and predictable. But some days the universe throws you a Padded Cat and you're living someone else's life."

Suzan then told me that her purpose for coming to New Mexico hadn't turned out well, but that she was leaving with a good feeling about *our* visit, that I, in fact, was the magical and joyous change agent of the trip, its Padded Cat! Saying this was a comical—and remarkably kind—act, and our merriment resounded as she stepped into the freshly fallen snow and made a dash for the warmth of the hotel lobby.

A curiously muted theme threads through this humorous tale, and this is Suzan's undying dedication to the generations preceding her and those that will follow, a consciousness that members of the future-leaning dominant society have failed to inherit or value. In an essay she wrote for the book *Past, Present, and Future: Challenges of NMAI,* she poignantly depicts the shameful history most non-Natives are aware of—at least in broad strokes—regarding the peoples who greeted the first settlers, the presidents, and military leaders: they were violently driven off their homelands, murdered in genocidal sweeps, molded into "reputable" citizens of "civilization," lied to, made fun of, and discounted as "savages." But Suzan rewrites this same history via the personal stories of her ancestors—and she does so as a way of honoring what her Muscogee ancestors Faulena and Yaha Fixico, her mother's Tsistsistas great-grandfather Chief Bull Bear and Buffalo Walla, her mother's great-uncle Chief Starving Bear, and her mother's grandparents Chief Thunderbird/Richard Davis and Nellie Aspenall did for her. Likewise, she bases her lifelong work for Native American rights on the simple fact that she is a granddaughter, daughter, and mother.

According to their stories, the Tsistsistas people hark back to the Morning Star, from which they were transported to be Bears in the Beautiful Land. When they learned prayer and ceremony, they were changed into humans. The Morning Star Woman came too—bearing her gifts of squash, corn, beans, and tobacco. The tradition of burial is to place the bodies on scaffolds just above or just below the surface of the ground—from whence each will return to the Morning Star and then be sent to another beautiful land as food or light or a sound—or even a star.

In the 1990s—as the planet began to show the worrisome signs of climate change, global warming, environmental destruction, mass extinctions, and the persistent spread of nuclear weapons—I began to think about death. And about the traditional story Suzan had shared of death being merely the time to return to the Morning Star. I decided to press my luck. Heaven knows, I was already The Padded Cat! What more could I possibly want? Nonetheless I asked Suzan if, when my time came, I might go back with her to the Morning Star.

She said she didn't know if such a decision would be up to her, but promised she'd ask. So far, as she reports, "No one's said no."

SIMON ORTIZ: WEAVER OF WORDS
(1941-)

It was a good sunny day to be out with the lilac
blossoms and the bees, butterflies, and ladybugs upon
them. The wonderful odor is so powerful, it feels heady,
and I can imagine how butterflies are afloat just from
the sweet wafts.

—S.O., LETTER TO CHELLIS GLENDINNING, APRIL 26, 1992

Indeed, 1992 was an extraordinary year for Native Americans; it had been exactly 500 years since the landing of the Niña, Pinta, and Santa Maria on a sandy Caribbean beach within throwing distance of the far greater Turtle Island—when the original inhabitants of the continent managed to sabotage the entire Spanish/U.S. governmental effort of what for those countries had been conceived as a public-relations coup, but what for Natives brought up the remembrance of an unspeakable and ongoing catastrophe.

It was an extraordinary year for me as well: I had the good fortune to come to know poet-philosopher Simon Ortiz (Aacqu/Acoma Pueblo). I first cast eyes on him in 1989 when he was honored at the New Mexico Council of the Humanities annual awards dinner in Albuquerque. I was there to receive a minor prize for a short story I had penned: he was the acclaimed recipient for the Humanitarian Award for Literary Achievement. He must be a very great writer, I thought, not slightly intimidated. But it was former SDS activist Mark Rudd who thought to introduce us. How we became close friends, I hardly recall. But we did. And 1992 became the timely witness to a rash of letters and postcards between Deetzeyaamah/McCartys in the heart of Aacqu and first Tesuque, where I was renting an adobe-plastered trailer, and then Chimayó of the Latino villages of the north; for his part, our communiqués were scrawled in between a demanding schedule of poetry readings, teaching jobs, and Native celebrations. On one letter, dated May 29, 1992, he wrote:

I got back from Germany, and I'm to be in New York June 2–4 for a Native American film festival. Then I'm going to Arizona for research on a film story dealing with the Native struggle to establish schools that are against the U.S. mentality of "education," or indoctrination as Indian people more commonly know it as. I'll be gone June 8–11 on that. Then I'll write and write fast (I hope) as I have a deadline of mid-June. I will be in Santa Fe on June 22 evening for a brief appearance at the CCA. Then back here for more writing until July 7–9 when I'll be in Oklahoma. . . .

Amid all that rampant packing and unpacking, Simon proceeded to propose we spend the day of June 23 together. I learned that, despite a schedule that a humming bird would have difficulty keeping up with, he is a man who values good conversation and, most of all, friendship.

We drove south from Santa Fe in my antiquated International Scout. The freeway cuts through Cochiti, Kewa/Santo Domingo, Katishtya/San Felipe, and Napeya/Sandia pueblos, revealing side-by-side mountain chains and horizons of desert sand that reach beyond vision; through Albuquerque, just east of the Cañoncito Diné/Navajo rez and Ka'waika/Laguna Pueblo—and finally to the village of Deetzeyaamah. Here Simon lived in a humble adobe house surrounded by his prized apricot, peach, and pear trees. In the tiny living room I noticed a signed photograph of him shaking hands with President Ronald Reagan at the White House's annual Salute to Poetry. We sipped Lipton tea. I watered the trees. And we talked, endlessly talked. About the uranium mine where he had toiled to put himself through university. About my work with miners of Ka'waika and the Diné. About his recovery from alcoholism. About gratitude and joy for being alive. And he invited me to someday join him on the annual hike up the sacred Lukuchai Mountain.

That was our beginning.

Simon is a member of the Eagle Clan of the Keres-speaking Aacqu; his real name is Hihdruutsi. His mother was a homemaker, his father a pueblo singer, woodcarver, railroad worker, and keeper of the spiritual knowledge and customs of the pueblo.

Architect Douglas Cardinal (Siksika/Blackfoot) offers a morsel of wisdom that is essential for any non-Native seeking to understand indigenous people. In *The Native Creative Process* he writes: "It is imperative that people understand the separate reality of Native peoples and the rest of society." Simon grew up speaking the Keres language and didn't know that a different world existed outside his own until he was twelve years old and U.S. law ordered that he attend a Bureau of Indian Affairs school, in his case Saint Catherine's boarding school in Santa Fe. There, forbidden to speak his own language under the nun's threats of castigation, he was being abruptly molded to assimilate into the U.S. mainstream. Instead of seething in a state of cynicism and paralysis, the cultural dissonance that resulted challenged him; he studied with a voracious hunger, in the end mastering English and gaining a love of language itself—and an ability to write.

The day after graduating, Simon began work as a laborer at a Kerr-McGee uranium processing plant near Aacqu—starting as a typist, rapidly demoted to working on the assembly line as a rock crusher, and later promoted to machine operator. After serving in the U.S. Army for three years, his grasp of the English language became even more fluid. He enrolled at Fort Lewis College in 1964 and two years later, the University of New Mexico. Here, despite the political upheaval exploding on campus, he was shocked to find that the Native voice was nearly unheard in the halls of academia! "There were really no models at all that were Native American," he explained to radio producer David Dunaway in a 1988 interview for KUNM-FM in Albuquerque. "The models that were there were the popular American ones, at least that we were taught in school: Hemingway, Faulkner, the poets Carl Sandberg, Robert Frost, and Whitman, who I felt spoke of a real America. I think that socially conscious and socially committed writers—Theodore Dreiser, realists like Hammond Garland, Steinbeck, Sinclair Lewis—these people were my models." He attributed the deafening silence to the repression in BIA school policy—and to the government's desire to wipe out all traces of the existence of original cultures. "'They're all a vanishing race, right?' 'There are no Native Americans east of the Mississippi,'" he said, explaining to Dunaway the prejudices Native People face. "In fact, the Native Americans in the United States are not real 'Indians,' they're Indians who aren't 'Indians' anymore because, well, they don't ride the painted ponies and live in tepees. That was a method of repression: a non-acceptance, non-recognition, much less respect, non-sensitivity to Native American people and culture and ways of life."

Simon decided to contribute to improving the deficiency and to pursue writing; he received a Masters of Fine Arts from the University of Iowa's Writer's School in 1969 and launched the poetry, short stories, and creative non-fiction that have placed him at the heart of the Native American Renaissance of the 1960s and '70s. By now he has written, edited, or had his work included in some twenty-five-plus books and anthologies. These include: *A Good Journey; Fight Back: For the Sake of the People, For the Sake of the Land; From Sand Creek: Rising in this Heart Which Is Our America; The People Shall Continue;* and *The Good Rainbow Road.* He also created a segment for the 1992 PBS film *Surviving Columbus: The Story of the Pueblo People.*

Simon's offerings are described as traditional storytelling; as gentle, caring, bold, exuberant, hopeful, despairing, angry, defiant, militant; as models of the Native voice holding its own in the modern world; as reflections on a land-based sense of time and space; as tales of survival and continuity; as passageways into the spirituality offered by the natural world; as a thriving form of preservation of the old ways. To me the writing appears remarkably simple and straightforward—replicas of the way Simon "talks Indian" in everyday life—but such a quick interpretation belies its inherent complexity and integrity of structure.

To the western thinker, a most revealing passage—and one of my favorites:

When my father has said a word—in speech or in song—I ask him, "What does that word break down to? I mean, breaking it down to the syllables of sound or phrases of sound, what do each of these parts mean?" And he has looked at me with an exasperated—slightly pained—expression on his face, wondering what I mean. And he tells me, *"It doesn't break down into anything."*

—S.O., "Song/Poetry and Language," 1977

Resulting from this dedication to translating what originated as oral culture into the written word was that New Mexico Humanities Council award in 1989. But that's not all. It also led to a National Endowment for the Arts Discovery Award, a National Endowment for the Arts fellowship, the Lila Wallace *Reader's Digest* prize, a Pushcart prize in poetry, an honorary Doctorate of Letters from the University of New Mexico, the Lifetime Achievement Award at the "Returning the Gift Festival of Native Writers"—and perhaps needless to say, a photo op with Ronald Reagan! Along with such contemporaries as the Kiowa novelist/poet N. Scott Momaday, A'aninin/Blackfeet poet Jim Welch, and novelist/poet Leslie Silko from Ka'waik/Laguna Pueblo, Simon has indeed fulfilled his desire to bring respect for Native perception to a wider audience.

Simon's first question to me via post sprung from his curiosity about my roots, my lineage, my responsibility for the land: in short, my sense of community and place. Not my job, not whatever accomplishments I might have garnered along the way. No, rather from a Native perspective *this* bit of knowledge is what is most revealing about a person: one's identity in relation to the history of people and land. "I'd like to know about your sense of home, ideas about it, and such. Am I being nosy? Maybe, but I think it's okay." I wrote back to say "northern Ohio." His conjecture as to my answer—which he revealed via postcard while waiting for a plane at the Albuquerque airport—was nearly spot on: upstate New York or Michigan, he had originally guessed.

From the start Simon wrote his letters and postcards in a style reflecting the lyrical and spacious character of his desert homeland. "Wind, they say at Aacqu, cleans and sweeps away the litter," he wrote from Chicago. "Leave it be, they say, it's Wind's way." At times his letters were lengthy, complex, and soul-searching, reflecting his questions about life, about himself, about his very public struggle with and recovery from alcoholism. After a time, the postcards took a turn toward poetry. From Dallas on June 2, 1992—on one side an Edward Curtis photo of a Tewa girl with hair in two majestic buns and on the other, a quickly scrawled verse:

Within the clasp
of stone, a certainty
Water knows –
we come there, the women

the spirit seeks,
a certainty song quiets,

aware, always silent
as light—
reforming always
returning always
to stone and water.

Then one day in that banner year, I drove south to visit Simon in a tiny, windowless room in a compound where artists, musicians, and photographers rented studios. He was drunk, deliriously drunk. It seemed crucial to stay with him, lying there as he was writhing in a stark metal bed amid a chaos of papers, desert dust, and books; shrieking out pronouncements that made little sense, vomiting into a bucket—and so I sat by him and emptied the bucket when need be. I stayed and stayed and stayed, until the sun went down and he had found in sleep a modicum of stillness.

After that, Simon continued his struggle with those inner demons that the calculated "gift" of whiskey by European invaders had introduced into Indian Country. He continued to write important works reflecting both traditional storytelling and the Native experience of the modern world. He taught creative writing and Native American literature in prestigious universities like the San Diego State University, Institute of Native American Arts, University of New Mexico, University of Toronto, and Arizona State University—in what has to be a rewarding reflection of how Native art has, after all these decades, been accepted, even championed in academia.

And now, as the elder who gave of himself to contribute to that historic change, the poet has returned to his beloved peach, pear, and apricot trees in Deetzeyaamah to feel the wind—a man in recovery.

XIV. ELEMENTS OF REFUSAL: ANARCHISM

*Anarchism is not a romantic fable but the hardheaded
realization, based on five thousand years of experience,
that we cannot entrust the management of our lives to
kings, priests, politicians, generals, and county
commissioners.*

—EDWARD ABBEY, *A VOICE CRYING THE WILDERNESS*, 1989

*Direct action against the invasive, meddlesome
authority of our moral code is the logical, consistent
method of Anarchism.*

—EMMA GOLDMAN IN *RED EMMA SPEAKS: AN EMMA GOLDMAN
READER*, EDITED BY ALIX KATES SHULMAN, 1996

THE COMMON UNDERSTANDING OF the word "anarchy" as
"destructive chaos" and "unthinkable breakdown of order" presents yet
another example of the conquerors redefining history. In fact, anarchy
as a philosophy/politics has been associated through the years and varying social contexts with a multiplicity of ideas. For example, the artisanal
socialism of pre-industrial farm life; the mutualism of intentional

In two words, "No Gods" sums up the philosophy of anarchism. The logo
can be found on tee shirts, posters, buttons, etc. Public Domain.

communities; Henry David Thoreau's transcendentalism; non-violent
civil disobedience as practiced in the U.S. civil rights and anti-nuclear
movements; equal rights, birth control, women's suffrage, and free love
as a means to liberate women from "man-made law"; libertarianism;
communal living and consensus decision-making; animal rights; ecology;
pacifism; active resistance as propaganda; active resistance through the
destruction of life-threatening property; communism and radical trade
unionism; the rights of individuals; and the rights of communities.

The *American Heritage Dictionary* defines anarchism as a "theory
that all forms of government are oppressive and should be abolished,"
while Andrew Gavin Marshall of the research Hampton Institute adds
that it is "a heightened and radical critique and questioning of power and
authority: if a source of authority cannot legitimize its existence, it
should not exist."

Originally a proclivity among our Paleolithic ancestors, it would
appear that the urge toward personal liberty and communal sovereignty
emerged as a natural response to the free-flowing nature of survival in
small equalitarian groups. As an approach to social relations it lasted
for millennia—along the way, stamping its irreversible mark upon the
human psyche—that is, until the ever-expanding project of domestication took hold, initiating unprecedented population increases, owner-
ship/social stratification, and hierarchical governance. Yet the memory
of the more congenial state of freedom and communalism has remained
in our hearts and in our blood—resurfacing again and again throughout
history. Take, for instance, the Greek city-states where longing references to such impulses appear in the works of Homer, Aeschylus, and
Zeno. Beginning in the sixteenth century, as monarchy-ridden European

civilization was evolving into equally hierarchical urban-based nation-states, Francois Rabelais, the Anabaptists, the Diggers, Jean-Jacques Rousseau, William Godwin, Leo Tolstoy, Michael Bakunin, and Piotr Kropotkin reflected what they sensed to be humans' archetypal mode of social relations.

In the continent that fueled Europeans' utopian visions, North America, religious dissenter Roger Williams, rebel theologian Anne Hutchinson, the Albemarle community of the Atlantic coast, the Quakers—all advocated societies modeled on anarchist ideals, just as many of the Native American tribes around them lived them. These same values were carried forth through U.S. history by such brave and disciplined souls as Emma Goldman, Lucy Parsons, Alexander Berkman, Margaret Sanger, Johann Most, and Voltairine de Cleyre, as well as the International Working People's Association, the Federation of Organized Trades and Labor Unions, and the journal *Freedom: A Revolutionary Anarchist-Communist Monthly*.

Such vibrancy did not lose its foothold in the human imagination during the twentieth century. In 1907 the International Anarchist Congress of Amsterdam gathered delegates from fourteen countries to hone a radical approach to the relationship between anarchism and syndicalism. In 1912 the Labadie Collection, highlighting anarchism's history in

Republican anarchists during Spanish Civil War, Barcelona, 1936.
Public Domain.

the U.S., was founded at the University of Michigan in Ann Arbor. The anarchist wing of the Catalonian Revolution/Spanish Civil War of the 1930s inspired men and women from all over the planet to risk their lives and join socialists, communists, trade unions.

Mujeres Libres, Catholic clergy in "the Good Fight," Buenaventura Derruti, Mother Jones, Emiliano Zapata, Eugene O'Neill, Ricardo Flores Magon, Oscar Wilde, Lillian Hellman, Dorothy Day, Leopold Kohr, and Fredy Perlman—all were prominent twentieth century anarchists. Today's effort proposes that anarchism based solely on anti-statism cannot step up to the plate to meet global corporate-run society, current levels of militarism, and electronic surveillance; rather a contemporary definition *must* include opposition to authority in all its multiple forms, from the obscene power that corporations wield and the spread of nuclear weapons to the daily perpetration of sexism, poverty, and racism. It is kept alive by magazines such as *Anarchy: A Journal of Desire Armed, Green Anarchist, Dark Mountain, El Fuelle, Abolishing the Borders from Below,* and *Fifth Estate* and 'zines like *Black Clad Messenger*; thinkers like Noam Chomsky, Germaine Greer, Starhawk, and Andrew Gavin Marshall; offshoots such as green anarchy, primitivist anarchy, Black anarchy, and anarcho-feminism; computer hackers like Julian Assange and Edward Snowden; organizations like Britain's Direct Action Movement, Bolivia's Mujeres Creando, Spain's Federación Ibérica de Juventudes Anarquistas, and the Italian Anarchist Federation; as well as actions such as the rise of indigenous resistance on all continents and direct action at the 1999 World Trade Organization talks in Seattle. When FEMA failed to meet the needs of survivors of Hurricane Katrina, anarchists showed up to offer on-the-ground mutual aid. The Occupy movement, Black Bloc support of teachers' strikes in Brazil in 2015-16, and anarchist contributions to the Arab Spring ousting of Hosni Mubarak of Egypt—all have been part of the continuity of anarchism. As political scientist Devon Douglass-Bowers wrote in *Foreign Policy Journal* in 2013, "This global resistance is extremely important as it reveals to the elites that their facade of democracy and consumerism is falling rapidly apart in the face of lagging economies, high unemployment rates, and a political class that is more concerned with its own personal needs rather than that of the people they have charge over."

In 2016 even the International Monetary Fund, normally the staunchest of cheerleaders for corporate-heavy globalism, admitted the failure of its advocacy of unfettered trade policies, the elimination of all restrictions on capital moving across borders, and use of castigating austerity measures that slash government spending. As reports Columbia University economist Martin Uribe on what radical considerations the IMF is contemplating, "the idea of state-run wealth redistribution likely has the godfathers of neoliberalism like Milton Friedman spinning in their graves. For the IMF, though, [it has come to] represent a continuing drift away from rigid neoliberal dogma and toward a more 'eclectic' blend of policies."

A turn towards addressing the current tribulations—of inequality, ecological devastation, climate upheaval, and human suffering that have only worsened since the 1980s—with an urge that dates back to the Paleolithic?

(*top left*) Feria del Libro en Resistencia, Chile, 2017. Public Domain. Courtesy of the Book Fair. (*top right*) Anarchist Book Fair poster, Zagreb, 2017. Courtesy of QueenMob Collective. (*bottom right*) May Day Weekend poster, Wroclaw, Poland. Courtesy of QueenMob Collective.

JOHN ZERZAN: THE GREEN ANARCHIST
(1943-)

Leftism is going the way of the dodo, though there are
still some remnants around. . . . Anarchy means
"without rule." This implies not only a rejection of
government bust of all forms of domination and power.
—J.Z., INTERVIEW ON PRIMITIVISM.COM

I first heard of John Zerzan in the dark hallway of a bed-and-breakfast in Washington, D.C., during a Jacques Ellul Society gathering. Who else could join our group? was the question at hand, and John's name came up as an illustrious and articulate technology critic. But one breath away from the mention of said name followed a commanding dismissal. He was "too radical," spouted the naysayer. My eyes bulged. "We stood beyond left and right," I thought. "We were anti-progress, anti-mass technology, anti-imperialist, anti-oppression of any kind. Who could *possibly* be more radical than ourselves!?"

I was to find out when, due to the popularity among primitive anarchists of *My Name Is Chellis and I'm in Recovery from Western Civilization,* I was invited to join Muscogee/Creek/Cherokee writer Ward Churchill on the Woodmen of the World Hall stage in Eugene, Oregon. The event was scheduled to coincide with the first anniversary of their noted 18 June 1999 demonstration/rampage/clash with the police. Eugene was a central hub for those who were being called the "new anarchists," and Zerzan was their intellectual theoretician.

Well, upon meeting him, many people remark that he is surprisingly polite, mild-mannered, and soft-spoken. As interviewer Duncan Campbell of the *Guardian* put it, "It is hard to imagine that the slight, bearded soul in khaki shorts and a T-shirt bearing the legend 'What goes up must come down' is really the bête noir of technology and capitalism." The geniality that Zerzan emanates would not stand out if it weren't for his politics. In essay collections like *Elements of Refusal, Future Primitive,* and *Twilight of the Machines,* as well as in the anthology he edited, *Against Civilization,* he pulls no punches in delineating the parts played in the emergence of people-alienating, planet-destroying empire.

He writes of the projection of our once-shared and natural sense of the bond with the cosmos onto glorified "god" figures and leaders of organized religion whose usurped authority robbed people of self-confidence and agency. This change occurred in the Upper Paleolithic, he says, with the invention of shamanism, and has been in development ever since, right up until today, when it includes gurus and the Pope himself. He explains in his essay "Future Primitive" that appeared in 1994 in *Anarchy: A Journal of Desire Armed*:

> Ritual, as shamanic practice, may also be considered as a regression from that state in which all shared a consciousness we would now classify as extrasensory. When specialists alone claim access to such perceptual heights as may have once been communal, further backward moves in division of labor are facilitated or enhanced. The way back to bliss through ritual is a virtually universal mythic theme, promising the dissolution of measurable time, among other joys. This theme of ritual points to an absence that it falsely claims to fill, as does symbolic culture in general.

The ensuing division of labor in all aspects of human activity followed this early source of alienation, along with the invention of mathematical counting and its logical segue into the objectification of nature, allowing for its destruction, and the mass production of commodities. According to Zerzan, the consequences of such developments range from private property, the hierarchies inherent to the ownership/wage-labor dynamic, capitalism, sexism, racism, classism, government rule, institutionalized religion, and "high" art. Not to mention the gung-ho pursuit of mass technologies whose purpose is to aid and abet whatever needs to be corralled and controlled. In essence, this anarchist thinker emerges as a critic of the symbolism inherent to language, art, and number, as well as of the division of labor in all its forms. And of technology itself. "Tools or roles that involve division of labor," he reports in a primitivism.com interview, "engender divided people and divided society."

Such investigations into the contemporary condition do not just reside in the pages of Zerzan's books: as a speaker, educator, and radio host of the program "Radio Anarchy," he is screamingly blunt about the sickness of today's global stretch. A recent theme of his is the alienation that computer-cellular, "connecting" technologies proffer and the parallel rise in teen suicides and school massacres. He has been described as anti-civilization, anti-modernity, anti-postmodernity, neo-Luddite, and a post-leftist/green/primitive anarchist. He believes that any hope at this late stage of civilization's command resides in the demise of all forms of social and personal control, decentralization of global societies into human-scale community, a renaissance of sensual, face-to-face social relations, and re-skilling in survival practices so that our technologies are no longer the incomprehensible products of multinational corporations, but rather the artisanal creations of the very people who use them.

"What do you replace cancer with?" Zerzan asks, brandishing an edge of mockery as if to spout a resounding "Duh." The answer is "good food, human-scale community and human-paced daily life, meaningful work, love, joy, friends, nature, honesty, a healthy body."

Perhaps Zerzan would have remained a small-town hero and deep-head scholar of acclaim in anarchist circles were it not for his reaching out to the serial mail-bombing Unabomber. After Ted Kaczynski's "Industrial Society and Its Future" was printed in the *Washington Post* and *New York Times* in 1995 as a tradeoff to stop future bombings, and after the wild mathematician was subsequently identified and arrested, Zerzan traveled to Colorado to witness the trial. There, in between court proceedings, he had the opportunity to talk with Kaczynski. The association of a fellow technology critic at the trial sparked national media interest in Zerzan. In the end Kaczynski was hauled off to serve eight life sentences; Zerzan came away with a full-page interview in the *New York Times.*

In it he was quick to set the record straight: he agreed with Kaczynski's analysis of the failure of mass technological society, but opposed his tactics of killing and maiming. Perhaps adding too much complexity for the monochromatic perceptions of media-delivered comprehension, he clarified: "The concept of justice should not be overlooked in considering the Unabomber phenomenon. In fact, except for his targets, when have the many little Eichmanns who are preparing the Brave New World ever

been called to account?... Is it unethical to try to stop those whose contributions are bringing an unprecedented assault on life?" When asked
by the *Guardian* if there would be more Unabombers, Zerzan replied, "I
hope not.... I hope that isn't going to be something that people feel they
have to take up because they have no other way to express their opposition to the brave new world." (He has since split from any association
with Kaczynski because of the latter's anti-primitivist writing that Zerzan claims uses "dishonest sources.")

To his mind, though, his international infamy grew as a result less of
the Unabomber connection than for his participation in the1999 anti–
World Trade Organization protests in Seattle, where the Black Bloc of
anarchists in general, and Zerzan as an organizer of the infamous
Eugene group in particular, played a sparking role. He also became notorious for his subsequent and, to him, "absurdly inflated" appearance in
the European film *SurPlus*.

Zerzan grew up with his working-class Czechoslovakian parents in
Salem, Oregon. A fervent member of the National Rifle Association, his
father worked as a garage mechanic and an outboard motor salesman,
finally graduating to ownership of a Western Auto store. His mother was
a housewife. To the pride of his parents, he earned a B.A. at Stanford
University and a master's in history at San Francisco State. He completed
course work for a Ph.D. at the University of Southern California but
dropped out before completing his dissertation to hang out with the Diggers and Merry Pranksters in the Haight-Ashbury during the 1960s. He
made his entrance into politics with an arrest for civil disobedience in
protest of the Vietnam War and went on to organize a social workers'
union in the San Francisco welfare department.

Just as Bay Area Situationists were denouncing Zerzan as a "Leftist
Bureaucrat," he began to read the works of anti-authoritarian Marxist/
Situationist Guy Debord, who put forth the notion of spectacle as symp-
tom of late capitalism's deterioration. More importantly, he began to pore
over the writings of the German anti-fascist philosopher Theodor
Adorno. Instead of a Marxian notion of a "historical dialectic" marching
ever forward toward the inevitability of a worker-run, egalitarian society,
Adorno wrote of a "negative dialectic" that rolled backward in time to

smaller, sovereign communities. He attacked modern rationalization and philosophies of domination and did so in what Zerzan terms "piercing, beautiful style that inspired…, showing what one mind can perfect."

After a day of good conversation with Ward, Zerzan, and Zerzan's partner, museum curator Alice Parman, the evening of our lectures arrived. Ward had left something essential to his presentation in the guest room of Zerzan's cottage in the health-food-freak/fair-trade/anarchist neighborhood of Whitaker, but upon arriving there, we found that Zerzan had already left for the Woodmen of the World Hall. The idea of breaking in seemed appropriate to the rebel atmosphere of the place, so I pushed Ward's butt up the side of the house while he reached to the window and jacked it open. I gave one last shove, and he fell into the living room with a thump befitting his body size.

The W.O.W. building had been opened in 1932 as the fraternal lodge dedicated to providing health benefits, life insurance, and burial services to working people, as well as recreational activities for their children. Elegantly modernist in style, it was dark with crafted mahogany on the inside—and crammed with so many young people (and police informants) on its rock-hard maple floor that every space to put a body was filled and the crowd spilled over into two anterooms where our voices were to be piped in.

Zerzan was calm as he cruised through the throng and, at the suitable moment, climbed on stage to introduce the evening. The crowd went wild with enthusiasm for their very own deep head, and he was in his element.

A thriving correspondence followed. In it, like a comet soaring across the night sky, Zerzan burst with aliveness and left a sparkling trail; even his handwriting exuded vigor. At the same time he was as sweet as a puppy wrapped in a blanket. He sent me descriptions of whatever book he was working on (*Running on Emptiness, Twilight of the Machines*, etc.). We batted back and forth about whether *The Nation* magazine was anti-anarchist and, as Zerzan put it, "torn between the Democratic Party and Nader"; if Che Guevara was a Stalinist apologist; what constitutes violence. He forwarded flyers for events put on by the Northeastern Federation of Anarcho-Cannibalists ("They Say Health Is

Wealth, We Say Let's Eat the Wealthy"), Future Political Prisoners of America's Subversive Pillow Theater, and Earth Liberation Front's Eco-Defense Night—and always he wrote postcards from the various locales of his travels.

Then in 2002, three years after our meeting in Eugene, Alice and Zerzan came to visit me in New Mexico. It was the peak of summer. We shared red-chile enchiladas and more good conversation at Rancho Chimayó, but to my mind the most memorable moment occurred when I took them to meet the award-winning lowrider painter Lowlow Medina. We pulled up to the apple tree outside the dilapidated adobe house. Multitudinous aging cars in varying states of disrepair sat helter-skelter about the yard. Lowlow gave us a tour. The white limousine painted to emphasize its aerodynamic shape had always been my favorite, but Zerzan went like a moth to an incandescent bulb to a dusty Buick whose hood was festooned with a painting showing Christ rising toward the sky just as flames, suffering, and chaos were erupting on Earth. Lowlow revealed his evangelic Christian zeal as he described the scene, and given that Zerzan was patently against all religion, I cringed to think what he might blurt out.

Left to right: John Zerzan; Aleksa Golijanin of anti-civilization Blok 45 publishing, Serbia; Enrico Manicardi, Italian anti-civ author of Liberi dalla Civiltá; and anonymous permaculturist, Northern Italy, 2011. Courtesy of John Zerzan.

But instead—brow rumpled, head thoughtfully nodding, index finger pressing against lips—he was enchanted. Here was Lowlow, whose imagery and language were poles apart from his own, yet this small-town New Mexican knew what was happening so clearly that his art highlighted it. *I* was enchanted that Zerzan was so open to a parallel vision.

In 2001 a fresh phase of Zerzan's work was born: to speak to and with anarchists around the world. He said to me once that he had conducted an inner debate as to whether he should spend the rest of his life wielding the Sword or the Word, and he had decided that his best venue was the Word. The next years were packed with speaking gigs, often traveling across vast distances in shabby buses with threadbare tires, sleeping on floors, and meeting his *camaradas* in Italy, Spain, England, India, Poland, Hungary, Brazil, Finland, and other locales. His conclusion: people all over the planet are enthusiastic about primitive anarchism and are seeking to know how such ideas might serve as guides in navigating these precarious times.

Alice and Zerzan got married in 2003, and back in Eugene, he continues with his weekly program "Radio Anarchy" and general rabble-rousing through words and actions.

EARTH LIBERATION GIRL: PALEOLITHIC AND PROUD
(1974-)

Why don't you just dump your house and car and
become a nomad like me?
—E.L.G., COMMENT TO CHELLIS GLENDINNING, 2009

We could call our anonymous/composite Earth Liberation Front activist Mountain Peak. Or Bone Wrath. Or Solstice. The name could be almost anything really, as out of dread of the U.S. government's invasive tentacles and retaliatory manacles, these folks change their monikers at the drop of a pine cone. But for purposes of identification, we will call her Luna.

Luna joined the underground movement to Bring the System Down in 1992 when she was eighteen. Much to the dismay of her hard-working, workaday, working-class parents, she boasted matted blonde dreadlocks and was known to sport waxed Filson logging pants and a halter top that she had scrounged at a garage sale that originally came from the street-fashion, but waaay off-the-charts expensive Free-the-People mail-order catalog. Her skin was baby smooth and nearly always burnt by the sun due to lengthy hikes into the Cascade wilderness of central Washington.

Luna was not just an anarchist; she was a primitive anarchist. Like many of my colleagues in the ecology, ecopsychology, and neo-Luddite movements, she believed that civilization itself was the culprit. Going one step farther, she felt that the true way to live was by the philosophies and practices of pre-Neolithic peoples. She herself was a graduate of some dozen primitive skills workshops. She carried a fire-sparking flint chip strung by deer gut to a two-forked deer horn and, on her arrival to my house, sported her ceremonial buckskin jumpsuit fashioned of road-kill hide that she had brain-tanned herself. She was a sight to behold, a modern-day Ayla who had stepped through the millennia from the original Bear Clan.

In part Luna's visit stemmed from the scattering of her people after the jail sentences wrought upon Jeff Luers and Chelsea Gerlach for acts of what she called "sanity," but what the post-9/11 U.S. government was categorizing as "terrorism." Luers had been convicted of setting fire to the Romania Chevrolet car lot's gas-guzzling SUVs, Gerlach of arson at a Boise Cascade office and of blowing up a Bonneville Power transmission tower. They were their generation's sampling of those willing to risk their lives for change: the Ethan Allens, the Mahatma Gandhis, the Juana Azurduys, the Emma Goldmans, the Geronimos. The agreement among them had always been that if the shit hit the fan—which it clearly had with this new classification of their actions as equal to those perpetrated by shoe bombers, aero-suicides, and people with the word "Al" in their names—they would break apart, never communicate again, essentially disappear.

I'm not so sure that coming to my house accomplished that directive. Luna had sought me out for another reason: I was the author of *My Name*

Is Chellis and I'm in Recovery from Western Civilization. The book had gained notoriety among ELF and Earth First! proponents for its analysis of the human/nature split that had jumpstarted humanity's downward spiral, or at least became evident, during the Neolithic. Just as I had sought to meet my intellectual mentor Lewis Mumford, this earnest young woman at my doorstep was seeking some guidance, some sustenance ... *something* from an elder.

In a parallel universe, known as Susan P., Luna had grown up in Long Beach where her father, Dirk P., worked at the Douglas Aircraft factory assembling wing parts and her mother, Susan P., at a drugstore selling pantyhose and ibuprofen. They had inculcated in her a strong dose of fear; her mother was a despotic Neat Freak, her father a belt-wielding disciplinarian, the two of them horror-film buffs. She had done well enough in high school, but her real flare had been the acrobatic precision of cheerleading. A turning point in her political consciousness was the senior prom: the school's lesbians had shown up as the couples (and triads) that in reality they were—some donned in men's suits, pointy shoes, and skinny ties; the others in slit-up-the-side cocktail dresses and fishnet stockings. Inflamed by such in-your-face dissent, the day after graduation she bolted.

After pulling my phone cords from their plugs to ensure that unwanted ears were not listening, Luna confided in me. This I will not forget. Once she had broken into an animal-testing laboratory and let loose the caged dogs. But her true expertise was setting modified egg timers that ticked until the minute hand crossed wires that then lit a fuse set next to its target. It didn't matter what those targets were—a seven-bedroom second-home McMansion, the base tower of a high-tension electric line, a U.S. Forest Service cabin. Her hand steadied by the somersaults and leaps of cheerleading, she could do it all.

Then, explaining that she was a practitioner of "Random Acts of Kindness and Senseless Acts of Beauty," Luna asked if there was anything she could do to help me. I was on the verge of my once-a-decade wipe-down of the refrigerator's innards. Somewhat red-faced that the contents consisted of straight health food fare rather than morning-glory tendrils and fresh-from-the-land elk thigh, I set her upon the task. Her neat-freak training not so far in the past, she attacked the job with meticulousness. I sat at the kitchen table, and so near to her, I could feel her lovely, youthful lightness as well as all the traumatic terrors etched into her body.

Luna stayed just one night—on the living room floor wrapped in a womb woven of moss-stuffed ripstop. She didn't want to linger any longer as her trail had to be as intricate as that of a pagan labyrinth and as fleeting as a puff of marijuana smoke.

JULIE HERRADA: LABADIE'S DAUGHTER
(1961-)

If we, the keepers of history, collect and protect only what is appealing, socially acceptable, or politically correct, we are hardly doing our jobs.
—J.H. "LETTERS TO THE UNABOMBER: A CASE STUDY AND SOME REFLECTIONS" IN *ARCHIVAL ISSUES*, 2003-04

When Julie Herrada showed up at my front door sporting two mini-braids and multiple dangling earrings, she looked to be about twenty years old. In fact she was forty-seven. We were going to the Che Guevara Dinner I had set up to take place at Rancho Chimayó in honor of her, the Mexican/Irish curator of the Labadie Collection at the University of Michigan. And indeed not one attendee—not the Latino farmers, the Mexican immigrants, the anti–Iraq War activists, nor the Green Party candidate for governor—could quite believe that this "youngster" commanded such a position of knowledge and responsibility.

It was Stephanie Mills who first told me about Julie. I was looking for a place to park the archives documenting my life's work before I headed south to live in Bolivia. I had already checked out Steph's alma mater Mills College, my alma mater at Berkeley, and the University of Texas, when she told me about the Labadie Collection. Although it would pay less, she warned, Labadie was a very special place. It had been founded by labor-movement anarchist Joseph Labadie in 1912. Housing some 50,000 books, 8000 serial titles, and countless recordings, buttons, photos, and sheet music, it was described as "the largest collection of anarchist and social protest literature in the country." Its focus: the history of radical movements in the United States going back to the 1800s.

Julie was only the third curator to direct it. Under her sharp-eyed tutelage, it had grown to include contemporary feminist, labor, animal-liberation, bioregional, sexual freedom, civil-rights and Black Liberation, peace, and gay-rights movements. Archived there, among others, were the documents of Emma Goldman, the Industrial Workers of the World, Kay Boyle, the Fifth Estate, Women's International League for Peace and Freedom, Boris Yelenski, Yippie activists Stew Alpert and Judy Gumbo, Fredy Perlman, and Tom Hayden. Steph herself had placed the records of significant ecology, anti-technology, and bioregional conferences there, and the Labadie now holds the largest collection of transgender research materials in the U.S.

Events bubbled up from the archives as well. Like "The Port Huron Statement and the Making of the New Left" fiftieth commemorative conference in 2012; Hayden, the author of the statement and a UM graduate, had returned to Ann Arbor for that. 2012 also marked the one-hundreth anniversary of the collection, celebrated with a stunning display of some of its favorites. It began with all the items that Labadie himself had donated, including a portrait painted in the 1880s and inscribed in his hand: "Liberty is the solution of all social-economic questions." Also on display were: a "LABOR DAY 1899" badge; an envelope containing Joe Hill's ashes (1915); photos of the Sacco and Vanzetti death masks; the memorial service program for Peter Kropotkin (1931); a photo of Paul Robeson in Valencia during the Spanish Civil War; a "Where Is Oswald When We Need Him?" button from the Reagan years; an "I'm a Fucking Queer" button from the 1990s; and a 2011 "I Used To Live In a Democracy" bumper sticker.

The most controversial collection Julie ever sought out contained the papers of mail-bomber Ted Kaczynski. Between 1978 and 1995 his bomb-laden packages sent to people engaged in the design or building of technologies he deemed murderous killed three and injured twenty-two others. A library such as the Labadie Collection that gives such presumed honor to such a "parasite on society," particularly alongside the papers of others considered to be heroic, was so controversial, and so delicate a legal matter, that after she had initiated contact with Kaczynski's lawyer, university officials took the negotiations out of her hands. In 1997 the Kaczynski Collection was acquired, including his own writings as well as personal letters written to him in the "Supermax" federal prison in Florence, Colorado.

Needless to say, Julie was barraged by journalists, both national and international, and she skillfully took the opportunity to herald and, for the politically conservative or "neutral," expand the concept of library archivist. In an article "Letters to the Unabomber" she wrote for the professional journal *Archival Issues*, she dubbed herself and colleagues "keepers of history" and highlighted the responsibility they carry to preserve materials—"*especially* if they are controversial." And she tells what she learned from gaining access to Kaczynski's papers: "I try to remain objective," she writes. "I don't condone that behavior, but I feel I have a responsibility to researchers in the future so they have access to that kind of material."

Julie grew up in Detroit, the daughter of a Mexican father and an Irish-German mother. It is said that what is submerged in the unconscious by one generation is unearthed and revealed by the next. In 2001 Julie, along with a cross-border group, formed Fronteras Norteñas. The goal was to document the pained history of the enticement to Mexican workers to cross the border and work in Detroit's auto industry, followed by their brusque deportations. The Immigration Act of 1917 had the specific goal of excluding immigrants from China, India, Japan, and the Philippines, but because U.S. agricultural and factory employers were desperate for cheap labor, Mexicans were exempted from many of the requirements for entry—and so began the northward *México de afuera* diaspora. With the promise of $5 a day, sky-scraping pay compared to what could be earned in post-revolution Mexico, Julie's grandfather left his home in Aguascalientes to work at the Ford Motor Company. Twelve years later, in a Depression-inspired policy about-face, the government ordered the "repatriation" (read: deportation) of some 500,000 to one million workers; this, despite the fact that most of them were born in the U.S. and were legitimate citizens. Julie's father was sent south to a Mexico disassembled by poverty and social disorder.

Julie's father, Alfredo Herrada, at the Chrysler factory where he worked for 43 years, Detroit, 1950s. Courtesy of Julie Herrada.

Fronteras Norteñas set out to interview participants in this sad history. Due to shame and suffering so great that few—including Julie's father—dared to recount the experience, the stories had largely been shoveled out of memory. The interviews took place both in Michigan and in Mexico. The trip south was the first time Julie had had the opportunity to experience her heritage firsthand, and out of the project came a thirty-minute documentary, *Los Repatriados: Exiles from the Promised Land*, broadcast on PBS and now used in history curricula around the country.

For Julie, the project became an intense personal journey, providing insight into her life as an activist and an archivist. "I wonder if my choice was subconsciously influenced by my family's desire to stay under the radar and not be noticed," she recounts in a 2011 essay, "Mexicans in the Midwest." "[The memories of immigrants] are far more than lamentable tales; they are crushing events embodying the shame of poverty, illiteracy, humiliation, rejection, and fear. . . . I don't attribute my career path to any particular familial or parental influence, but I can say that my becoming an archivist has figured powerfully in my zeal to understand and preserve the authentic history of my own family."

The Che Guevara Dinner grew out of an inspiration I harbored as the date marking the fortieth anniversary of the *guerrillero*'s death neared. A group including the director of the Española Farmers Market, a New Mexico historian, a Nicaraguan *curandera*, and ten other participants met in 2007 at the Rancho Chimayó, notably in what was called The Red Room. After ordering tacos and *trucha*, each took a few minutes to share feelings and insights about Che or the Cuban Revolution. An exercise that might have taken a half hour turned into a three-hour fest of political intimacy, and even then the restaurant had to kick us out when they closed and the fervent discussions continued on in the parking lot.

I realized how hungry we all were to locate ourselves in the flow of collective events. I continued throwing Che Guevara dinners, but now expanding the theme to *any* moment in history that each invitee had participated in or been affected by. The new topic drew just as much interest, and for five more dinners we were regaled with the tale of a Guatemalan woman's escape from the military, what it was like for a Latino to grow up in racist New Mexico, a 1960s anti-war demonstration on the Berkeley campus, a young Jew shepherding her concentration-camp survivor grandmother to the Holocaust Museum, etc.

The year of this last U.S. Che Guevara Dinners took place in 2009—and here was Julie, in all her youthful glory, downing enchiladas and clinking glasses with twenty-three of northern New Mexico's finest. Because we were such a large group, we "picked straws" in the form of cards, most of

Julie and Chellis. Che Guevara Dinner, Chimayó, New Mexico, 2009.
Courtesy of Chellis Glendinning.

which were blank, six of which contained the rubber stamp of a 1957 Chevy to indicate that that person would be a speaker. And then there was Julie's formal address. She likes to think of herself as a quiet scholarly type, a person behind the scenes and out of sight, but her ability to energize the group was in full evidence with her story of growing up as an inheritor of Detroit's history of Mexican workers and deportations, her subsequent emergence as an archivist of social movements, and the various collections preserved at Labadie. The clincher came when someone—harboring great expectations what with being in the presence of a real expert—asked Julie, "What is your definition of anarchism?" She was quick to answer. "I don't have one," she said—and everyone burst into hilarity at the parallel between her surprise response and the very essence of anarchism.

The next day she and I sealed the deal for my papers, citing a thematic emphasis on my writing as well as my relationship with my activist mother. Since then I've had the opportunity to witness, from the southern continent, the creativity she has let blossom and the pioneering work she has accomplished in her role as a keeper of history.

With fiancée Michael Johnson. Detroit, 2014. Photo Credit: Andrea Gietzen. Courtesy of Julie Herrada.

XV. INSIDE THE BELTWAY

*The tree of liberty must be refreshed from time to time
with the blood of patriots and tyrants.*

—THOMAS JEFFERSON, LETTER TO REPRESENTATIVE WILLIAM
STEPHENS SMITH, NOVEMBER 13, 1787

FROM THE MARGINS, THE streets, and the waste bins of power—
where the bulk of our political movements tend to begin—Washington,
D.C., too often appears to radicals as the U.S. once-and-future swamp of
a throng of opportunists, narcissists, hype promoters, sellouts, and
slight-of-hand jugglers. It is where—by birthright, excessive exertion, or
magical intervention—people with a taste for clout slog away in the labyrinths of pabulum bureaucracy and behind-the-scenes cooptation.
Mostly this is the way things go … but every now and again there emerges
an uncompromising, clear thinker who refuses to be changed by political
pressure or exigency. A Ron Dellums, an …

ABIGAIL MCCARTHY: CATHOLIC PEACEMAKER
(1915-2001)

Responsible dissent is the essence of democracy.

—A.MCC., *PRIVATE FACES, PUBLIC PLACES,*1972

My mother was enamored of Abigail McCarthy in the same way she had been of the daring First Lady Eleanor Roosevelt and of suffragette Josephine Irwin, who in 1920 had ridden down Cleveland's Euclid Avenue on a white horse. All three were great feminists, but only the Senator's wife received the honor of having the Glendinning family dog named after her. It was the early 1970s, and Hooker dubbed her new pound puppy "Abigail."

I met Abigail McCarthy through Marc Kasky. He had been a student coordinator in the 1968 Eugene McCarthy run for president and, having been extraordinarily creative and principled in his approach to the New Hampshire primary, had been invited to watch the election returns with the McCarthy family in the Wayfarer Hotel of Berlin. He arrived thinking that the room would be filled with other student coordinators, but lo and behold! *he* was the only one they had invited. Abigail reflected on why in her 1972 book *Private Faces/Public Places*, calling him "a symbol of . . . all that was good in the new politics." And this is not to mention that their special affinity for each other was enhanced by the fact that their birthdays fell on the same day: 16 April—hers in 1915, his on the same day twenty-nine years later.

In 1986 she was in San Francisco to promote a new book, *One Woman Lost*, a novel she had written together with another Senator's wife, Jane Gray Muskie. But, while the publishers had arranged a book tour complete with readings in West Coast cities, they had not made sure that any books would actually *be* in those places. Ergo, Abigail had enjoyed an all-expenses-paid trip to San Francisco, but there was nothing for her to do until some books showed up. Marc gave her the five-star tour of Fort Mason Center where he was director, and then she stopped in at our North Beach flat for a cup of tea.

She was exactly as I would have expected. Of course I already knew what she looked like, but it was those familiar mannerisms of class and generation that made me feel at home in her presence: the sweet smile, the formality of etiquette, the thoughtful responses—plus the flaming, eyebrow-raised sense of irony and, as her former editor at the Catholic magazine *Commonweal,* Margaret O-Brien Steinfels, has proposed, "unflappability." Sitting around the oak table in the kitchen, my most delicate cups brimming with good English leaves, I felt something akin to a déjà vu, as if I had been catapulted back to the 1950s to sip Lipton with my Great Aunt Mary. Abigail was marvelous.

And dedicated. She had graduated Phi Beta Kappa from St. John's College in Minnesota in 1936, went on to earn a master's from the University of Minnesota, then did post-graduate work at the University of Chicago and the Middlebury School of English—all feats of courage and intelligence for a woman of her generation and for anybody, really, during the Depression. She met Eugene while teaching in North Dakota. Both were devout Catholics and educated intellectuals who sought to make their lives count. They got married in 1945 and set up housekeeping on an agricultural commune shared with other idealistic Catholic couples.

Elected in 1948 from the Minnesota Democratic-Farmer-Labor Party, Eugene had been a U.S. Representative for five terms when he moved up to the Senate. His time was marked by any number of progressive acts. In 1960 he delivered a dynamite speech in favor of Adlai Stevenson as the Democratic choice for the presidency and in 1964 met *guerrillero* Che Guevara secretly in New York City to discuss repairing U.S.-Cuban relations.

He had been a Senator for three terms when he and Abigail engaged in some solemn soul-searching and decided that the escalating war in Vietnam was morally wrong. Together, for she was always by his side, they stepped into the public eye of a country raging with conflict not only from racial tensions exploding in urban riots, but also from the widening chasm between generations as the student anti-war movement leapt across the continent like a fire through a desiccated woodland. Remarkably, he gained 42 percent of the vote in the New Hampshire primary and won in Wisconsin and Oregon, but lost the candidacy to the Democratic Party machine's namby-pamby choice, Hubert Humphrey. As we know too well, the election left the country saddled with Mr. Cloth-Coat Nixon. *The Pentagon Papers*, the secret bombing campaign in Cambodia, the disclosure of My Lai, the killing of four anti-war activists at Kent State, Watergate, and Nixon's resignation followed. In the end, one benefit of the McCarthy shot at the presidency was that the war became a national issue to be considered and debated until its final bomb was dropped in 1975.

In *Private Faces/Public Places* Abigail penned her wrap-up of the campaign: "Despite the fact that the campaign brought almost unbearable emotional strain and disaster to our family, I cannot wish that the campaign did not happen. Through it I crossed the barrier into the world of my children and of all the young people to whom this world really belongs. I see the world now as they see it. I feel a sense of surprise that it is so easy to lay aside what once were rocklike basic assumptions as I look at injustice in the fierce light of their outrage. But I do not wish to have crossed this barrier having brought nothing from the other side. . . . What I would like to bring with me is a sense of the past, its continuity to the present, and a sense of identity stemming from the past which enables each one of us to withstand the assault of change."

After the campaign, to her surprise and heartbreak, Eugene fled the marriage. "He wanted to cut off everything and that is what he did," she wrote. "He had to be against his party, against his home state, people—and against his wife. It was a dividing point in his life—and he had to divide from so much to do it . . ., so many things that mattered."

I went to visit Abigail several times in Washington at the Connecticut Avenue apartment she moved into after the separation. The first time was in the early '90s during one of my social-movement trips to the capital. We didn't go up to the apartment; rather, we ate lunch next to a fish tank in the Chinese restaurant immediately below the building. There, amid sonorous bubbles and swishing orange fins, she revealed her generosity of interest in others by granting an inordinate amount of attention to my life—Marc and I had by then broken up and I had moved to New Mexico—and she confided her agony that her daughter Mary Abigail, who was about my age, was struggling with pancreatic cancer.

The last time I saw Abigail was in 1996 the day after a Jacques Ellul Society meeting in D.C. This time I took the elevator up and silently floated across the padded carpet to her door. Inside was a home so much like my mother's or aunt's or grandmother's that I had to blink. Déjà vu number two. Oriental rugs, foot stools in front of winged arm chairs, everywhere photos of family members in silver frames. She told me that, at age eighty-one, she was still writing her column for *Commonweal,* with the occasional book review for the *New York Times* or *Washington Post;* she was also still active with the national organization she had founded, Church Women United. Then she proposed that we walk across a nearby bridge to a favorite restaurant of hers. We walked very, very slowly to make it across, her every brittle step an opportunity to award her a Congressional medal for heroism. But the trek was exactly what she wanted. Seated at a table, she explained that indeed her daughter had died of cancer and that the loss had been the most painful of her life. I asked what it was like to be in her eighties. She replied that she had to be extra careful because, mysteriously to her way of thinking, her body wouldn't do the things it had always done before—but that inside, in her spirit, she felt as if she were twenty years old.

Abigail died in February of 2001—thankfully, before she had to endure the upset imposed by the 9/11 Twin Towers and Pentagon attacks. There is no question in my mind that she would have been one of the few in Washington to admit that the assaults stemmed from the U.S. government's own hubris in trying to command the rest of the world; it was an example of what the C.I.A. refers to as "blowback." In her honor the Abigail Quigley McCarthy Center for Women was established at her alma mater, now called St. Catherine University. I take sustenance from her strength of character and, as the years pass and I inevitably follow in those same brittle steps into old age, from her observation that at eighty-one she felt as if she were twenty.

XVI. IT'S THE LAW, THE ECONOMY, AND WAR—STUPID!

The only interesting answers are those that destroy the questions.

—SUSAN SONTAG, "THE AESTHETICS OF SILENCE" IN *STYLES OF RADICAL WILL*, 1969

"IT'S THE ECONOMY, STUPID!" arose as a satirical catchphrase in the 1990s anti-globalization movement as a take-off on the slogan invented by Bill Clinton's campaign-for-president strategist James Carville. "The Economy, Stupid!" he had scratched on a scrap of paper to take to the podium at a campaign speech. As the story goes, the purpose of that original expression was to remind the candidate which issues to mention, but for activists its adaptation pointed a spotlight on the unfortunate fact that every aspect of human existence—from bathroom tissue and DNA to tree bark excavated in the Amazon rainforest—has been reduced to and defined by its monetary worth in the global corporate economy.

One might just as easily print "It's the Law, Stupid!" on bumper stickers and political buttons. Let's talk about the legal arena: legal decisions are neither objective nor value-free; they reflect the language, prejudices, and ambitions of a place and an era. A plethora of U.S. laws that still dictate how things are done hark back to the seventeenth and eighteenth centuries when corporations were merely a means to achieve a one-time public work like a bridge or a road; the laws created to accomplish such projects give those entities the same freedoms that individuals have—and as entrepreneurs discovered in time a right to do whatever they damn well please in order to garner profit like cut-off mountain tops or turn Chinese farmers into wage-slave factory workers.

And lest we forget to remind the presidents of the world: "It's the War, Stupid!" In a world of weapons of mass destruction and daily acts of terrorism, war itself is stupid, and in the ultimate case of flamingly illogical juxtaposition, President Barack Obama won the Nobel Prize for Peace just as the new President's U.S. was continuing to conduct its exploitative attacks on Afghanistan and Iraq.

As Thomas Jefferson warned lo these many centuries ago, "The tree of liberty must be refreshed from time to time with the blood of patriots and tyrants." These are words befitting today's reality: the tasks of challenging unjust economic mechanisms, the class-based biases behind legal phrasing, or the decision to commit collective violence is ongoing in a world overpowered by corporate empire, ecological ruin, waning food sources, social chaos, and weapons capable of extinguishing the planet.

RICHARD GROSSMAN: BE STRONG
(1943–2011)

Is it really true that the majority of the American people over the last twenty years didn't want a major transition in energy to move to efficiency and solar, didn't want universal health care, but wanted pig genes in fish?

—R. G., LETTER TO CHELLIS GLENDINNING, 2011

Richard Grossman became a strong presence in my life in 2006 when he blew through New Mexico to offer his latest invention, Democracy

School. His arrival was an exemplary case of how, in our social movements, a ready community exists even though you don't personally know everybody in it. You have heard of a person's work, perhaps admired it—and, if need or desire be, you stand but zero degrees of separation from them: you can just call them up. Richard called me up. The night after his workshop in Santa Fe, he drove to Chimayó with his young sidekick lawyer Tom Linzey, as he explained, to further Linzey's education by introducing him to activists of our generation. What Linzey learned by meeting me, I don't know—but what he became witness to was two older activists who were thrilled to get together.

Three things linked us: we had both dedicated decades to making social change; we were both adherents of wild ideas and the written word; and, springing from his enthusiastic guidance, I joined him in the unlawful activity of growing opium poppies. A cross-country correspondence was launched that grew to include one lengthy phone conversation per week and a bevy of hand-penned letters between upstate New York and northern New Mexico.

Painting of Richard Grossman by Robert Shetterly for Americans Who Tell the Truth. Permission of Robert Shetterly.

Richard Grossman: a tall presence, a towering intellect, and an irrepressible go-getter. Determined. Dogged. In-your-face. And surely one of North America's staunchest adherents of the Zapatista ethic of using every waking moment and every available occurrence to challenge the system. One tale to appear in print after his death told of a scene revealing his edgy sensibility: he was walking along a street in New York City and came upon a stretch limo parked at the curb. Without a moment's thought he stuck his head in the open window and barked something to the effect of: "You should be ashamed of yourselves! Flaunting your riches while so many others suffer in poverty!"

Activist/author David Bollier was more sober about this aspect of Richard's methods. "Richard Grossman was one of those activist eccentrics who took democratic power so seriously that he knowingly marginalized himself," wrote Bollier. "Mainstream political culture regarded his positions as crazy or tactically unwise—but eventually the world began to catch up with him."

After graduating from Columbia University in 1965, Richard served in the Peace Corps in the Philippines. He began his forty-plus years as a political activist in the movement against the Vietnam War, signing the Writers' and Editors' War Tax Protest pledge to refuse to pay war taxes, and went on to found Environmentalists for Full Employment, a group seeking to bring environmentalists together with unions. He started the Stop the Pollution/Save the Planet program at the Highlander Research and Education Center in Tennessee and from 1988 to 1993 was executive director of Greenpeace USA.

In 1993 he and Ward Morehouse cofounded the Program on Corporations, Law and Democracy to deepen and teach the work on the topic he became most known for: corporate personhood.

The mission of the POCLAD collective was to pursue historical/legal research for the purpose of contesting the excessive power "legally" allotted to corporations. At base lay the insight that we live under minority rule of people who today might be called the corporate class—but some 200 years ago were known as the slave master class and one hundred years before that were the propertied nobility in England. Corporate personhood was the legal mechanism built into U.S. law that allowed business entities to enjoy the same rights that individuals do and therefore have the freedom to do whatever they want without constraint. This insight was startling news to many activists, but Richard called its singular popularity "the corporate personhood fetish." His concern was broader, he insisted: *all* the laws, regulations, and mechanisms by which government builds and sustains the dominance of a minority class play this role, giving it privileges and protections to do as it pleases for profit's sake—all the while veiling this reality from the public behind myths of George Washington's cherry tree and Benjamin Franklin's kite-flying in a thunder storm; about honesty, ingenuity, equality, and democracy.

The consequence? "You want sanity, democracy, community, an intact Earth?" he is quoted in Jim Craven's blog on June 17, 2007. "We can't get there obeying Constitutional theory and law crafted by slave masters, imperialists, corporate masters, and Nature destroyers. We can't get there kneeling before robed lawyers stockpiling class plunder precedent up their venerable sleeves. So isn't disobedience the challenge of our age? Principled, inventive, escalating disobedience to liberate our souls, to transfigure our work as humans on this Earth."

Not long after I met Richard a notable meeting took place in a highway restaurant. I needed a ride to the Hartford, Connecticut, airport after giving a workshop at Rowe Camp in Massachusetts. Richard drove over from West Hurley, New York; picked me up, and we headed south. Kirkpatrick Sale arrived from Cold Spring, New York, and the three of us settled into a booth amid salads, spaghetti, and sandwiches. Richard and Kirk knew of each other's work but had never met. Both were devoted to

"We the Corporations" image POCLAD found via Google
and used widely in its publications.

their particular politics, and both had reputations for being crusty warriors. They shared something else; each harbored the daring but rarely admitted realization that our social movements had *lost*—an insight Kirk articulated in a 2009 conversation with Stephanie Mills and myself printed in *Counterpunch* and stated publicly by Richard in a 2011 interview with the D.C. weekly newsletter *Corporate Crime Reporter*.

After the briefest of introductions, they plunged headlong into the inevitable: a heated Demolition-of-the-Classist-Constitution versus Secession-from-the-United-States debate. Richard was hot for his plan to defang corporate/government minority rule so that sovereign, self-governing citizens could reinvent the structures defining how decisions are made. Kirk had launched the Middlebury Institute to foster the then twenty-five-plus secession movements in the United States, explaining that the U.S., and therefore its institutions, was too grandiose; the government could neither effectively respond to a storming by the voters nor maneuver its hefty complexity toward meaningful reform. After an hour of intense back-and-forth, I suddenly looked at my watch and, sadly, butted in to remind the debaters that I had a plane to catch.

Richard was many things besides a giant of a political philosopher and an irrepressible mover and shaker. He loved his home in a village in the Catskills. He reveled in his vegetable garden and had plans to build a rock bridge across a creek on the land. We spoke of a battle that we shared against an enemy even more cunning than multinational corporations: gophers. And when he had my confidence, he impishly sprung upon me the existence of the blossom whose cultivation gave him the most pleasure, describing it in a hallowed whisper that highlighted its fragile, fleeting—and illegal—attributes. He proposed that he send me seeds so that I too could grow opium.

As the author of a book about the devastating impact of heroin addiction on the Latino communities of northern New Mexico—where our county held the record for the most overdose deaths per capita in the nation and my village, Chimayó, boasted the biggest dealers—I felt ambivalence about such a horticultural experiment. He mailed me an in-depth article on the topic, whose only point I can recall today is a relevant (albeit strange) one: if a gardener doesn't know what the flower is, it's lawful to nurture it in her soil; if she does know, it is illegal. And so, illegally, Richard mailed me seeds and, illegally, I planted them in the New Mexico dirt. When at long last the flowers blossomed, he was right. They were delicate, of an almost neon orange, their petals as thin as fairy wings—and, like life, they lasted but a very short time.

I was stunned to hear of Richard's 2010 diagnosis of metastatic melanoma. His wife of forty-plus years, Mary MacArthur, had spent the year before battling cancer, and so it was with extra sorrow I learned that he, Mary, and daughter Alyssa would have to endure that same chilling journey once again. He underwent three surgeries, the last being more like what he called "an excavation," plus countless medical tests, scans, and biopsies. "I've been dealing with the industrial cancer behemoths, trying to get a clear picture of my situation," he wrote on November 6, 2011. "Meeting with drs in NYC this week, which I hope will elucidate.... Being industrialized sick can be a full-time job."

But when he could muster the energy, he spent his time on the things that mattered. In October he traveled to Sweden to visit Alyssa, her husband, and his new grandson. Back at home in the Catskills, he had set out to write a book that would present the legal history of the U.S. government to show the inherent bias behind laws favoring the corporate class and making it possible for them to usurp power, plunder resources, devastate ecologies, operate all over the planet without regard for citizenship, take advantage of workers, and swindle consumers. Tentatively titled *Rethinking the Corporation, Rethinking Strategy*, it would nudge activists toward re-conceptualizing goals and tactics commensurate with this fresh reading of history. As he put it, "How do we move beyond resisting one corporate state assault at a time—over and over and over again—toward undoing accumulations and structures and habits of the past?"

His last public act was to propose two new laws. The first would criminalize the act of gas-oil fracking in the state of New York as a Class C felony. In an email to me dated November 7, he wrote: "Law & strategy. . . . soo central. And yet, LEGISLATURES make laws, and so do courts. They make the laws for MAKING and UNMAKING laws. And we the rabble, we the many, have no remedy in those basic realms of governance. . . . So here in NY state, we've drafted a law 'criminalizing' fracking and corporate frackers, and public officials who aid and abet. . . . I've been a bit surprised that this simple step to criminalization seems to carry so much transformational clout."

The second piece of legislation was bolder. It would criminalize the corporation as it now stands. In his interview with *Corporate Crime Report*, he explained, "All existing charters for incorporated business entities would be null and void. . . . This law would strip away 500 years of Constitutional protections and privileges. No more limited liability for shareholders. No more perpetual life. No more Constitutional protections."

His last act in regards to our friendship was an email written two weeks before his death. For some mysterious reason, perhaps by some inner knowing that the end was approaching, in early November we found ourselves communing almost every day. He reported that although the doctors had proclaimed him free of cancer, he had lost trust. "Seems to be consensus: no evidence of spread. But beware of consensi among health professionals. . . . with this most 'capricious' and aggressive cancer, never final."

And he reminded me to "Be Cool."

PETER BARNES: THE PRETEND BANKER
(1942-)

America today is on the brink of losing its
historic vision.

—P.B., *WITH LIBERTY AND DIVIDENDS FOR ALL*, 2014

A photographer snapped a picture of a lineup of anti-war activists sitting cross-legged under Sather Gate on the UC Berkeley campus—faced by an opposing lineup of National Guardsmen boasting bayonets and gas masks. The year was 1969, and perhaps the demonstrators should have taken better notice of the particular gear the soldier were wearing that day; we at the north end of Sproul Plaza could not see that *all* the entrances/exits were similarly blocked, and we entrapped within them. Moments later, in a policing experiment derived from counter-guerrilla methods used by the military in Vietnam, a helicopter flew over the plaza

The author is on the left with braid. The woman to my immediate right told me she was on LSD. UC Berkeley campus, Berkeley, California, May 1969. Photo credit and courtesy of Peter Barnes.

spraying CS gas. Most of the protesters fell to the plaza's concrete floor writhing and vomiting, while the Guard moved in to beat the shit out of them. By a stroke of luck, my husband and I fled through the cafeteria and down the spiral staircase to escape into the lower plaza.

The photo appeared in *Newsweek* the following week.

And as the accompanying article reported, "police have also gone on a riot, displaying a lawless brutality equal to that of Chicago, along with weapons and techniques that even the authorities in Chicago did not dare employ: the firing of buckshot at fleeing crowds and unarmed bystanders, and the gassing—at times for no reason at all—of entire streets and portions of a college campus."

Nineteen years later, in 1988, I needed a place to stay for a few weeks in the Bay Area. Friends recommended a San Francisco writer who was looking for a house trade in some beautiful place where he could concentrate solely on his work. They gave me Peter Barnes's phone number. He arrived one day before I left so each of us could explain the inevitable quirks of our abodes. Right off, just as the sun was throwing pink and orange streamers across an evening sky, we headed into the desert. According to Peter: "The whole experience was electric. Your house, the desert, you and your amazing wardrobe and car. I was blown away."

On my next trip to San Francisco, we became lovers. He wrote me afterward: "Now that the dust is settling, I want to say that I still think there was a 'higher reason' our paths crossed.... I want to plunge (or at least briskly walk) ahead." At first, we traveled back and forth to see each other. I particularly enjoyed staying at his 28th Street Edwardian in Noe Valley where we were within walking distance of cafés, natural-food stores, and movie houses. We went on a few jaunts in northern California and, when apart, madly scrawled letters.

Before one such visit, I was getting ready to appear in the film *Berkeley in the '60's*. Director Mark Kitchell had told me to bring a photo that could be blown up to serve as a backdrop for my interview. I chose the shot that had appeared in *Newsweek*. I pulled out the tattered magazine featuring that photo from my files, and lo and behold! the photographer was ... *Peter Barnes*, the author of the accompanying article. (In the end my part was dropped from the film when the filmmakers decided they had signed on too many interviewees.)

After five or six months, Peter confessed he was "not in love with me." I was surprised but taken by his candor, and so what was I to do? We became lifelong friends. As of this writing we have been linked by a political tableau for fifty years, by friendship for more than thirty.

Peter is a gentle soul, a vulnerable man who questions himself at every turn, yet has the courage to live in a state of spiritual wonder and carry through his passions to completion. Plus, he is rakishly handsome, boasting a chiseled face and penetrating eyes. He is also one of Harvard University's post-Beatnik, early-'60s graduates who include Adam Hochschild, Todd Gitlin, Michael B. Katz, and Elizabeth Holtzman, all of whom have made key contributions to U.S. social-change movements.

Read: Peter is a Rebel and a Deep Head.

And he has made much of his intelligence. He grew up in New York City, the elder of the two children of Leo and Regina Barnes. Leo's parents had emigrated from Odessa to the United States in 1905. Regina's had traveled to the U.S. from Bucharest, Romania. Leo was an economist, Regina an English teacher at the High School of Art and Music where she helped organize the teachers' union—and together they managed to save enough money to send their son to Harvard. He did them well, graduating summa cum laude in history and later earning a master's in government at Georgetown.

From 1966 to 1970 Peter worked at *Newsweek* in a position he likes to call "their House Lefty." He then worked as the West Coast correspondent for the *New Republic*. He also wrote a book that was daring for its time: *Pawns: The Plight of the Citizen-Soldier*, illustrating that soldiers are not nasty perpetrators of war, as so many erroneously saw them during the Vietnam War; rather, they are the pawns of higher architects of war. In 1976 Peter cofounded a worker-owned solar energy company, The Solar Center, but after Governor Jerry Brown and President Jimmy Carter were replaced by Republicans, tax breaks for solar energy were eliminated and the entire industry went down the tubes. He then cofounded one of the first socially responsible money funds, Working Assets, whose credit card donated to social justice, environmental, and human rights groups each time a cardholder made a purchase. As an originator of Working Assets, he humorously referred to himself as a "pretend banker." By the early '90s, he could have added "pretend telecommunications entrepreneur." In 1982 the monopoly of AT&T was broken into multitudinous "Baby Bells," and Peter set out to form his own phone company. Now as friends, I would receive late-night phone calls while he was trying to convince investors to risk money on what deep inside he suspected was a harebrained project. "I must be mad!" he would moan from a hotel room. "They're going to think I'm crazy. *I am, I AM!*" Working Assets Long Distance turned into a financially successful alternative for people with a social conscience—with a portion of each phone call's earnings going to social-change groups.

In 1995 Peter was named Socially Responsible Entrepreneur of the Year in northern California.

He felt the urge to become a father in the mid-1980s. Still reflecting the Bohemian tone of the'60s, all manner of possibilities to go about such an endeavor were exploding in San Francisco's neighborhoods. Threesomes were living together, gay couples raised sons and daughters, serial monogamy was popular, open marriages abounded. Peter got together with a lesbian living down the street, Pam Miller; he provided the sperm, and she gave birth. Zachary arrived in 1987, and he began his young life going back and forth between the two houses, with a bedroom he could call his own in each. Peter liked being a father. In 1998 his then-wife Leyna Bernstein got pregnant, and Eli was born.

As Peter was approaching the age of sixty, he was struck as if by lightning with an electric idea. Flush with the psychological task of older age to pull together the disparate threads of his life into a coherent whole, he wrote *Who Owns the Sky?* Inspired by the patriot Thomas Paine, his answer was that every one of us owns the sky—from which it follows that we could limit the amount of carbon big polluters pump into our air by charging them for putting it there and giving the returns to everyone equally—one person, one share. The sky then becomes The Commons in the sense of that concept in eighteenth-century, pre-industrial English village life. The work thrust Peter into the public forum in a new way. He promoted his "sky trust" idea in the halls of government, and indeed bills were introduced in the House and Senate to create a "cap and dividend" system for carbon. (Cap and dividend is not to be confused with "cap and trade," a loophole-ridden contrivance that would largely benefit polluters and Wall Street.)

After that, he penned another visionary treatise, *Capitalism 3.0: A Guide to Reclaiming the Commons.* Unlike many of his cohorts who see capitalism as beyond redemption, Peter believes that capitalism is flexible and worth fixing. To him, its two flaws—ever-widening inequality and unending destruction of the planet—can be repaired by charging for private exploitation of The Commons, like natural ecosystems, and paying equal dividends to everyone.

Notice for E.F. Schumacher Lecture, Great Barrington, Massachussets, 2014. Courtesy of Peter Barnes.

One thing can be said for sure. For all his shyness and self-doubt, Peter Barnes is a thinker of one-of-a-kind ideas and an adept at using them to stir things up. And he has *definitely* recovered from the writer's block he perennially claimed to be suffering from.

Yet another book popped out in 2014: *With Liberty and Dividends for All: How to Save Our Middle Class When Jobs Don't Pay Enough.* Conceptually an extension of his previous two books, it argues that America's considerable middle class needs not just jobs, but also non-labor income if it is to survive the twenty-first century. And where might such non-labor come from? From charging corporations when they use common wealth and paying dividends to everyone. "Would dividends from co-owned wealth mean the end of capitalism? Not at all," he argues. "They would mean the end of *winner-takes-all capitalism,* our currently dominant version, and the beginning of a more balanced version that respects all members of society, including those not yet born. This better-balanced capitalism—perhaps we could call it *everyone-owns-a-share capitalism*—wouldn't solve all our problems, but it would do more than any other potential remedy to preserve our middle class, our democracy, and our planet."

As the years rolled by, Peter became financially stable, and he realized a dream: he bought land along Tomales Bay north of San Francisco. The idea was not just to have his personal sanctuary, but to offer it as a haven for writers who otherwise would not have unobstructed time to concentrate fully on their craft. Peter quotes poet Mary Oliver: "No one has yet made a list of places where the extraordinary may happen. Still, there are indications. It likes the out-of-doors. It likes the concentrating mind. It likes solitude. It isn't that it would disparage comforts, or the set routines of the world, but that its concern is directed to another place. Its concern is the edge, and the making of form out of the formlessness that is beyond the edge."

"I have seen time and again how true these words are," Peter adds, "how a few weeks of writing 'beyond the edge' can be transformational for emerging writers, and rejuvenating for established ones." He built cottages overlooking the bay as it reached north to the Pacific Ocean and in 1997 began the Mesa Refuge writers retreat. Residents since then have included Michael Pollen, Terry Tempest Williams, Daniel Ellsberg, George Lakoff, Francis Moore Lappé, Wes "Scoop" Nisker, Wolfgang Sachs, and Carl Anthony—in all, over 600 established and budding writers. He is quick to add: "So far."

Meanwhile, in his house nearby, Peter keeps a collection of items related to our porcine kin, at its peak containing over 200 pieces. Pink pigs. Brown pigs. Polka-dot pigs. Clay pigs. Plastic pigs. Pig magnets. A pig weathervane. Pig slippers. Aprons adorned with pigs. Although some friends refer to the collection as some sort of Freudian manifestation, he maintains he is lampooning himself as "a capitalist pig."

I visited Peter one evening in Tomales and got a glimpse of the animals festooning several shelves in the kitchen, *too* many shelves, as Peter insisted of his run-away menagerie, and he politely explained that he had put away the bulk of the sounder and made it clear to friends that he did *not* care to receive any more porcine donations. And yet some years later, I am remorseful to confess that, in a market in Cochabamba, I stumbled upon a baby spoon boasting a handle shaped like a fat piglet. Unable to hold myself in check, I mailed it to my dear friend. Always the gentleman, he received it with aplomb.

ANDRE VLTCHEK: A DAY IN THE LIFE
(1963-)

What Germans did, gazing at the chimneys of the
concentration camps that were regurgitating thick
smoke of the victims of Holocaust and then claiming that
"they did not know," was exactly what all Europeans did
for centuries and millennia when their troops and
"investments" into all sorts of Crusades were looting and
brutalizing everyone on the surface of our Planet.

—A.V., "IGNORANCE AND INDOCTRINATION OF WESTERNERS KILLS MILLIONS," *GLOBAL RESEARCH*, NOVEMBER 17, 2015

André Vltchek moves faster than the speed of light, and for one day in 2012 I had the opportunity to soar alongside him. We began corresponding after

André in Goma, East Kiju, Democratic Republic of Congo, 2009.
Courtesy of André Vltchek.

I had read an article called "In Defense of Paper Books" that he wrote for *Counterpunch*. In it he analyzed the loss of cultural depth by the onslaught of e-books replacing hold-in-the-hand, turn-the-page volumes. He also linked the presumed demise of "our best friends for many centuries" with the global corporate market, insisting, "Books are some of the mightiest weapons in revolutionary struggles and in resistance. To abandon them, to let them be captured would mean that everything is lost. It would be an acceptance that market fundamentalism and imperialism should be now allowed to possess, digitize, and manipulate all knowledge, all verbalized dreams and the hopes that our humanity has created throughout the centuries." I wrote him in praise. Mostly authors respond to such missives with a quick note of thanks, but in this case André initiated an ongoing exchange.

I learned that he is a photographing-filming-writing war correspondent. Bosnia, Peru, the Democratic Republic of Congo, Timor Leste, Sri Lanka, Syria, Nairobi, Indonesia, Rwanda—he's been there. Clearly, André sleeps little to not at all and accomplishes the bulk of his work while strapped into an airplane seat. Sometimes his essays appear every other day in *Counterpunch*. Also in *Asia Times, People's Daily, Asia-Pacific Journal, Der Spiegel, Newsweek, ZMagazine*, etc. He makes documentary films for Venezuelan TV, Telesur, as well as for Russia Today, Press TV, and UNESCO. He speaks six Western languages and two Asian, and while he tends to write in English, his books have been translated into fifteen languages.

Needless to say, they cover some hefty subject matters. *Western Terror: From Potosí to Baghdad* was published in 2006. *Oceania* is an analysis of the Pacific Rim in the context of its history of colonization. *Indonesia: Archipelago of Fear* came out in 2012, a view of the country and its struggles of the last forty years. *Fighting against Western Imperialism* and *Exposing Lies of the Empire* take on uprisings against Western hegemony.

André has also compiled two books based on conversations with people he admires. The first is *Exile*. Put together with Rossie Indira, it highlights various chats with Southeast Asian writer Pramoedya Ananta Toer. The second, *On Western Terrorism: From Hiroshima to Drone Warfare*, is a dialogue with Noam Chomsky on the power and propaganda wielded by the United States and its European allies. According to political scientist Richard Falk, André "consistently and calmly held his own during the conversations, speaking with comparable authority and knowledge about an extraordinary assortment of topics that embraced the entire global scene, something few of us would have the nerve to attempt, much less with such verve, insight, and empathy." After Falk finished the book, he reports that he felt "a sense of how much even those of us who try to be progressive and informed leave untouched."

When I met André in 2012, he had written several novels. One commentator, Tony Cristini, wrote that *Point of No Return* is "one of the great novels of the twenty-first century." I thought: well, this couldn't be, the author is moving at too clipped a pace to pen a great novel. Made curious by such unabashed praise, though, I bought it. The book, I found, daringly hurdles the standard barricades between fiction and non-fiction. Like a postmodern rampage between fragmentation and longing, it juxtaposes a war correspondent's crossings into those conflict zones that mainstream reporters shun with his craving to establish a stable love life and home. In the denouement, a brutal battle between U.S.-trained Mexican paramilitaries and guerrilla defenders validates that André knows war as intimately as Hemingway did. I was regretful when I had to turn the last page, and I have to admit: the book vies for a place on a list of the great novels of the twenty-first century.

To me, André looks Russian. Blonde, bearded, with eyes set close together so he can gaze across the open Russkaya Ravnina. Indeed, he was born in Leningrad in the year of the Cuban Missile Crisis, arriving in time for the Soviet-U.S. face-offs of the Cold War. His mother is a Russian/Kazakh/Chinese architect and artist, his father, a scientist from Czechoslovakia. Despite auspicious beginnings in the country that would hold numinosity for him for the rest of his life, the family moved across the border to his father's land. Here his unusual racial makeup turned childhood into, as he describes it, "a living hell." As wintry temperatures gripped the small city of Pilsen, packs of classmates urinated into his shoes and threw them into the icy street; he had to "fight for survival after each class at elementary school."

He now spends his life endeavoring to ensure that, in the battlefields and war zones of the world, someone is present to witness in order to help—and to reveal who the perpetrators are.

Knowing something of André's fervor for far-flung ventures, one can only guess that he has graced the tattered upholstery of the most rickety single-prop planes in the world and chocked up a surfeit of free miles on the leading commercial airlines. It was that surfeit that ferried him to South America.

The thing that troubled me the most as the day of his arrival neared was that I did not know *how to pronounce his last name.* V-L-T-C-H-E-K. No matter how hard I tried to wrap my tongue around the mash of consonants, a decent articulation simply would not manifest. So, after he hailed my Jeep down on Cochabamba's Avenida Heroinas, the first sentiment out of my mouth was my sorry admission. The first out of his was graciously crafted to put me at ease: *no one* knew how to pronounce his last name, and I should just forget he had one.

Next came his admission. Instead of the several days he had promised, he had but a half day to spend in Bolivia. Such a pace turned out to be emblematic of this globe-trotting journalist; he had a plane to catch in six hours—and, before anything, would we be able to grab a cup of coffee?

With a high-speed swirl of a visit in the works, my mind went as vacant as a campesino's bank account. It was Sunday. Not much happening. We walked to Plaza 14 de Septiembre, and lo and behold! it boasted a health fair with booths touting free tastes of yogurt, brochures explaining the rights of the disabled, lessons on how to cook *calabasas*, charts explaining the nutritional pyramid—and at each stall throngs of neatly dressed campesinos in ... ahem ... tidy lines.

Tidy lines? Hello? Bolivian campesinos do not—I repeat, *not*—stand in tidy lines. No, push-and-shove bedlam is the norm, particularly if there is something to be had. In this case, a free amaranth-quinoa-honey bar, a blood test for diabetes. And, as if it were the day of a village wedding, everyone's costume was outstandingly clean and put-together. In between his ooohs and aaahs of glee, André went wild taking photos.

I had seen campesinos bussed into the city before. For show of the overwhelming political support that existed in the *campo* for the Evo Morales administration. As with all village association events, participation is not by individual choice; it's mandatory. Each participant might even be paid. Or the community could receive a tractor and a cell-phone tower. Clearly, these folks had been given lessons in more than cooking calabasas, including what sort of personal etiquette to bring to an orderly queue.

"This is a theater piece, you know," I quipped, reflecting a certain realism about what had developed in Bolivia since the 2006 inauguration that Tom Hayden and I—and Bolivians—had felt so enthusiastic about. "It's propaganda." After the government had taken a bite out of freedom of the press in 2010 by establishing a legal process by which it could shut down chosen venues; after Gasolinazo, in which Vicepresidente Álvaro García Linera announced (on Christmas Eve) that the price of gas was to be hiked up by as much as 82 percent; after the 2011 police attack on *indígenas* marching peacefully to protect their sovereignty and homelands from the administration's brand of neoliberal development; after many affronts Bolivians saw as unjust—the administration was not popular at the radical cafés Co-Café Arte and Caracol that I frequented.

"Maybe it *is* propaganda," André replied.

"Look at how organized the campesinos are."

"Listen." He touched my arm to emphasize his point. "I don't care who's putting this thing on or why. It's a service."

"Ya, but..."

Now he butted in with urgency. "Compared to the tanks and land mines, dead corpses, rubble of bridges blown to smithereens, and utter social breakdown I'm normally confronted with in the Third World, *this* is progress!"

André had a point. I went silent and have been mulling over his perspective ever since.

Next stop fell at the other end of the class spectrum: a restaurant on the green lawn of a wood-and-rock residence in Tiquipaya. The chef had recently returned after a successful career outside of Bolivia; the food is a lip-smacking blend inspired by the ingredients of his home department, Oruro, and the olive-oil-drenched dishes of Italy. We positioned ourselves at a table on the grass, and as a gaggle of geese waddled by, André excavated a cell phone from his bag. In between mouthfuls of cooked calabasas, pasta smothered in tomato sauce, and roast beef, he devoured e-messages, madly sent texts back, and made international calls.

When his second espresso arrived, he placed the phone on the tablecloth. "I must explain," he said … "I'm on this trip to document how things are going in the leftist anti-imperialist countries of Latin America. It's for my film/book project with Noam Chomsky, and there are endless travel details that have to be arranged right away." With a self-awareness I was learning was one of his endearing attributes, André apologized again for the flash visit—and asked forgiveness for his lack of attention to the brief moment we were sharing.

After hurling praise upon the chef, we hightailed it down the Reducto to Avenida Blanco Galindo and, from there, Wilstermann airport. André Vtlchek disappeared into his airborne office—and I was left to contemplate the life of a dyed-in-the-wool war correspondent.

XVII. *PLANETA O MUERTE*: LATIN AMERICA

*The division of labor among nations is that some
specialize in winning and others in losing. Our part
of the world, known today as Latin America, was
precocious: it has specialized in losing ever since those
remote times when Renaissance Europeans ventured
across the ocean and buried their teeth in the throats
of the Indian civilizations.*

—EDUARDO GALEANO, *THE OPEN VEINS OF LATIN AMERICA*, 1971

LATIN AMERICA HOLDS A special place in history; the region
proudly presents its emblematic richness of cultural development just
as it remains the archetypal victim of pre-colonial, classical, and neoliberal exploitation. In the thirteenth century a gluttonous Incan Empire
thrust itself upon the indigenous communities that stretch from the
Peruvian Andes to the southern beaches of Chile—in the process creating an early system of extended military rule, convoluted bureaucracy,
and large-scale agriculture. To the north, in what is modern-day Central

America, the Aztecs were similarly lording over Mesoamerica, while the Mayans held the Yucatán.

The 1500s saw Spain making its play at conquest, posing as the region's liberator but in reality voraciously exploiting resources and turning workers into slaves. Into its coffers poured the precious metals that Iberian myth had long promised; the revelation of unfathomable reserves of gold and silver beneath the Cerro Rico in Potosí, Bolivia, provided enough riches to make Spain the first world power. It is said that enough precious metals were excavated at Potosí alone to build a bridge made of gold between South America and the Iberic Peninsula.

An imagined arrival of Christopher Columbus' campaign to the "New World." Engraving by Theodor de Bry, 1594. Public Domain, Courtesy of Special Collections, University of Houston Libraries.

After the Bolivarian revolution of the early 1800s—led by such as Simon Bolivar and Juana Azurduy de Padilla and highlighted by the founding of new countries —the nation state emerging as a global power to the north, the U.S. of A., began to look at its neighboring territories to the south with the covetous eyes of a wolf gazing at prey. Invasions by fundamentalist Christian missions touting capitalism and individualism buttered the bread, while wars of aggression, domination via CIA-sponsored assassinations/dictatorships, and outright theft of natural resources followed.

As a result, Latin Americans are strikingly attentive to the machinations of power. By the 1990s said awareness found its moment, startling the world as a Marxist-informed people's "revolution" burst forth through the election of *más-o-menos* democratic/*más-o-menos* socialist leaders such as Hugo Chavez, Inácio Lula da Silva, Michelle Bachelet,

Néstor Kirchner, Cristina Fernandez de Kirchner, Evo Morales, and José Mujica—many of whom had been imprisoned or tortured, or had lost a loved one during the dictatorships. In this process Latin America attempted to transform itself from the poor, victimized, almost invisible continent it had been into the region most earnest about decolonizing itself from a horrific past.

Unfortunately, colonization is not over; in these times of spreading uncertainty and fear, in the face of corporate globalization and loss of cultural identity, nuclear/genetic/biological/electromagnetic war, ecological collapse, unprecedented weather disasters, and terrorism—just as elsewhere in the world—the electorate is giving over all possibility of democratic participation to "father/savior figures" whose promises offer an illusion of control.

But also like anywhere else, Latin America isn't just its heads of state and the "leaders" of right or left governments; it is full of people who are passionately engaged in fighting, living, and creating the future. Here are some of them who might inspire you . . .

JORGE BAYRO CORROCHANO: *GUERRILLERO URBANO*
(1950-)

We are the generation chosen to live an exceptional age of rebellion— that of the revolution by the students of May 1968, the hippie movement, the Cuban Revolution, uprisings for national liberation, [the movement against] the war in Vietnam, Che's army . . .
—J.B.C., "CARLOS BAYRO, DESAPARECIDO," *BOLPRESS*, 2006

Bayro and I had a portrait sketched together in one of those European-style sidewalk cafés. It was the end of the day; cars were streaming past on the tree-studded Prado just as workers were carting home sacks of just-baked bread. Bayro was sipping a Huari, I *unacopa de vino tinto*. Our portrayer was Nicolás Block, a street artist who frequents the *boliches* of Cochabamba scouting out opportunities to

Pencil portrait of Chellis and Jorge, "Los Revolucionarios de la Vida"
by Nicolás Block, 2013. Photo credit: PhotoMark, Sucre, Bolivia.
Courtesy of Chellis Glendinning.

render his distinctive caricatures. For this one, he sketched us in exaggerated form and then scrawled the phrase: "REVOLUCIONA-RIOS DE LA VIDA."

No matter from what angle you look at him, Bayro is one magnetic character. Strangers in the street still call out to him "¡Ramirito!"—his underground handle from the post-Che, *volveremos-a-las-montañasguerrilla* uprising in the lowland jungles near Teoponte—and he boasts a booming, deep voice that speaks the language of revolution. On a darker side, he still has a hard time finding work due to his reputation as an unrelenting freedom fighter. His predicament is ironic in today's Bolivia, where buses proudly boast decals of Che Guevara and it's no secret that President Evo Morales broke through the dictatorships/neoliberal governments on the coattails of the revolutionary/social movements that came before him. Like Teoponte. But maybe it's also because, after all these years, Bayro has not softened his ardor one iota: an issue arises, the fist soars toward the sky of his ideals.

The guerrilla movement of Teoponte meant to give proof that the anti-totalitarian movements in Bolivia had not died out just because Che and his band of *rebeldes* had been gunned down. It was 1970, and this new fighting group was made up of sixty-seven budding fighters, all men—fifty-three Bolivianos, eight Chilenos, two Argentinos, one Peruano, one Brasileño, and a Hispano-Norteamericano. They were Christians, Communists, and Trotskyites: the majority from the middle class, many students, while a few were *obreros* or campesinos. With heroism pumping through their veins, they took their boots, jungle fatigues, and Uzis to the *selva* in the east, not far from La Higuera where Che had been shot dead in a schoolhouse and then transported by helicopter to Vallegrande. These new soldiers were idealistic. When the brother of my friend jazz-musician Javier "Pajarito" Caballero, announced that he was joining the revolutionaries, his mother requested x-rays of his teeth so the family could identify him in the morgue. He would hear nothing of their concern; he *had* to go. It was the same for Bayro's brother Carlos. A promising twenty-two-year-old artist and *dirigente* in the Movimiento de la Izquierda Revolutionaria, he too answered the call to fight against the repressive Junta Militar of Hugo Banzer Suarez.

The plan was three-tiered. First, to hike the terrain so the soldiers could become acclimatized to the unforgiving landscape. Second, to confront the Bolivian military in the field to test the pluck of the neophyte band of *guerrilleros*. Third, to reach the zone of operations of the miners in Caranavi and Tipuani, where they could lend support to the miners' revolutionary efforts.

Just as with Che's army, though, there were not enough of them, they didn't have enough armaments, they didn't know the terrain, etc. But perhaps the most significant factors in what happened were the cocky self-importance of Bolivia's military *jefes* due to their recent triumph in having done away with the most notorious revolutionary in the world and the anti-guerrilla experience they had gained ferreting him out. They were gung ho to squelch this nascent uprising, and so they did. In one campaign the army mounted more than 1000 soldiers geared and voracious against the by-now dwindling cadre of starving rebels. It was a massacre: in all, fifty-eight mowed down or dead from malnourishment—with only nine survivors escaping the carnage. Those who were taken captive were forced to dig their own graves before being machine-gunned into them. Pajarito's mother did

Military roundup, Bolivia. Photo credit: Lucio Flores Archive.

indeed trudge to the morgue carting Carlos's dental x-rays to identify the body.

Every rebel campaign headed to the mountains needs a support organization in the city—to infiltrate the opposition class as Tania Bunke had done during Che's effort, to raise funds, to gather food and craft/find arms, to provide safe houses for returning/arriving compañeros. He who was known as Ramirito did his work underground—in the back alleys, basements, and shadowy bars of Cochabamba; by 1969 his mug appeared on a WANTED poster all over Bolivia and the authorities were on the lookout for him.

By necessity the guerrillero fights with a wide variety of weapons, whatever can be made at home, captured, or supplied from outside connections. Bayro forged himself into an expert in armaments and explosives. At first he and his companions made their own. "Together with two comrades, both of whom were killed in Teoponte," he tells me when we talk in the plush-carpet hush of an old Cochabamba hotel, "we assembled all the material needed for explosives for both the battle in Teoponte and in the cities. All of it was crafted by hand—copying methods garnered from the Vietnamese—using cast-off metal waste, tin cans, whatever. After we lost our storage places, we also sewed the backpacks, the hammocks, the plastic ponchos, everything." Boasting an ironic smirk, he attributes his aptitude in such areas to his education at the prestigious Catholic high school, el Colegio San Agustín, where he learned not just literature, math, philosophy, and science—but also carpentry, metal work, and shop skills.

The organization of the effort was typical for uprisings in danger of infiltration; it consisted of a centralized nexus of decision-makers at the top rung with small cadres enacting policy from below, often unknown to each other. The Luddite rebels fighting against industrialism of their villages in the early 1800s, Georgios Grivas's Greek freedom fighters of the 1940s, the Algerian National Liberation Front of the 1950s, the U.S.'s Earth Liberation Front of the 1990-2000s—all shared a closed-system hierarchy in which tight-knit cadres gave focus to specific tasks, while a strict policy of full-blown confidentiality kept members from knowing who worked in parallel cells or those at other levels.

Bayro describes the general atmosphere of the urban arena in an essay about his brother Carlos. "Riding around in white Toyota jeeps and brandishing threatening rifles, the police patrolled the streets in search of resisters against a non-constitutional government. The militants sustained their attitude of resistance through networks of comrades like a wall against death. Sheltered in safe houses, they survived—rejecting flight, defending the principles of life and the future of Bolivia." About his brother's disappearance, he writes: "Carlos was detained for a 'crime,' the same one that groups of paramilitaries were using to ambush other militants. Resisting inevitable death Carlos ran for three blocks, he against eight thugs. He fought until he fell unconscious. Then they carried him to the Ministry of the Interior where by torture they murdered him."

Cochabamba is a city with a proud history of resistance. The 2000 Guerra del Agua stands out, wherein for three months cholos, campesinos, students, professionals, the middle class, and international supporters sustained an uprising against U.S. multinational corporation Bechtel, feverishly fighting the military and police in protest against an already signed contract to privatize the valley's water. As one of the earliest post–World Trade Organization challenges, the event—and its startling success—blew the minds of pro-democracy/ anti-globalization activists from all corners of the planet.

Today the city boasts two cafés frequented by Cochabamba's cadres of such activists. Co-Café Arte, run by Emma Abasto Rivera and Guido Capcha Campos, is located at the corner of Calles Ecuador and Antezana; here, amidst posters of Frida Kahlo's monkey and Picasso's gray panorama of *Guernica*, you will stumble upon debates about politics, the most enduring topic these days being whether or not the Movimiento del Socialismo and Evo Morales are good for the country. Four blocks to the west on Mayor Rocha lies the other hotbed of debate, the Caracol. Filled with the smoke of Cuban Habanas and the songs of Mercedes Sosa, its tiny rooms display sepia-tinted photos of Cochabamba in the 1930s. I happened upon Jorge Bayro at Caracol.

It was a moonless night in 2012, and I spotted a friend at the bar. Fernando "Boxer" Machiceo was one of the most committed urban supporters of the *indígenas* who were fighting the Morales government's global-economic plan to cut a superhighway through their constitutionally protected Territoria Indígena y Parque Nacional Isiboro-Secure, the traditional and Constitution-protected lands where they still practiced hunting-gathering. Also home to the nation's richest biodiversity, including species in immediate danger of extinction. Indefatigable, Boxer had made both three-month-long protest marches from Trinidad to La Paz and was forever traveling from the reserve to the city to raise funds, sell videos, and speak on the radio. Upon seeing me, he stood up and, with his old compañero Jorge Bayro, moved us to a quiet table in the back hall. Bayro was perceptive, honest, engaging—and immediately launched a rap on the importance of insurgency.

A passion for rebellion had been nurtured in his middle-class family in an old estate on Calle Tumusla. His parents, art collector Luis Guillermo Bayro Fernandez and homemaker Gladys Corrochano Ramos, had nine sons, each of whom has carried on the family dedication to strong education, love of free thinking—and boasting a penchant for *rebeldía*. Luis Guillermo is an architect. Carlos was an up-and-coming artist and key *dirigente* in the MIR before his disappearance. Jorge came next. Mauricio escaped the lack of educational opportunities in Bolivia during the dictatorships and is now a successful painter/sculptor in Mexico. José followed Mauricio's footsteps, as an artist of unusual talent. Fernando is a psychoanalyst in Paris, while Ramiro creates gourmet cheeses in Cochabamba. Roberto passed away too early, and the youngest, Eduardo, is a computer scientist who designs robots for use in medicine.

Jorge grew up in an atmosphere of questioning and insurgence. He explains the origins of this mutineering nature. "Cochabamba was a small city in [the 1960s]," he told me during a 2016 interview. "We all knew each other and were comfortable families, middle class, while relationship with poorer people did not exist; each class lived in its own world. In the case of my family with my eight brothers, we were just beginning to mature in the '60s. We grew up with the memories of the family, of the fathers, the grandparents who had lived through the Revolution of 1952. The majority of the middle class was the enemy of this revolution because they had property, they had haciendas, houses, they were the owners of Indians.... Then came the experience of the Guerrilla de Che, the arising of Latin American literature with its grand writers like Gabriel Garcia Marques, Borges, Julio Cortázar. We began to read history and develop a critique, and we were as avid as any human who chooses to search for truth. Take into account that we had no relation with the miners, the factories, the campesinos, but we were looking deeply at ourselves—and at them with respect, sensibility, feeling.... There were organized parties, the communist party, the first organizations of the left like Movimiento Nacionalista Revolucionario, the Trotskyites had a strong presence, the Frente Revolucionario Universitario.... We questioned religion and its complicity with the injustices. [There] arose movements of rebel Catholics, especially the Dominicans, the Augustines, the Jesuits."

After their parents died in 1960 and 1961, the Bayro brothers turned their house into a living tribute to the socialist-anarchist experiment they admired. Living without adult supervision, they sold the old colonial furniture, made their own out of wood cartons and hung their own paintings in a style of "universal art." Emulating the Japanese, they left their shoes at the door out of respect for the brother whose job that week was to clean the floors. They replaced the old books with those of Marx, Lenin, Che, all the great Latin authors, and "everything that was part of the polemic of the era, everything that was prohibited." They grew their hair long, and they studied in a disciplined fashion so they would both learn and do well in school. This liberated zone became a hotbed of fellow artists and activists where theories were hashed out and friendship abounded, while the neighbors looked on with crooked eyebrows.

After the Teoponte massacre and subsequent countrywide repressive measures, some of the survivors attempted to disappear into normal life. Not Jorge Bayro. He went to Chile where Salvador Allende was the newly elected progressive president, and given his stature as a Teoponte guerrillero, was offered a Chilean passport, free university education, work, whatever he wanted. Instead he chose to continue the struggle, joining the Junta de Coordinación Revolucionario and working in Peru, Argentina, with the Tupamaros, the Ejército Revolucionario del Pueblo, and the MIR in Chile—essentially becoming an internationalist participating in operations he still feels he cannot speak about.

Upon his return to Bolivia, he vanished into the dank labyrinths of the mines at Llallagua "with my lantern, my boots, like a Halloween get-up. The entire world knew me. . . . They searched for me high and low, sky and land—and here I was. In the mines you could pass under their very noses and they had no idea you were the one they wanted." Not merely seeking to escape detection while in the mines, Bayro organized the column of miners known as Juana Azurduy de Padilla that trained, garnered weapons, and engaged in actions.

Sometimes when I am with him now—despite nearly four decades of electoral democracy in Bolivia, despite the fact that he walks the streets of Cochabamba freely, I notice that a gnawing, desperate need to remain under the radar hangs on. He moves from low-grade hostel to residential dive with regularity, no one knows exactly where he sleeps, and yet people on the street still call out "¡Ramirito!" "Until the day I die," he tells me, "my dedication is to keep history alive. Everything my compañeros did, I survived not because I was in a comfortable position. I carried the same risk as they did. But I survived. My job now is to rescue the memory. I'm not out there speaking at conferences, I'm not at the rallies, I'm not marching in the streets, I'm not armed, but in my intimate moments, like now with you, I expound, I fight, I spread the word."

He bellows that bottomless laugh of his. "Like a complete LOCO!"

IVÁN NOGALES BAZÁN: *LIBERTAD POR TEATRO*
(1963-)

[The body] is the physical, spiritual, sexual, and creative energy of a human being; it is the sanctuary of one's culture. To reestablish the energy of the body it is necessary to regain one's dominion over space (territory) and time (history).

—I.N.B., *LA DESCOLONIZACIÓN DEL CUERPO*

I picked up Iván in the oval driveway of the Hyatt Place. He emerged through the glass doors of Santa Fe's hotel and sheepishly looked around for his designated ride. I could see that he was shorter than I, boasting the rotund ribcage of the altiplano and the lucent face of a full moon in October. The year was 2004, and he was in New Mexico as part of a U.S. Embassy grant for social-change activists. Home base: El Alto, Bolivia, and given that we had a common friend in that country, Appalachian folksinger Jack Herranen, that is how I came to be given the task of shepherding Iván's visit and introducing him to the Norteño desert. I took him to lunch at a Mexican restaurant on Cerrillos and then out to my house in Chimayó. When we parted, he handed me a copy of *El mañana es hoy*, his book about the theater group he founded, Teatro Trono. Its actors, designers, dancers, and costume makers: all former glue sniffers and street ruffians. I believed I would never see him again.

Fast-forward to 2006. Fate stepped in—unexpectedly shepherding *me* to the inauguration of Bolivia's first indigenous president, Evo

Morales—when I ran into him again in La Paz's jam-packed Plaza de San Francisco, where thousands upon thousands of ecstatic voters were gathered to welcome their newly sworn-in leader. After hours of spontaneous celebration, Morales marched in along with Uruguayan writer Eduardo Galeano, the new vice president, ex-guerrilla fighter Álvaro Garcia Linera, and a host of supporters from the winning party, el Movimiento al Socialismo—all madly waving the colorful, emblematic *wiphala* flag representing the diverse cultures of Bolivia. And there was Iván—alongside his theater troupe with their painted faces and rainbow of costumes, many on stilts, adding rhythm and drama to the moment as they beat on hide-and-gut drums.

This time, on *his* home ground.

El Alto is the "satellite" city that grew up on the mesa above La Paz, built by the anguish of campesinos who, no longer able to survive on their lands, had migrated to the city to find work in construction, as *taxistas*, as maids, as garbage collectors. Ever the gentleman, Iván proceeded to show me the seven-story building he had built in El Alto. It was a monster of a structure housing a theater, dance hall, cinema, museum dedicated to his father who had been killed by the army in the post-Che Teoponte uprising, and his own apartment on the top two levels. Listen up you believers in recycling: the place was constructed *entirely* from cast-off and upcycled materials he had come upon in the street, scrounged from construction sites, or begged from corporations.

There—amidst Chaco War–era wood window sills, fancy glass doors from some company that was upgrading its headquarters, circular staircases fashioned from used rebars, and mismatched linoleum flooring—I was introduced to one mind-blowing space. Iván's apartment was a museum bursting at the seams with Victorian mirrors, Daguerreotype-era camera equipment, copper kettles, sepia photos of important moments in Bolivian history, ships' lanterns, tattered posters of theater events, an autobus door, portraits of Lenin, umbrellas, miniature metal-soldier armies, puppets dangling from the ceiling from their strings, and—what caught my eye—a marvelous faux Louis-XIV gilded table that was so tacky it was, as we say in the U.S., "camp." ("¡*Yo tengo un ojo!*" he joked: I have an eye for treasures.) And books. Books all over the place: history, sociology, theater, architecture, art, you name it.

Ivan in his home above Teatro Trono, 2014.
Photo credit: Alex Ayala Ugarte. Courtesy of Ivan Nogales.

I then knew I was in the company of a master curator, and I admit: I fell in love. Not so much because of his accomplishments as an internationally respected theater director. Or his writings linking theater work with societal liberation. Or his social vision and dedication to carry it through. Not even his non-stop creativity in the service of making life better for others. No, I fell in love because of this marvelously wacky and insightful testimony to our sad, splendid, decidedly surrealistic world.

Iván Nogales Bazán was born in 1963 to Claudina Bazán Nogales and Indalecio Nogales Caceres. His mother was, as Iván calls her, *"una verdadera guerrillera de la sobre viviencia"* (a true guerrilla fighter in the battle for survival); in other words, she did whatever was required for the good of the family. Indalecio also performed that duty, but on a more collective scale; he was a carpenter-plumber-mechanic who in the 1960s became a leader of the syndicate of the SAID textile factory. After the military coup d' état of René Barrientos in 1964, he was forced to go underground, and in 1970 he joined the post–Che Guevara guerrilla effort that was named for the locale of its most extreme massacre: Teoponte. Since his body was never identified, he is considered to this day desaparecido.

As a psychotherapist I have found that each person's life story is like a novel: it brings to the fore its own special symbolic images, movements, actions, and outcomes. Its own myths, really. Iván presents a superb example of this phenomenon.

The story is this: his father had a steamer trunk, painted red and stashed with all manner of documents, tools, and memorabilia. He used it as his own special space, his "office." When Iván was six and the eldest of the three siblings, without explanation Indalecio ceremoniously passed the Caja Roja (red box) on to his son. He then left to join the Ejército de Liberación Nacional to bring down the dictatorships—*never to return*; by 1972 almost the entire rebel force had been slaughtered, some forced to dig their own graves before being shot into them. Suddenly thrust into poverty, the family was left destitute. Iván became both a street kid and the "man" of the house. It was then that he began to perfect the fine art of scavenging. He brought home wooden matchboxes, aluminum pots, old shoes, whatever he could get his hands on. He was shaping himself into a go-getter in service to the family.

After graduating from La Paz's Universidad Mayor de San Andrés in sociology, Iván designed and built the humongous house in El Alto where he then lived with six other chicos who were, like him, street kids. To stay alive, they began to perform on street corners. "It was marvelous, very hard, complicated, tragicomical, poetic, a little of everything really," Iván told *La Razón* reporter Alex Ayala Ugarte in 2014. And out of this survival tactic came a voracious appetite to teach himself the performing arts and build what would become La Comunidad de Productores en Artes and its theater project Teatro Trono. By now the troupe of rehabilitated street-kid actors has trucked its sets and costumes all over Latin America and traveled to Europe to the tune of some 200,000 miles, adding up to more than seven voyages around the planet.

Iván had built and filled his own Caja Roja.

With all the flamboyance of vaudeville and Charlie Chaplin, with all the innovation of Bertolt Brecht and Antonin Artaud, Teatro Trono

Teatro Trono bringing Bolivian culture to Germany.
Courtesy of Ivan Nogales.

has performed original plays like *Hoy se sirve* about dictatorial/ authoritarian governments and *Hasta la última gota* on Cochabamba's 2000 Guerra del Agua against privatization of water. They have also mounted innovative renditions of known stories like *Romeo and Juliet*. In the process they have been awarded distinctions and prizes given by municipalities, universities, and festivals. Now COMPA has member centers in Cochabamba, Santa Cruz, and Berlin. In the process Iván has been recognized as an authority on people's theater in service to the psycho-political liberation necessary for recovery from centuries of oppression and dictatorship.

In 2013 he wrote a book called *La descolonización del cuerpo*. Herein he reveals the educational thinking and methods he has used for almost thirty years. Just as in parallel work by psychoanalyst Wilhelm Reich and psychologist Peter Levine, the connection between the private life of the body and the vicissitudes of societal demands is underscored. In essence the book is more than a guide for theater directors; it amounts to a theory of psycho-corporal-social change. In the swing of the atmosphere of a much-pained past and the expectation of decolonization that Evo Morales's MASistas have attempted to infuse, Iván writes of a revolution not so much via economic and legal models, but of citizen participation and cultural creation. As former Brazilian Secretario de Ciudadañía Cultural Célio Turino writes in the preface, *"Empezar de nuevo presupone actuar en el campo simbólico. Descolonizar."* (To start anew presupposes acting on the symbolic realm to decolonize ourselves.)

Witnessing the *"negación corporal"* of his comrades in the streets of El Alto, Iván set out to liberate his budding artists from colonized auto-repression, stimulate their memories of both personal trauma and social possibility, and inculcate communal values. He uses theater and bodywork exercises, self-disclosure, dance, acting classes, involvement in Teatro Trono's outreach programs like Radio Trono, and travel. *"El cuerpo es pasado, presente y futuro"* (The body is the past, the present, and the future), he writes. *"El cuerpo habla. Con la lengua, y las otras lenguas como las huellas digitales, las plantas de los pies, las orejas. . . ."* (The body speaks. With the tongue, and the handprint, the bottom of the feet, the ears. . . .)The result: several generations of focused youth—still vulnerable to slips into isolation, depression, and antisocial acting out, for sure—but also with qualities of integrity and possibilities for a better future; historically/politically aware artists involved in imaginative creation making a cultural contribution to Bolivia they could never have imagined.

In 2010, after I made my decisive move to Bolivia, Iván and I met up again. Providential for us was that, in 2015, Evo Morales was holding his third installation as president in La Paz. We arranged to meet in the Plaza de San Francisco, where we had originally connected nine years before.

But unlike in 2006, the plaza was strangely empty. Intuitively, we headed up Calle Genaro Sanjines to the presidential palace in Plaza Murillo, and indeed this was the site of the action. But there was little joyous solidarity this time; instead there was frustration at the police line that prohibited citizens from entering the plaza. We situated ourselves at the top of Sanjines and watched waves of people puff and pant up the steep street, encounter the blockage, turn around, and descend. A lone miner in his best for-show hardhat. Here and there an *amauta* (healer) in traditional dress, his magic stick in a tube on his back. Whole branches of bananas and wooden boxes full of tomatoes were heroically lugged up, only to be turned back. There was no connection between people, no music generated from the celebrants; this time the government was in charge. We stood eyeball to eyeball with the police.

Then something out of the ordinary took place. I cannot give details as to how it happened—perhaps as the result of a *curandero*'s magic stick?—but Iván and I were inexplicably swept through the olive barricade *to the other side*. And suddenly we were charged with carrying the Comité Cívica Juvenil de Oruro banner and—a cadre of red-coated military musicians blasting trumpets, trombones, and drums at our backs— we were marching *straight into Plaza Murillo*, where Evo Morales, Álvaro Garcia Linera, various Latin American presidents and Bolivian officials awaited the exhibition of citizen support.

After all the excitement, Iván was pensive for a moment. "You know, I don't usually go in for marching. It's too regimented, too militaristic for me, you can understand given my father's death," he mused. "But this . . . this was special. Evo Morales is the *best* president Bolivia has ever had."

We retired to El Alto where we regaled ourselves with his seventy-three-year-old mother's cooking on the top floor of the COMPA building, gazing out at the majestic glacier Illimani in the distance and a graying horizon of the architectural hodgepodge of the million-resident city of El Alto built largely of materials scrounged in haste.

In his fifties, Iván's passion is to complete the building of an artist community in the tropical Yungas called Pueblo de los Creadores. He has been dogged in his dedication to this, his most ambitious project, since the 1980s. With the help of local building masters, the group has constructed a main house, two work sheds, several compost toilets, and a plaza. The objective, he tells me, is to create "a political reference point" for artists of all stripes and temperaments to employ concepts of decolonization in their work, "a laboratory for alternative methodologies in which art is the central action of the search for community."

He talks about this vision at length and earnestly. But what remains unspoken is a personal dream he admitted to me in the Plaza de San Francisco at Evo Morales's first inauguration. "I want to do a solo performance as Charlie Chaplin's Tramp." He twinkled with delight as he spoke—and this, *mis compañeros,* we await.

JESÚS SEPÚLVEDA:
POETA CONTRA LA DICTADURA
(1967-)

Every morning mom turns the corner
Dad works in the back
The drill and the emery make me nervous
The hair dryer and the lighter
I like to curl up under the blankets as if it were winter
Now father is sick
There is a curfew and helicopters
—J.S., "THE DRUM"

My first encounter with Jesús Sepúlveda took place in the seam between known reality and Another World. In 2004 what looked like a galley version of his anarchist essay, *The Garden of Peculiarities,* appeared in my mailbox, but without a note indicating who sent it or why. Granted, I'm used to getting books in the mail; fellow authors send them as gifts, press agents request that I provide a promotional blurb—but this was neither.

I launched into the text. The thin tome was a superbly penned prose poem addressing the essential qualities of anarchy, biodiversity, cultural diversity, and home-grown community. Up my alley, for sure. Plus, my work—alongside that of friend John Zerzan—was mentioned in an early segment. But something didn't feel right, something was off. My mind began to spin and float, spin and float in a kind of Platonic rendition of vertigo: real vertigo is fully embodied while this "lite" version felt more like its giddy ghost. I looked to the author's bio on the inside flap of the cover. It read fine. He was said to be a Chilean poet who had escaped the country after Pinochet's dictatorship fell. In the United States, it read, he gained his doctorate in literature and was now teaching at the University of Oregon.

But the photo . . . it wasn't a photo at all, it was nothing but a crude pencil sketch. At that moment I felt as unhinged as Alice tumbling down the rabbit hole: I had been "had." Oh yeah, I get it, I thought. This was another of those postmodern tricks wherein a nonexistent author is invented to lampoon accepted ideas or ridicule the academy's rules. This so-called Jesús Sepúlveda, why, he didn't actually *exist!*

A year later, a fully embodied Jesús Sepúlveda pulled up my driveway in a vehicle packed to the gills with knapsacks and food, alongside his U.S. wife Janine Sepúlveda and their two-and-a-half-year-old son Indigo. After John Zerzan convinced me that indeed Jesús was a flesh-and-blood human—and a veritable comrade in our struggle for a world free of domination—Jesús and I became correspondents. And now he was in New Mexico for a visit.

We headed north up the winding Río Grande to Embudo to call on fellow writer Estevan Arellano. Sitting in the living room of Estevan's hand-built adobe, Janine and I became witness to a veritable encounter. As Jesús describes it in a letter to me:

"What impacted me the most was his Spanish, a language that survived through generations in his family—since perhaps the old *conquistadores*—in that remote region of the planet and that he carried with his whole body.... He used expressions that my father used, and he accented words in such a way that were familiar to me—now unused idioms and language archaisms according to the dictionary.

"He mentioned that he had Spanish and Apache ancestors through whom he learned Spanish. Meeting him made me realize he was a truly Hispanic American writer. The only difference between him and me was that he was born on the northern side of the Río Grande. That changed my geography and gave me a new perspective about Latin American writers; that is to say, we sometimes write in a language of old, unsuccessful expeditions trapped in remote places. The survivors of those expeditions lost everything except their language, which between Estevan and me became a sort of secret code that connected us.... Centuries of dreams and struggles were encrusted in that code."

As we took our leave, Estevan scurried to his library and returned to give Jesús a copy of *Palabras de la vista/Retratos de la pluma*, a memoir that, in Jesús's words, "linked his life, the long concrete road (a common metaphor for life?), and poetry."

Jesús's poetic work springs from perception. He believes in the value of experience (as opposed to that of ideology) and claims anarchy as his abiding philosophy in work and life, as well as in politics. Perhaps this tendency was fortified by the time and place of his formative years. He was born to Olga Rosa Salas Valdés and Mario Sepúlveda Garay in a lower-class neighborhood in Santiago. Olga claimed Sephardic, Basque, Spanish, and, it is said, Native Mapuche bloodlines. She worked at the Bacteriological Institute of Chile for twenty years but, with the overthrow of President Salvador Allende's democratic socialist government on September 11, 1973, and the onset of Augusto Pinochet's right-wing, totalitarian regime, was forced out for being a member of the Communist Party–controlled syndicate. She was also a believer in magic and the

Los Bárbaros, Santiago's post-Pinochet poets, 1988. Left to right: Állvaro Leiva in black tee shirt; Jorge Lagos Nilsson behind Leiva; Tomás Harris; Alexis Figueroa; and Jesús Sepúlveda. Courtesy of Jesús Sepúlveda.

supernatural powers of the Catholic saints.

Mario shared her Sephardic and Basque bloodlines. A veteran of the Mambo/Cha-Cha-Cha scene in old Santiago, he crafted musical instruments—congas, bongos, *cajón peruano, bírimbao*—and played violin. One night the police picked him up in the streets after curfew and he was beaten to a pulp; his hips remained mangled until his death.

Perhaps as a way to express pain and carve out a space for what inner peace could be had, Jesús began to write at age twelve. This was in 1979—six long years into Pinochet's regime. He describes this initiation in a 2008 *Crítica* interview with Julián Gutiérrez: "I believe in many cases the propensity to write is born when an external situation suffocates one's ability to express, gagging one from the highest spheres of political power down to the very ambiance of the family. When I was in school, my mother told me that, to avoid political repression, we must not speak of anything that has been said at home. I grew up in an environment that was censured and self-censured, that spoke a truncated Castellano. . . ."

Today Jesús is liberated from censure and fully literate in two languages. He is recognized as one of the Generation of 1987, otherwise known as Los Bárbaros—those who erupted into poetic/artistic expression in the new-born freedom of the end of Pinochet's reign, taking to pen and paintbrush to admit, tell, and heal the vile experience so recently shared by all Chileans; to facilitate its passage out of self-repression and into the safe-keeping of memory. Supported by this cohort of like-minded youth engaged in an outburst of creativity, Jesús launched. Through the years his freedom to use language has been transformed into a torrent of literature. He is the author of, as he puts it, "more books than the ones I have published." Those that have been published include *Hotel Marconi, Escrivania*, and *The Garden of Peculiarities*. The latter has been translated into six languages and—a true literary tribute—boasts pirated versions in Spanish and English. He is coeditor, with Chilean poet Amado Lascar, of the anthology *Rebeldes y terrestres* and has written dozens of essays and articles, as well as served as editor of the magazines *Piel del leopardo* and *Helicóptero*. In 2013 a collection of his selected poems was printed as *Poemas de un bárbaro*. To Gutiérrez, Jesús's writing "expresses the profound sensibility of one who has taken on Existence as a radical search for liberty."

In 2008 Jesús and I came up with a project: a dialogue. (When completed, it was published as "In Service to the Deities: Chellis Glendinning and Jesús Sepúlveda Talk Across Continents," in *Sacred Fire*, No. 9, Summer 2009.) Such an idea sprang from a hope that our conversations could be of interest to people beyond ourselves, particularly because we would be speaking to each other over the divide between South and North America. Plus, I could never be sure what Jesús might say next, and I saw this uncertainty as an advantage for an exploration of a challenge for which no one had answers: how to *BE* in the context of a world spinning out of control from ecological disintegration as well as rampant species extinctions, potential financial collapse, Peak Oil, incessant wars, social chaos, terrorism, and widespread governmental tilts toward fascism. I also sensed that, what with his recent journeys into realms offered up via the Amazonian jungle psychotropic ayahuasca, Jesús might reach beyond how our readers were taught to think.

And indeed he did.

"The emergence of different realities, in the context of the uniform life of mass society, interests me a lot," he began.

"We are defined and controlled by the process of socialization, inscribing in us an identity as well as a sensorial perception of the world, which must be homogenous to all individuals if the modern machine is to

function. Everybody must play a role to be part of the gears. Either you
play this role willingly or the role is imposed. But the consequence is the
same: you become a standardized subject who has to accept the industrial illness that this society produces in your body as well as in your
mind and spirit. Then you have anxiety, rootlessness, depression, anger,
frustration, emptiness—alienation—as a result of the disconnection
from personal experience. And by this I mean, *direct* experience—not
the one filtered through commercial consumption.

"But against this one-dimensional aspect of reality emerges the perception of multidimensional realities embedded in indigenous culture,"
he continued. "It has to do with life here and now on the Earth and under
the cosmos. This multiversal dimension, which is inhabited by spirits
and other invisible forms, is generally part of the daily reality of
non-modern peoples. The extrapolation of this sense into modern life
is a political act. But it is also, as you know, a way toward healing. And
shamanic practices can be crucial if an individual wants to cross the
threshold of modern life into a more natural, direct, and sensual experience. . . . Experience is magical always."

One matter we validated through the conversation was Frantz Fanon's
notion that people in colonized cultures experience the trauma of political domination in their shared public world. They therefore largely hold
that tyranny in the conscious mind; they know it is happening. On the
other hand, trauma perpetrated within the empire is typically accomplished in secret, often within the family—father beating up son, uncle
violating niece—and that experience becomes holed up in reticent,
unconscious fragments. Both Jesús and I are survivors of trauma just as
Fanon described: he of political violence, I of brutality within the family.

He spoke of his experience. "I remember my hands sweating when
crossing any checkpoint or even airport controls," he said. "Trauma is a
kind of paranoia that accompanies you for a long time. . . . I still break
down whenever I read news about the disappeared in Chile. . . . [Today]
I see trauma in the faces of people whenever I walk in the neighborhood
where my parents lived."

Of his friend Chilean writer, journalist, and publisher Jorje Lagos
Nilsson, Jesús reports that he "escaped [the military] by jumping over

the wall of the Mexican embassy, while his wife and daughters made it to Mexico days later not knowing if he was alive or not. Meanwhile, his nephews and niece—who were children at the time—were walking around the city with no direction or home, until someone took them to the Australian and Swedish embassies. They grew up in exile trying to make contact with their uncle. Their mother, Gloria Esther Lagos Nilsson, disappeared months after the coup in torture center Villa Grimaldi. She was three-months pregnant.

"Families, couples, neighborhoods, entire countries are traumatized by the political machine. As Chilean poet Juan Luis Martinez said: 'The nation-state is the only one that is allowed to sacrifice its children in the name of the political father.' And this is also true for the 'Fourth World'—as Ward Churchill puts it—in the sense that indigenous peoples were sacrificed in the name of 'progress' and 'civilization.'"

At the conclusion of our conversation, I propose that our task at this fragile moment is to "ride the bucking bronco of the ancient prophesies" and, always, to nurture our connection to Creation. Jesús concludes with the vision that, to be fully human, we must all become like shamans. "We all have shamanic capacities to connect with nature," he offers. "We can all heal ourselves, and by doing this, we heal others." "The shaman can hear the message of the planet," he goes on. "That is the main difference between the sick modern existence and the magical Shamanic life. The shaman can heal with plants because s/he hears what the plants have to say. The shaman knows when it is time to close the loop because he lives in cycles instead of being patterned by the dead-line of 'progress.' The shaman perceives the direction of the wind, the energy that trees have, the moon cycles, the health of the soil, the language of animals, the aperture of dimensional portals—or electromagnetic fields. The shaman is in contact with the world of presences and apparitions who function as allies in the process of unveiling the illusions of the modern world." To Jesús the illusion of the modern world leads him to seek the authenticity of other realities—filling him with the courage to heal, to write, to teach, to raise his son, to journey into other realms and, like the shaman, bring back the wisdom that is revealed there.

RAÚL: HOW TO CROSS THE BORDER
(1973-)

I came to the U.S. because in my ejido *in Chihuahua,*
there isn't enough money to buy toilet paper.
—R., ANSWER TO DINÉ/NAVAJO ETHNOBOTANIST DONNA
HOUSE'S 2004 QUESTION "WHY DID YOU RISK EVERYTHING
TO COME TO THE U.S.?"

Raúl has forged the border between Mexico and the U.S. so many times
he has the passage down to a craft. "They chase us down in the desert,"
he told me. "They put up twenty-five-foot walls, they add airplanes that
fly without pilots, they make fences that sting like bees—but we always
find a way to get through." He and his band of *indocumentados* in our
village in northern New Mexico were always regaling me with their experiences, ideas, and opinions. They had pioneered the journey north in
tight groups and, upon arrival, called their cousins back at the *ejido* so
they too could launch using the same, now-proven routes.

Raúl first arrived in Chimayó in 2002, and in the eight years I was
around him, I learned that his breaking point came like clockwork at a year
and a half. After that, he would feel like bursting if he could not hug his
wife Gabriela, his sons Raulito and Bryan, and his parents. And so he would
head south for a few months—only to be challenged once again to retake
the walls, hide from the drones, and slither under the electric-shock fences.

His choice story about the journey centered on the twenty-five-foot concrete wall that separated the U.S. from Mexico. Dauntless as always, one
man hopped onto the shoulders of another, a third onto his back, a fourth
onto his, etc.—until the last man reached the summit of the wall. Then, to
bring up those at the lower levels, they repeated the action in reverse:
instead of scaling the body of a compañero, he who had reached the upper
rim pulled the highest man up using a "rope" made of a sweatshirt, then
with two sweatshirts tied together the next-to-highest—until finally, using
every shirt they had, the man at the bottom. Another time, one dark night
under a crescent moon, he jumped a freight train traveling from Tucson,

Opening a bank account, New Mexico, 2007.
Photo credit and courtesy of Chellis Glendinning.

Arizona, into New Mexico—riding the whole way clinging to iron girders underneath a car, enduring the thunder of the engine and screeching of wheels, with grease splattering his body until he turned black.

Raúl is an intellect with a philosophical bent. He delights me with his original insight that existence inside the human body is one intense proposition. Springing from the near-absolute power his government has wielded during the whole of his thirty years, plus the poverty he knows by heart, his philosophy is Buddhist without ever having heard of Buddha: he believes that suffering reigns in this life and we have to make the best of it by transcending the pain and living a life of meaning. His meaning, as he explained to me, is to fulfill his role as a man; his greatest desire is that his sons grow up to be *trabajadores* like him. Once, as he was packing a van he had bought to resell in Chihuahua, we decided that, to stay connected no matter which side of the border each of us was on, we would look to the full moon—and feel the presence of the other in its silver reflection.

The work that Raúl and his compañero Jorge found was indeed a job, as stipulates immigration requirements for working legally, that not one citizen of the United States wanted to do: they worked at a septic-tank service, sometimes upwards of seventy hours a week. On Sunday they would trundle to the laundromat in Española and sit on the plastic chairs while the machines clunked and spun. Then to the Shop'n Save to buy enough tortillas, tomatoes, hamburger meat, and chiles to last the week. And finally back to the trailer to watch telenovelas.

The high point of their week also took place on Sunday: to use my telephone to call home. I papered an entire desk with their used *tarjetas prepagadas* boasting depictions of Mexican women in off-the-shoulder blouses, San Juan Diego at his magical moment, and Superman looking like a Mexican wrestler in purple tights. Once Jorge was talking loudly on the phone in the office, as was his wont, and I overheard his description of El Día de los Muertos we had attended the night before at the Museo Cultural de Santa Fe. Let's get one thing straight: el Museo is not in any way a fancy museum boasting managed temperature, camera surveillance, and sealed cases; it's a down-home warehouse that lies on the razor's edge of paying the rent—and is run by northern New Mexico Latinos with a beautiful vision. Nonetheless, from my office telephone came Jorge's booming voice: "You're not going to believe this," he squealed with pride. "I went to a . . . a *MUSEUM!*"

While Jorge was dialing up Sinaloa, Raúl and I sat in the living room browsing a book of Augustín Casasola's photos of the Mexican Revolution. Here were his *paisanos*, even his ancestors—and yet these images of federal troops in pointy felt sombreros, women boasting *bandoleras* strung across their breasts, and Zapatista soldiers entrenched in cornfields were new to him. Irony of ironies, they were well-known to me. Yes, many experiences I regarded as normal, even ho-hum, were startlingly novel to Raúl, and so I became witness to a plethora of his "firsts." Like the first time he drove on a freeway. His first taste of tofu. His first glimpse of a computer screen. His first trip to Wal-Mart . . . Jazz, however, did not present a bona fide first. Upon popping a Miles Davis CD into the stereo, I asked Raúl and Jorge if they had ever heard such sounds. I was looking forward to regaling them with the origins and history of a truly "American" music. Raúl listened for a spell, looked to Jorge in a moment of mutual recognition, and then responded, "Oh yes, yes. Of course. We know this music! It's the music from the limousine between Phoenix and Albuquerque."

Raúl plots breathlessly. "I'm gonna get a really big truck with double tires and a major CD player." "I'll haul fish from Sinaloa to restaurants in Chihuahua." "I'm ready to bring Gabriela and the *niños* over and we can live together in a little adobe with a corn field and a rose bush and the boys can go to Chimayó Elementary and learn English and become proud *trabajadores* like me." On his paltry salary and given the fact that he AFEXes ninety percent of it in a southward direction, I can't see the truck happening soon. Or the fish business. But I can see a family reunion. Others have pulled it off, and given the general lack of toilet paper on the *ejido*, it's a viable answer to the dead-of- night misery Raúl feels in the trailer with the other guys and the telenovelas reminding them of home. I can also see the potential tragedy. Bristling with Nike knockoffs and *American Idol*—with the suffering of their father in full view—the new generation grows up to leave the older in the dust. The thought of Raúl hurting because his sons dis their father's life's meaning claws at my chest like an eagle's talon.

I send out a plea to friends and friends of friends via the internet. It's 2003 and one never knows what will fly anymore, but while the U.S. psyche is digesting the dizzying disempowerment flung upon the land by George W. Bush's pronouncements proposing the futility of activism, the economic slam of corporate globalization, and September 11's shockwaves, the prospect of helping *one family* appeals: the bucks roll in.

And so Gabriela and the boys take a bus to Nogales. They ferret out a *coyote*. They set off across the blistering sands. Raulito has taken on the job of being son-husband-father. He puts on a brave face, but Little Bryan is four and has diarrhea. They sweat. They trudge. The *migra* (border patrol) appears from behind a saguaro like a mirage and marches them back to the border. They sweat and trudge again. The *migra* catches them again. Bryan's pants are soiled with crap, and he's bawling like a lost cat. There's no place for them to stay in Nogales except under a bush. Gabriela hears about the rapes. They give up, take a bus home, and spend the money on a doctor.

To divert his attention from the disappointment, I take Raúl to his second museum: the Museum of International Folk Art in Santa Fe. The exhibition consists of artsy photos of Mexican buses decorated with tricolor banners, plastic statuettes of Nuestra Señora de Guadalupe, and gold tassels reminiscent of shrines, and on the way home I foolishly ask if he's ever been to a museum in his homeland. He puffs up and proclaims, "Yes, *of course*." I ask what they were exhibiting. The silence that ensues goes on a tad too long. No, way too long.

Then, like a kernel of corn popping into the air, he blurts out his answer: "Photos of Mexican buses!"

After Raúl honored me by asking me to be *madrina* (godmother) to his sons, he came to visit with regularity. It was during these quiet times together that I learned about his early life. He grew up on the *ejido* San Lorenzo Viejo near Ahome, Sinaloa; it had been established after the revolution as a way to "give back" land to the people. One downside of such redistribution was that formerly indigenous peoples were randomly stirred in with others and eventually lost knowledge of their particular cultural roots. When we had gone to the Museo Cultural, Raúl and Jorge had spent an inordinate amount of time in front of a map showing the pre-revolution outlay of Mexico's indigenous cultures, explaining to me that they truly did not know who they were. "Maybe this group, maybe that one" was about as clear as they could get.

His parents are Alvino and Guadalupe; his father, he proudly related, is ten years older than his mother. At his dirt-floored school he learned both modern skills like reading and writing, as well as ancient skills like planting seeds with a stick. He danced the traditional steps through the streets of his pueblo and, upon seeing a young woman ten years his younger at a cantina, he knew immediately that she was the one he would marry.

His first job, at age twelve, was selling oranges from the tailgate of a pickup truck. This was a worthy exchange for having to give up school, he explained, as he got to ride in the back of the truck, eat as much citrus as he could devour, and get to know all the pueblos around Sinaloa. Next he assembled seat belts in a *maquila* at the border and weeded industrial watermelon patches—and, indeed, married the woman he had seen in the cantina.

Now he puts in sixty or seventy hours a week scouring porta potties. And now, due to the devaluation of the peso and the North American Free Trade Agreement that has supplanted Mexico's communal corn-fields to make way for Fritos's hegemony, he is part of history: one of

somewhere between twelve and twenty million undocumented immigrant workers in the U.S. in the early 2000s. As such, he wears his thin-
ning ponytail under a series of baseball hats festooned with words he
can't read. NYPD. MOUNTAIN DEW. GET A GRIP. Soon after I meet
him, he announces in perfect Castilian that he will never, *ever* deign to
speak English.

Except for one word he has learned on the job: *whatever*.

Perhaps it is this word that best sums up Raúl's philosophy. After all,
he has forged hundreds of miles in thin huaraches through 100-degree
saguaro desert, bedded down with cockroaches and feces, been deported,
trudged hundreds more miles in thinner huaraches, been kidnapped by
pirates, held for ransom on one hard-boiled egg a day, and pressed into
slavery to pay back the *coyote*.

On one unbearably hot August afternoon in Chimayó, I figure it's good
for such a hero to go over to the waterfall in a bathing suit. You can wade
in, stand inches from the river crashing down, inhale a great big breath
for courage, and spring through to the other side. There lies a pocket of
air just big enough for one person—and once in its sanctuary you can cop
a feel of God's glory.

But on this day the river is but a trickle.

Raúl and I plop into a shallow pool and, border policy never far from
mind, set out to build a symbolic bridge. A miniature rendition of the
Santa Fe Bridge linking Juarez to El Paso, it will be. We each know the
exact place in the middle where the brass cap marks the boundary—Raúl
from a recent enforced journey to the other side of that cap (read: depor-
tation), I from staying in a $14/night motel in El Paso (the kind where
the cashier sits on the other side of iron bars) and walking across the
bridge so I could see what was so important to Raúl's life.

He will build the Mexican side; I, the U.S. The distance between us is
a foot and a half. Raúl gets right to work gathering pebbles, twigs, soil,
and leaves. I put a branch in place, but I can see right off that I don't know
what I'm doing. He lays the tiny rocks as a foundation, covers this with
leaves and dirt, extends sticks toward the U.S. side. I try to imitate.

"Raúl." The laziness of the river tilts me toward the deeper side of things.
"What's it like being here?" It's not as if I haven't been party to the buying

of cars without license plates, the telenovelas at the end of the day, the September *gritos de libertad*, and New Year's midnight handshakes.

But I mean something else.

He's placing twigs between the long sticks like *latias* between *vigas*. "I miss my children and wife and my parents and brothers and sisters and cousins," he muses." I miss the *quinceñeras* and the dances at the *ejido*. Over there I know exactly what to do, when to do it, and how." He drips wet sand and pebbles over the sticks to make pavement. *"Pero . . ."*

"Yeah? What?" I ask.

"Pero . . . I'm a different person here. I go shopping for myself. At Club Lumina I can dance with anyone. I do what I want, when I want, how I want."

"Freedom?"

"Sí, sí... freedom."

It's an odd toss-up: the bonds of family and culture on the side of tradition; the one rootless person on the side of global capitalism's benefits. I want to protest, to insist that tradition and culture are superior, but I myself am a raging sample of what he has now tasted. Until I was named *madrina* to his children and given entrance into the formal world of Mexican social relations, Raúl and his compañeros didn't know what to do with me. I, a woman, owned a car. I showed up when I felt like it. I paid for myself. I could drive to El Paso and stay in a motel just to see what it was like.

"How is it for you to have me here?" he asks.

"I admire your courage."

Once, after his cousin finished a day laying adobes at the upscale Las Campanas condo-golf-club and returned to regale us with tales of pet dogs boasting their very own indoor bathrooms and horses whose hooves are toasted by sub-floor radiant heat, I asked Raúl how he deals with the discrimination and inequality. "I know why I'm here," he stated with pride. "I know what I must do. Thanks be to God, I know who I am."

By now, the Mexican side of our bridge reaches halfway across. The U.S. construct is a tad rickety, but I pat a last finger of sand on to solidify where the two sides meet in the middle. And together we cop a feel of one and a half feet of God's glory.

In 2009 the time arrives for me to tell Raúl that I myself will soon be an immigrant—in Bolivia. ¡*Ay, mi compadre!* Poor soul, he harbors the constant possibility of upheaval. A policeman's glance in the direction of a nonexistent license plate. An immigration raid. An accident. He's not expecting *this* upheaval. But there it is for all to see: I'm packing my books into boxes. Selling futons and bookcases. Clearly, *something* is going on.

Tears pool, then spill over like the Chimayó waterfall on a big-river day . . . but *NO!* Raúl has a better plan. I can move to his house on the *ejido* in Chihuahua! Live with Gabriela and Raulito and Bryan in two-room splendor with a boom box that holds fifty-two CDs at once! He would build me my *own* room! Not with a dirt floor, but a *concrete* floor! And, *Dios Mío*, I'm a woman of a grandmotherly age: *I won't have to work!*

In the face of such generosity my head begins to whirl like a drunken dervish on a *migra* drone flight over the *frontera*. I can't imagine that anyone I know in the U.S. would ever offer the same. No, in this North American country, a single woman is on her own. But with Raúl—to him—I'm family. I gasp for breath. What can I say? I thank him. "Wow . . . This is unbelievable . . . We don't know what will happen . . . Maybe . . . Can we wait and see? . . . I'm aiming for Bolivia, but who knows?"

Raúl's teeth glisten like the bubbles on the surface of a freshly poured Corona. "*Sí, sí,* Che," he chirps. "We will wait and see." And then, brandishing the kingpin of his grasp of the English language, he says it: "Whaat-é*fff*-er."

ANITA RODRIGUEZ: PAINT AND MYLAR
(1941–)

If you contact death on a daily basis, that dialogue will give you great personal power.
—A.R., SPEECH AT THE "CREATIVITY AND MADNESS"
CONFERENCE, SANTA FE, NEW MEXICO, 2009

It was El Día de los Muertos in Guanajuato, Mexico, and Anita Rodriguez put on her seven-foot-tall Spirit attire just as the traditional festival honoring those who had passed to the other side was in full swing. Out in the streets mariachi bands filled the night air with piercing moans and yearning strums; clusters of solemn celebrants crowded kiosks to purchase the sugar-skull figurines known as *piestos*. Anita's get-up was different from anything else in the cemetery. Imposing with its Mylar fringes, white ribbons, macramé, and metal roofing discs, it made her look like a *fantasma* with roots in Moorish, Spanish, and Mexican soils.

The first time I encountered this mestiza was at an art happening at her hand-crafted home on the *llano* right before you get to Taos, New Mexico. Just to walk through the vestibule was a passage through Middle Eastern–influenced symbols and goddesses whose presence unraveled the everyday mind. Once inside, a magical cocoon revealed straw-inflected adobe walls festooned with paintings in the flash-vivid colors of Mexico of skeletons in all manner of activity, from cooking and cruising in lowrider cars to having sex. Aforementioned Spirit costume accented the merrymaking from the living-room ceiling like a supernatural being, adding to the tone of otherworldliness. And exuding from the kitchen, aromas of lamb slathered in chile and home-baked bread textured the flavor of this woman's creativity. By the time she read her short story to the admiring crowd of friends and family—a journey into the normal, abnormal, and paranormal—I was stupefied.

Other meetings followed. She drove down from the Taos mesa to a literary gathering I was hosting in Chimayó. All the other writers shared a poem or a story, but her presentation was a theatrical enactment of the *Envidia*/Jealousy Problem so persistent in the Latino community of northern New Mexico, where the advance of any individual is viewed as suspect. Her character was an aging *vecino*—cranky, jealous, and resentful of his neighbor who had somehow secured something that no one else in the pueblo could possibly get their hands on: black paper to be nailed to the inside walls of the hen house.

Another time Anita insisted that my life-size (stuffed animal) gorilla companion Roosevelt should visit her for a week. Since Roose's raison d'être is to bring joy to anyone and everyone within her presence, I agreed. What resulted was a madcap fest of photographs shot in emblematic locations on the mesa. Here, in one photo, she is munching on bananas atop the fruit display at the Shop'n Save. There, our simian friend is looking expectant with napkin draped over her chest, before a table of Talavera plates, blue-glass goblets—and Anita's finest cooking. My favorite is the shot of a Taos policeman pulling her over for a traffic infraction.

Yet another time Anita and I sat together on the veranda of a Mexican restaurant smack on the main highway into Taos—cars and trucks whizzing by like shooting stars—and she regaled me with sad tales of how these new, "not-from-here" commercial outlets had contaminated the core of what Taos had once been. And, by contrast, what the town had been like when she was growing up in the 1940s and '50s.

Anita Rodriguez was born in 1941 to Alfredo Antonio Rodriguez and Grace Graham King. His heritage harked back ten generations on the Taos mesa. He ran the drugstore in the plaza, and as Anita comically describes, he was "a terrible photographer" who on weekends took the family out in his '39 Studebaker to document the outhouses of New Mexico. Grace was a serious Anglo artist from Texas who passed her fascination with European art and literature on to Anita.

Her childhood, then, was infused with many cultures: Hispanic folk and religious art, Mexican mysticism, the rebel styles of the realists at the original Taos Art Colony, Native American ceremonialism, traditional *curanderos,* and the living presence of Taos painters like Mabel Dodge Lujan and Andrew Dasburg—all together marking her young psyche with a confluence of perspectives that streamed into everyday existence like a wild river. At the same time, her childhood was a thorny terrain for the chaos and violence she could not escape. Not only did her parents regularly explode into conflict over cultural and class differences; they drank.

The combination presented Anita with a classic psychological blueprint. She was all too well acquainted with the terror and inner shattering that brutality can provoke, yet instead of freezing her development, she became propelled by a striving against all odds to *become.* Her story is the tale of a psyche courageously combining what it senses to be supportive, such as traditional knowledge and personal creativity, with raw awareness of the ugliness to which humans can devolve. And, as with so

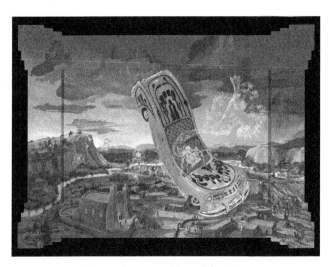

"Love, Lace, and Lowriders."
Artist, photo credit, and courtesy of Anita Rodriguez.

many survivors of childhood ordeals, she possesses the knack for passage into shamanic realms.

The upshot is an art visited by supernatural forces. Her painting— on canvases, in wooden *nichos*, on paper—gives glimpse of a surreal landscape injected with magical realism, Jungian symbolism, Mexican mysticism (with a tip of the sombrero to illustrator/printmaker José Guadalupe Posadas), and northern New Mexico humor. As she wrote in a 2010 speech delivered in both Santa Fe and Taos: "I learned at an early age that parallel worlds coexist wherever people speak different languages and believe in different ways of life. The crypto-Jew paintings especially play with this concept—many of them are painted in *nicho* form [niches with doors that open and close, derived from Mexican folk art], inviting the viewer to step into the reality of another world. The physical act of opening the doors commits the viewer to participate in the story. . . . When one becomes expert in crossing boundaries, psychic boundaries are a snap. In my 'artist mode' I can cross over into a world where the saints are alive . . . [and] there are the dancers—perhaps it is the archetypal dancer, or the dance of the cosmos, the dance of atomic particles, the sensation of dancing."

In August of 1996, about the time when Norteños begin to comment (way too early) that summer is almost over, I met up with Anita on her patio. We sipped *cota* tea and spoke of dreams, Jungian psychology, the Tarot . . . and her decision to move to Mexico. Yes, the woman was going to rent out her adobe studio; pack up her hermaphrodite street dog Orlando and all her paint tubes, brushes, and easels; even her Mylar Spirit getup—and she was going to head south to the land of her ancestors. No amount of recitation of my grief at the loss could dissuade her.

In Guanajuato she rented an apartment with light streaming in through its tall windows, and large enough to provide both living quarters and studio. She set out to paint. Previously she had showed at Santa Fe's prestigious Spanish Market, the Mexican Fine Arts Center in Chicago, the Mizel Family Cultural Arts Center of Denver, and other northern locales, and now she was landing one-woman shows and places in group exhibitions in galleries and museums across Mexico—at Casa de la Cultura in Quintana Roo, Casa de Redonda in Ciudad Chihuahua, and in Guanajuato at the distinguished Alhondigas. The Gene Byron Museum in that city, where she had a one-woman exhibition, acknowledged her as a genuine *"pintora guanajuatense."*

And yet, despite her success, she was besieged by financial worries. With characteristic big-view perspective, she wrote me: "I am but a drop in a wave of desperate people, masses without a place to fall dead, facing the inevitable tightening of the noose by the police state, all the money sucked into the killing machine, on a planet in ecological crisis—LET ME OFF!" And, with her need to understand the human condition speckled with her typical wry humor: "I found a website by Human Rights that translates the news into whatever language from all over the world! Shocking to read newspapers with content translated from Arabic. If I am going to be hit by a train, at least I want to know its make, model, velocity, and the name of the engineer. Let the rest of the people never know what hit them."

Mexico was changing. Its importance as both narcotic producer and conduit state between Colombia and the United States brought in (as well as induced) drug cartels, drug production, and drug addiction. Cocaine, mainly—but heroin too, an originally homegrown industry dating back to the arrival of Chinese migrants in Sinaloa in the 1880s. Suddenly the barrios where streets were once burgeoning with families until late at night turned into deserted tracts. It became dangerous to be an *extranjera* for fear of kidnapping and extortion, and the letters changed in tone from delighted to fearful. "I don't know a Mexican whose family has not been impacted by the violence," she wrote. "Every day rumors of some new atrocity sweep the neighborhood, and whether true or not, they serve to thicken the paranoia we swim in like fish in water." In 2010 Anita packed up her easel and paints and, hiring a man to protect her along the long drive from the south of Mexico north to the border, made the trek back to Taos.

On the mesa she lives in the house she built. Aside from painting, her talent as a writer has reemerged. She authored and illustrated *Coyota in the Kitchen: A Memoir of New and Old Mexico, with Recipes.* Published by University of New Mexico Press, it weaves fantastic myths and true tales from childhood with instructions for how to prepare *chicos* in an adobe *horno, cáribe,* and other New/Mexican favorites. In her mid-seventies she tells of running into old friends in the Shop'n Save, only to listen to lengthy recitations of their health woes. But, Anita . . . well, whether her bones creak or not, she remains an exceptional voice of her generation—ever alive, wildly creative, and undeniably out of this world.

SAUL LANDAU: ONE SHOT
(1936–2013)

*I came out of Madison (University of Wisconsin) with a
passion for social justice and the idea that you only get
one shot at participating in the history of the world.*
—S.L. AS QUOTED IN *CAPITAL TIMES*, MADISON, 2006

Saul Landau lived at the border between life and death: due to his unrelenting political stands, he endured threats to his existence as if they were the morning delivery of the newspaper. At some 15,000 documents, his FBI files constitute a stack worthy of measurement, albeit not by a mere wooden ruler, but the copies available to the public are so disjointed by black marks deleting phrases and paragraphs—read:

classified material not available to the citizen eye—there is practically *nothing left to read*!

I first laid eyes upon Saul in San Francisco where he was speaking on a panel about the Third World Debt Crisis. It was the mid-1980s, and the Institute for Policy Studies in Washington, D.C., was spreading the facts regarding the global financial disaster perpetrated by the International Monetary Fund/World Bank's neoliberal structural-adjustment (read: austerity) "loans." These were given only if the recipient country would abide by certain conditions—that it would privatize all public industries, including telecommunications, water, and gas; deregulate control of exports/imports to favor foreign multinational corporations, engage in massive construction projects that only big-time foreign transnationals had the expertise to build and maintain, impose blatant raids on local resources like minerals and metals, water, and forests; inflict social asceticism through slashes to health, social services, and education; and enforce high interest gouges with resultant skyrocketing inflation. As the panel members spoke, it became obvious that the disappearances, massacres, and dictatorships ravaging Latin America at the time were a direct consequence of such sadistic means to push neoliberal capitalism, make the rich richer, and boost their self-serving global economy. My mind was reeling like a whirling carnival ride. I knew little of the background to the horrors being perpetrated in Uruguay, Chile, Argentina, etc.—and, like the day I emerged from the movie theater showing *The China Syndrome* an anti-nuclear activist, I felt as motivated as a mother cow in a pen ready to charge.

At the same time I felt charged by the lucidity of this speaker with the broad smile and short black hair just launching its retreat from a freckled forehead. He was as bushy-tailed as the stickball-playing eight-year-old he once had been. I don't recall how I came upon the phone number of the place where he was staying in San Francisco—it was clearly one of those six-degree connections—but I called to tell him I knew a TV producer in Los Angeles whose raison d'être was getting political issues before the small-screen-viewing public. Amazingly, he remembered me from the audience and, after chatting for some minutes, asked me to lunch. His time crunch eclipsed that plan, but we began to exchange letters across the continent, needless to say sharing political perspectives and our writings, but also our deepest feelings about being alive. In one letter I told him that my mother was dying, and I was in an airplane on my way to Cleveland. He wrote back that the grieving never stops; it wells up at the most unexpected moments . . . again and again and again.

I am besieged by that same inundation of grief right now. After suffering from cancer, Saul passed on in September 2013—and the sorrow, like a stone weighing down my heart, engulfs me again and again and again.

Saul grew up a few blocks from Yankee Stadium in the Bronx among Central and Eastern European Jews, Puerto Ricans, Russians, Blacks, and Irish. His mother, Sadie "Sue" Frishkoff, was a teacher; his father, Leon Landau, a pharmacist who had escaped pogroms in the Ukraine. While working as a fry cook in the Catskills the summer after his high-school graduation, he met the teen-aged Bohemian Nina Serrano, and they began a life together that would lead to a twenty-year marriage, much political action, and jointly produced films, plus two children and a host of grandchildren and great-grandchildren—all of whom followed in their parents' footsteps as fighters for a just world. He later married Rebecca Switzer, who collaborated with him on projects and bore three more children devoted to social justice.

In describing the adult who came out of this promising launch, one might gravitate toward a phrase like "Renaissance Man." In an obituary written for *Counterpunch*, his long-time comrade University of New Mexico professor emeritus Nelson Valdez found a way to articulate the complexity of the task: Saul was a "universal man," Valdez proposed. He authored fourteen books, produced and directed some fifty documentary films, and wrote hundreds of essays and investigative articles in magazines and journals. His books covered such topics as the injustices caused by U.S. interventionism, guerrilla war in Central America, and the Pinochet-backed murders of Chilean ambassador Orlando Letelier and colleague Ronni Moffitt. That book, *Assassination on Embassy Row,* written with John Dinges, won the Edgar Allan Poe Award.

Saul is perhaps best known for his work regarding the politics and social issues of Castro's Cuba. Cuba became a passion for Saul the year after the revolution when he read a report in the socialist

Saul with Fidel Castro in Havana, 1989. From www.SaulLandau.com.
Courtesy of Greg Landau and Valerie Landau.

magazine *Monthly Review* by Leo Huberman and Paul Sweezy. Ever
curious, he hitchhiked through the island so that he could see what a
revolution looks like. U.S. Federal Bureau of Investigation tracking
of Saul's actions had actually begun while he was a student at the
University of Wisconsin, but now its frequency and intensity were
stepped up. Still, he didn't miss a beat. A second tour of Cuba took
place along with friend/collaborator sociologist C. Wright Mills.
Then, while working as a reporter at KQED-TV in San Francisco, he
went a third time to make a news documentary. Castro was impressed
by its positive slant and invited him back to the make another film,
which became *Fidel*. A hasty chronicle shot in 16mm with a handheld
camera, it documented an in-depth interview and a weeklong Jeep
trip Castro took through the countryside. Outraged by the potential
of its impact, anti-Castro exiles attempted to prevent its screening—
bombing New York's Fifth Avenue Cinema and burning the Haymar-
ket Theater in Los Angeles to the ground. The death threats intensi-
fied, but Saul was pleased: he was gaining what became a lifelong
friendship with Fidel Castro, as well as access to the inner workings
of a Communist government. He produced five more films about the
island nation, even as Castro's political choices were not always 100
percent to his liking.

Another impactful film that he produced/directed was the 1971 *Brazil:
A Report on Torture* about the atrocities committed against civilians who

opposed the dictatorship. Perhaps his most popular film was *Paul Jacobs and the Nuclear Gang*—codirected with journalist Jack Willis, with camera work by cinematographer Haskell Wexler—about barefaced governmental suppression of the health dangers of the radiation flung across the country from the Nevada Test Site. Jacobs had worked with Saul on various projects, including the books *To Serve the Devil* and *The New Radicals*; just as the filming was completed, Jacobs died of cancer he suspected was from exposure to radiation. The film won an Emmy Award, the Hefner First Amendment Award for journalism, the Mannheim Film Festival Film Critics Prize, and the George Polk Award for investigative journalism on TV.

Saul had begun his organizing work by joining a University of Wisconsin group advocating the recall of Senator Joe McCarthy, went on to participate in the launch of the leftist magazines *Studies in the Left, Ramparts,* and *Mother Jones,* and became a fellow at the Institute for Policy Studies, plus both senior fellow and director at IPS's Transnational Institute in Amsterdam. Cuba's longtime ambassador to the United Nations, Ricardo Alarcón, said of Saul as he was awarding him the Medal of Friendship in 2013: he is "a real combatant with no other weapons than his talent and intellectual integrity."

And: humility. I'm talking about the kind that springs from genuine inquisitiveness. Our original lunch long since having vanished into the realm of non-happenings, we decided to share a dinner during one of his following trips to San Francisco. We met at a restaurant in North Beach. The darkness, highlighted by pervasive cigar smoke and mahogany-wood paneling, was illuminated by white-linen tablecloths, the clinking of glasses, and the exuberance of conversations. The place was the hangout of movers and shakers in San Francisco's business and government circles, and so our exchange fit in. Well, *somewhat*—as we were focused less on specific urban matters and power juggling than on the global overview. Amid all the topics two people can cover in a few hours, it's curious what remains in memory. I don't recall if we drank wine or not, what we ordered for dinner, or if we even spoke about our personal lives. I do remember that he jokingly told me about his monstrous FBI file with all the juicy parts deleted. Deep into the anti-nuclear movement, I talked about my work involving the impacts of the arms race on the human psyche and psychologically informed methods for helping citizens break through what psychiatrist Robert Jay Lifton had termed "psychic numbing." He went on to insist that the world had *not* been made safe because of nuclear weapons, which had been touted in the 1950s as a menace horrific enough to squelch all armed conflict; more wars, he said, had been waged in the previous four decades than in any equivalent stretch of time in history.

But what I remember best was Saul himself—not just his intelligence and dedication, but rather his caring for the well-being of people. He seemed the spot-on expression of the infamous statement by Che Guevara: *"Al riesgo de parecer ridículo, dejeme decirle que el verdardero revolucionario está guido por gran sentimientos de amor."* (At risk of appearing ridiculous, allow me to venture that the true revolutionary is guided by great feelings of love.)

He had clearly fulfilled his "one shot at participating in the history of the world."

Nelson Valdez has commented that Saul had thousands of friends. I don't doubt it—and I count myself as fortunate to have been one among those numbers. But as it became clear that his passing was nigh, the multitude had to be narrowed down. During the last weeks, those who sat at his bedside included his most beloved: his five children who took on the daily tasks of caregiving, Rebecca, Nina, his sister Beryl Landau and her family, plus his grandchildren and great-grandchildren.

Hasta la victoria siempre.

JOHN ROSS: HUMAN SHIELD
(1938-2011)

I came here [to Iraq] just to be bombed!
Bush already has a bomb with my name written on it.
—J.R., CLAIM TO HIS NGO HOST WHILE BEING OUSTED AS A
HUMAN SHIELD, DAURA OIL REFINERY, IRAQ, 2003

John Ross was bigger in spirit than a human body could contain. He was a "red diaper baby," a Beat poet whose stronghold had been the cafés and cantinas of The Village, an uncountable-cups-a-day espresso freak, and a nonstop news-breaking, award-winning *periodista* informing the world about Mexican politics. Tom Hayden once told me that John was his favorite journalist—most likely for his razor-sharp reportage combined with witty double entendres and down-home phrases like "a rat's ass." The man had almost no teeth left after being beaten up for some political stand he had taken—and when I say "stand" I mean literally placing his bipedal body in the way of injustice. He was half blind, having lost one eye after being hammered for another political stand. He had a bad back and walked with a limp for having been clobbered for another couple of political stands. He was loud and sure of himself; he was a man of irony, outrage, and courage.

I say "was" because John was beaten up once and for all by liver cancer in 2011. All medical intervention that could be done had been done, and he asked to leave his rooms at the Isabel Hotel in Mexico City's Federal District and be shepherded to the Michoacán village where he had raised a family and lived on and off for fifty years. It wasn't that we hadn't had sufficient notice of the possibility of death, yet when I received the news, I sat in my chair for some time, as stunned as a baby bird slamming into a glass window.

I was overcome with the feeling that I could not imagine—nor *accept*—a world without John Ross.

John was born on March 11, 1938, and raised in an apartment in New York City. His parents were Hollywood show-biz Commies, and before the age of sixteen he had sold a joint to Dizzie Gillespie, babysat for Billie Holiday's dog, and gotten loaded at his mother's dinner parties with veterans of the Abraham Lincoln Brigade. From the moment of consciousness, just about every move he made was defined by politics and poetry.

He first went to Mexico in 1961, where he and his lover Norma Melbourne landed in a village in Michoacán and built a casita. He also hung out in the Mission District, which was the heart of the Latin community in San Francisco. He had torn up his draft card during the U.S. invasion of Lebanon in the 1950s, and he resisted the draft during the Vietnam years, for which he spent seven months at Terminal Island Penitentiary. Here he wrote his first tome, a pamphlet answering a crucial question for those incarcerated. It was called *What to Do in Jail*.

The truth is that John didn't really find his vocation until 1984 when he was fifty-six years old. He became a Spanglish-speaking news correspondent with a focus on Mexico, and Pacific News Service sent him south to report. The job was a perfect fit. He trailed the Shining Path through Peru's jungles. He reported on resistance to Pinochet's dictatorship. He shadowed Cuauhtémoc Cárdenas's run for president of Mexico. He also met up with composer/author Paul Bowles in Morocco and the Basque separatist Euskadi Ta Askatasuna in Franco's Spain. When the 1985 earthquake devastated Mexico City, PNS sent him to report on *los damnificados*. He checked into the Isabel Hotel—and did not check out until 2010 when he left for Michoacán to die.

His second book won the American Book Award in 1995, *Rebellion from the Roots*, a chronicle of the Zapatista uprising in Chiapas on January 1, 1994, the first day of the North American Free Trade Agreement. He became a regular at Zapatista events, braving the long and muddy trek to their jungle hideaway, and at all events involving Mexican politics. *The War against Oblivion*, *The Annexation of Mexico*, *¡Zapatistas!* and a novel based on voting corruption during Cárdenas's presidential bid, *Tonatiuh's People*, followed. He also penned ten poetry chapbooks.

When I saw that John was coming to Brodsky's Bookstore in Taos, New Mexico, to give a reading of Subcomandante Insurgente Marcos's children's book *La historia de los colores*, I jumped into my old Jeep and made tracks northward. The book had been commissioned in 1999 by the

National Endowment for the Arts to be published by Lee and Bobby Byrd's Cinco Puntos Press of El Paso, Texas. But when some of the anxious politicos of the Clinton administration got wind of the fact that U.S. taxpayer monies were bringing a "subversive" document into print, they nixed the project. After some tense weeks, the Lannan Foundation of Santa Fe came to the rescue, offering up the now-revoked $7500; the book came out in glorious colors, and John was trotting about the U.S. promoting it.

Somehow, in the commotion after the reading, I ended up in the same caravan with John and his ladylove of the moment, headed for a late-night dinner at some dowager's adobe, and it was here that our friendship began. It was nurtured across the distance—Chimayó, New Mexico to Mexico City—by none other than... the internet. Yes, John Ross was the guilty party who got this Luddite clacking away on a computer keyboard—and, for his wild notions, sleight-of-hand use of language, and utter dedication to friendship, it was worth every byte.

Our first poetry reading together took place at my house in Chimayó and went on into the night, lubricated by a bottle of red wine—I audience to his poems, he to mine. Our second was in El Paso. We were scheduled, along with publisher Bobby Byrd, to read at La Fe Cultural Center. The afternoon of the event John was all excited about an archeo-art exhibit made of Mexican *indocumentados'* used water bottles, dirty, ripped *cachuchas*; broken plastic shrines of Nuestra Señora de Guadalupe, photos of loved ones, and wayward underpants found in the Arizona desert. The source of John's devotion to the border was obvious; mine sprung from my labors as something of an underground railroad for incoming, deported, and departing immigrants in northern New Mexico. We set out to find the show. Of course, neither of us knew north from south in El Paso. We ended up driving around and around, only to find the building housing the exhibit locked shut—and an even worse tragedy: no espresso machine within sight. We stopped to down some chile-smothered hot dogs, which appeared to be the only semi-lifelike foodstuff available, and after our grueling search for something, *anything*, to eat, it seemed to me to make up the Official Cuisine of El Paso. Sitting in plastic chairs on the sidewalk, John regaled me with gritty tales of the down-and-out denizens of his 'hood in Mexico City and the 1997 massacre of peasants in Acteal as the government's cruel retribution for the existence of the Zapatistas.

With the arrival of the millennium, John went on to resist the incursion of Israeli settlers into Palestinian olive groves (where they bludgeoned him with clubs) and act as a Human Shield in Iraq to prevent the U.S. from attacking; upon their arrival Donald Rumsfeld threatened that if any of the Shields survived they would be prosecuted for war crimes for impeding U.S. bombs. In the early 2000s John also wrote a creative memoir entitled *Murdered by Capitalism* in which, while imbibing Gallo wine and smoking PCP-laced pot in a Humboldt County cemetery, he meets the ghost of anarchist Edward B. Schnaubelt (1901–1979), and together they compare notes on the burial of the Old Left of Schnaubelt's era and the New Left of John's.

Upon returning to the Isabel, he wrote what was to be his last book, *El Monstruo,* a monstrous tribute to Mexico City.

Through the years John identified himself as a "rebel reporter," an "investigative poet," a "left-wing Mr. Rogers," a "professional blurb writer," and, toward the end, a "corpse-in-training." During his last round of chemotherapy, he attended the traditional Day of the Dead celebration in San Francisco's Mission District dressed as a cancer-ridden liver. His last wishes echoed those of socialist Joe Hill—that his ashes would be scattered in a diversity of locations: in John's case, in the ash trays at the Hotel Isabel; along the #14 bus route through the Mission; mixed with marijuana and rolled in a joint to be smoked at his funeral.

In early 2010 John—half-blind and barely able to walk—braved the Rail Runner from Albuquerque to Santa Fe to visit me while on book tour. The mission was to swig espresso, buy a really cool, Pueblo-crafted cane to bolster his failing leg, and (needless to say) talk politics. I was on the verge of moving to Bolivia, and at a little café by the tracks he reached into the suitcases of memory to regale me with his encounters with Evo Morales before the man became El Presidente—the major theme being the clash between John's aspiration to discuss anti-imperialist strategies and Morales' obsession with ogling passing women. Although neither John nor I said a word, when he mounted the aluminum steps for the return journey, we knew it would be the last time we would be together. Hyper-focusing every cell of my body, from eyeballs to toenails, I clung to the vision of this valiant warrior as he hobbled to grab the overhead bar and plop his wiry body into a seat.

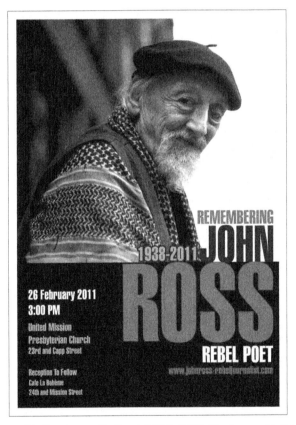

John Ross, a life flamboyantly lived (1938–2011). Photo credit: Peter Allen. Poster design: Carla Ross Allen. Courtesy of Carla Ross Allen.

AFTERWORD

IN THIS BOOK I have attempted to convey the soul of an era through the people who lived it, responded to it, made it what it is—and whom I had the fine fortune to know. The glory, and tragedy, of this book is that it could have been an encyclopedia. Or a symphony. Even a Busby Berkeley dance extravaganza! Or, shall I say? our historical times have been and *are* an encyclopedia, a symphony, and a mandalic dance production all rolled into one. I wish I had the time and space to include so very many other rebels and history makers. Beth Hallett. Troy Duster. Anne Kent Rush. Sandy Boucher. Ofer Zur. Ralph Metzner. Chris Wells. Godfrey Reggio. Jeannette Armstrong. Donna House. John Mohawk. Lorenzo Valdez. Kay Matthews. Roberto Roibal. Arthur Monroe. Libby Kelley. Blake Levitt. Arthur Firstenberg. Olle Johansson. Stan Cox. Nancy Caro Hollander. Luis Bredow. Juan Claudio Lechín. Raúl Peñaranda. Pedro Susz . . .

One might call all these folks truth-tellers. Or artists of life. They are perhaps independent scholars. And rebel rousers. They could also be described as "creatives," a relatively new term that proposes such qualities as unquenchable curiosity, love of beauty, mindfulness, risk-taking, belief that existence itself is a work of art, use of both intuition and intellect, and keenness to play. Whatever the term one prefers, it strikes me that the individuals I have chosen to write about are those who—like the poets, painters, performers, philosophers, and political activists of Greenwich Village, the Left Bank, and Taos, New Mexico—have given expression to their era while, at the same time, being immersed in it.

In reading the individual essays, you may notice a certain mutual recognition that is nurtured within such a grouping; each of these daring folk shares a carte blanche to get to know each other, no matter what particular focus each may hold. And it is true: a sturdy web, what we might call a non-geographic community, exists that connects people who are working to counter the negatives the system perpetrates and to make positive history. Lifelong friendships may begin simply with "We've not met, but I heard you speak/read your book/ saw your film," which is answered with "Of course! I've admired *your* work for some time."

You may notice another shared quality: they *never* retire.

One of the more profound lessons I have taken to heart by putting together these essays is that—no matter how wounded or healed each of us is, no matter if we hold a post-graduate degree or we barely made it through the sixth grade, no matter how heralded or anonymous we have been in our life's work—in the end, *each of us is a hero*. The word is loaded, of course: weighed down by its popular connotation that defines heroism as the high-flying acts of a Superman. I wish to use it in the frame that cultural anthropologist Ernest Becker meant when he introduced the notion that heroism is the sense of meaning one brings to the act of living. A hero can be a breadwinner or a stay-at-home mom, a practitioner of civil disobedience or a computer hacker exposing the corruption of a nation. I realized the truth of this definition via the deaths—one after another—of so many of my comrades. Through the psychic frame that the ultimate curtain call imposes, I could see the caring, passion, soul—and meaning—each brought to being alive.

It is such a frame that I wish to pass on to you, dear reader. Each one of us has the capacity to make of the times we are born into an expression of the humanity that—despite all the cruelty, inequality, and injustice in our flailing world—miraculously never gives up on us.

Every minute, a chance to change the world...
—DOLORES HUERTA, IN ESSAY FOR CARE2.COM, 2016

ACKNOWLEDGMENTS

I WISH TO EXTEND my thanks to Kinga Tomczyk, who early on, in the one-light-bulb obscurity of Sucre's Hostel San Marcos, valued the initial scrawlings of this generational memoir. Marc Kasky, Julie Herrada of the Labadie Collection at the University of Michigan, Kate Mack, Susan Griffin, Shepherd Bliss—all radiant Rebels, Bohos, and/or Deep Heads—provided details and set me straight on various blunders of memory. Rob Williams, Suzan Harjo, Whitney Smith, Anthony "Twig" Wheeler, and Mark Kitchell went beyond the call of duty in digging up old photos or taking new ones. Ben Camardi at H. Matson Company literary agency kept my spirits up in what, in 2012, started out as a post-2008-economic-collapse publishing environment manifesting zero interest in social delvings, an attitude that was only bolstered by the presence of young computer-raised editors whose single focus seemed to span from internet possibilities to computer breakthroughs. I wish also to extend gratitude to Lynne Elizabeth at New Village Press, who saw the possibilities of a memoir not just of one person's life, but of a period of history. She took the risk to publish it and throughout lent her extensive experience as writer, editor, designer, and publisher. And to Ignacio Choi, my genius editor.

Lastly, I am grateful to a very fine documenter of living history, Ramón Chao, whose *Le Monde Diplomatique* series on artists, thinkers, and writers in Paris in the 1950s inspired the form and value of this effort.

Any errors the reader may encounter are mine. I wish to add that I have done my very best to track down sources for every photograph and every image. Sometimes in the effort, though, I crashed into a dead end, so to any not fully acknowledged photographer or publisher, I thank you for your work; it enhances the impact of this book immeasurably.

THE AUTHOR

CHELLIS GLENDINNING is a psychologist whose practice for over thirty-five years focused on recovery from traumatic stress. She is also the author of nine books, a bilingual opera, and hundreds of essays and articles. Her books include *Off the Map: An Expedition Deep into Empire and the Global Economy* and *Chiva: A Village Takes on the Global Heroin Trade,* both winners of (U.S.) National Federation of Press Women book awards in nonfiction. Her most recent are *Hyper: An Electromagnetic Chapbook,* a poetry chapbook about the health impacts of wireless technologies, and the book blog *luddite.com* on technology criticism from Ned Ludd to Kirkpatrick Sale. Her first novel and first book in Spanish, *Objetos,* was published in 2018 by Editorial 3600 of La Paz, Bolivia. A northern Ohioan with mindfully tended roots in northern California and northern New Mexico, she lives now in an antique house in the southern altiplano of Bolivia. The archives of her life and work are housed at the Labadie Collection, University of Michigan. Her website is chellisglendinning.org

THE PUBLISHER

NEW VILLAGE PRESS is best known for books that animate emerging movements in societal transformation, true stories about collaborative community building, and the creative roles that artists and scholars, citizens and planners can play in public life. New Village Press Inc is a 501c3 nonprofit organization. Our books are distributed by New York University Press. Our website is newvillagepress.org

If you enjoyed *In the Company of Rebels*, you will appreciate the following.

RECENT MEMOIRS BY ACTIVISTS FEATURED IN
IN THE COMPANY OF REBELS

The Earth, the City, and the Hidden Narrative of Race
By Carl C. Anthony

*Openings: A Memoir from the Women's Art Movement,
New York City 1970-1992*
By Sabra Moore
Forewords by Lucy R. Lippard and Margaret Randall

FORTHCOMING MEMOIRS BY OTHER NOTABLE ACTIVISTS

Such a Pretty Girl: A Story of Struggle,
Empowerment, and Disability Pride
By Nadina LaSpina

Between Two Revolutions: Survival of an Artist in Iran
By Nasser Rahmaninejad

My Life in 100 Objects
By Margaret Randall

ALSO FORTHCOMING

Waging Peace in Vietnam:
The US Soldiers and Veterans Who Opposed the War
Edited by Ron Carver, David Cortright, and Barbara Doherty